THE TEACHER

A Study of Teaching in

THE TEACHER'S CRAFT

A Study of Teaching
in the Primary School

JOHN L POWELL

The Scottish Council for Research in Education

SCRE PUBLICATION 85

ISBN 0 901116 98 X Boards
ISBN 0 901116 99 8 Limp

Printed and bound in Great Britain for the Scottish Council for Research in Education, 15 St John Street, Edinburgh EH8 8JR, by Russell Print, Blantyre

Reprinted in 1986.

CONTENTS

LIST OF TABLES

LIST OF FIGURES

INTRODUCTION

Although this book is a report on a research study, priority has been given to presenting it in such a way that it may be both meaningful and helpful to practising teachers. This will, it is hoped, make it suitable for use in both pre-service and in-service courses for teachers, where the ideas presented may be useful both in themselves and as a basis for discussion.

In order to achieve this, some price has had to be paid. However, the interests of researchers have not been overlooked and as much data as practicable has been included to allow the work to be evaluated as research. Research issues have, indeed, been presented, though as far as possible using non-technical language. Since the discussion of these issues contributes to the understanding of the findings reported, they have been included in the main text, though much of the data is to be found in appendices. Readers without interest in procedures followed have, however, been given some choice in how they use the text, for indications are given as to what parts may be passed over—at the cost of some loss of understanding of how the conclusions have been reached. On the other hand, it has been made plain that profitable use of the book does require some effort on the part of all readers, notably in respect of gaining adequate familiarity with the SCOTS schedule and the thinking underlying each if its items.

For reasons explained in Chapter 3, judgements and related value judgements have not been eschewed, though every endeavour has been made to distinguish these from research-based evidence. Moreover, particularly in the final chapter, the conclusions reached are essentially the personal conclusions of the writer after he has undergone the educative experience of undertaking the research and thinking deeply about the issues discussed in the light of his own experience as a teacher and with close regard to the research evidence available to him. No claim beyond this to the 'rightness' of the conclusions is made.

Some researchers may disapprove of what has been done, preferring to make only highly qualified statements and to interpret data only in the most parsimonious way. The writer's view is that in order to be useful the researcher has to pass on what understanding he believes himself to have obtained, even though that understanding may be far from perfect. To pretend that research can provide clear-cut and certain answers to complex questions is to deceive oneself. The very questions asked and the evidence sought inevitably depend on judgements of the researchers involved, and all but the simplest data are capable of multiple interpretations. The researcher, like others, learns from experience: he differs from others only in having, through his research, enriched his experience and devoted more time to seeking to understand it. His training as a researcher helps him to look critically at all inferences he is inclined to draw and to test them, so far as he can, against such data as he can bring to bear. At the end of the day, however, the worth of his conclusions depend on the worth of his judgements. Others have both a right and a duty to question these judgements in the light of their own knowledge and experience and, in so far as they accept them, to act on them on the tentative assumption that they are right. If this book assists teachers to look critically at what they do, to question their objectives and their ways of achieving them, and to amend their practice is so far as they come to see amendment as necessary, it will have achieved its purpose.

General Note on Gender

To avoid endless employment of he/she, him/her, and his/her, teachers and pupils are referred to in this book by the use of masculine pronouns, except where specific individuals are (anonymously) referred to. (The alternative of using feminine pronouns was rejected on the grounds that it would serve to perpetuate the myth that almost all primary teachers are female.) The intention is to refer to teachers as teachers, wholly irrespective of their sex.

How to Read this Book.

This book is designed to be read in a number of different ways, each related to the needs of the reader. Some readers may wish only to acquaint themselves with the main conclusions reached (which are to be found principally in Chapters 8 and 11); some researchers, on the other hand, may wish to use every appendix in order to be able to examine in detail, and question, how the research was done. For the general reader, however, the best course may well be to read all the chapters, making appropriate references, as indicated in the text, to Appendices A and B, and perhaps E also. (Those especially interested in the tests developed are likely to wish to look at Appendices F, G and H also.) Those wishing to read the text selectively may choose to omit certain chapters—eg, 2, 4, 5, 6, 9 and 10—but they should scan them first so that their omissions may be the result of choice rather than accident.

ACKNOWLEDGEMENTS

The research described in this book took place in classrooms and involved exposing the work of the teachers concerned to the gaze of researchers. To the more than two hundred teachers involved— some in either or both of the main stages of the work and some in the pilot phases—great debt is owed. They and their schools remain unnamed because of the need to ensure their anonymity in the pages of this book.

A debt of another nature is owed to the Dundee division of Tayside Region for support in the developmental phase of the research and especially for the secondment to the project of Mabel Scrimgeour for approximately two and a quarter years in 1973-75. The assistance of Mr David Robertson, Director of Education, Tayside Region, Mr J M Scott, Divisional Education Officer, and Mr W Tait, Principal Adviser in Primary Education is particularly acknowledged.

The members of the research team are named immediately hereafter. Their contribution to the research is incalculable. They did moreover give unstintingly of their time and energy, not least when, during the field work, the relentless pressure of the timetable called for physical as well as mental endurance. That, despite all the difficulties encountered, they were not merely colleagues but friends says all.

Along with the researchers, must be named Ray Ramsay, who, though not a researcher, was certainly a member of the team. At the height of the research programme she not only met typing demands with miraculous speed but voluntarily gave many hours of her own time to ensure the continued flow of those test materials that required manual preparation. To her and to the many others who, whether named or unacknowledged, contributed to the work of the project, I give my warmest thanks.

January 1984   J L P

THE RESEARCHERS

1973-76 MABEL SCRIMGEOUR who shared with the author the conceptualisation of the research project and of all the research instruments developed for the project. In particular, she was joint author of the SCOTS schedule.

1974-77 CHRISTINE DARROCH who help pioneer the first use of the SCOTS schedule in 1974/75 and who contributed greatly, in the following year, to the development of research instruments. In particular, she played the major role in devising the 'puzzles' for the Application to Work test and in smoothing the hand-over to the second research team early in 1977.

1974-75 JAMES CALDERHEAD who was the third of the team of observers who pioneered the use of the SCOTS schedule in 1974/75.

1977-78 ANNE PROCTOR whose understanding of the dynamics of classrooms provided innumerable insights that have proved invaluable in the writing of this book.

1977-78 FINLAY COUPAR who devised (with Graham McAvoy) the observation system required for the Application to Work test and who was a most perceptive classroom observer during the 1977/78 observations.

1977-78 GRAHAM McAVOY who, in addition to being joint-deviser of the Application to Work observational system, programmed the initial part of the analysis of the 'Application' data; whose terse comments on individual classrooms so often cut to the heart of the matter; and whose meticulous record keeping was of lasting value.

1978-79 BET GORDON who patiently undertook the demanding coding of the scripts of the arithmetic computation test.

1982 JOHN HART who for two short periods assisted with the analysis of test data.

CHAPTER 1

DISCOVERING THE PROBLEM

The Teaching Strategies in the Primary School project was initiated with the purpose of exploring an area of concern that was the subject of much discussion in the 1970's, whether "progressive methods" in primary schools were having an adverse effect on standards. The present writer was given an open remit to examine this area of concern and to investigate as seemed to him appropriate. This provided him with a degree of freedom researchers do not often enjoy; it made it possible to follow a path of discovery.

An explorer who sets off into unknown territory cannot tell whether he will discover a malarial swamp, make some interesting and original observations, or discover El Dorado itself. In short, the risks are high, but the possibility of making real discoveries is there. Such it has been with the Teaching Strategies project. The approach has been innovative and questing; failure has been risked. The outcome has not been the discovery of El Dorado, but neither has the final destination proved to be a malarial swamp. The territory has proved rich and exciting and has provoked much thought. The traveller believes himself wiser for his travels. It is the purpose of this book to share this experience and the insights it has provided.

In his travels he was not alone, though only he has been fortunate enough to complete the whole journey. As is acknowledged on another page, he had successively two teams of travelling companions who contributed uniquely to what was achieved. One individual, however, must even among these receive special mention: Mabel Scrimgeour, who joined him soon after the commencement of the project. It was she who in the very early stages of the project—when the research tools were note-pad and pen—visited schools with him and observed and reflected and argued about the significance—or possible significance—of what was seen. In this way the research problem was defined and the strategy of exploration devised.

Our early observations convinced us that if standards of attainment were falling—and we had no reason to suppose that they were[1]—it was most unlikely to be the result of 'progressive

[1] A number of surveys conducted by SCRE had shown standards, in terms of performance at traditional computative Arithmetic and English, had indeed indicated the contrary—see *Rising Standards in the Primary School* (SCRE, 1968).

methods', since any teaching that could be described as 'progressive' in any extreme sense was difficult if not impossible to find at least in the parts where our initial work was done.

Of course we were faced with the difficulty that 'progressive methods' is not a term with any precise meaning. We took it in practice to include concepts and practices such as 'child centredness', individualised and small group learning, and pupil freedom (including, in its extreme forms, freedom to choose when and what to learn).

In the teaching we observed there was of course some variation in respect of some of these matters. Some did, for instance, make much use of group methods and others used predominantly class teaching; some classes were given rather more freedom of choice and action than others; some teachers did lay rather more emphasis on rote memorisation and some rather more on acquiring understanding. But the differences were typically not extreme. Certainly none left it to the whim of pupils what they should learn—though they differed in whether their control of, or influence on, pupil learning was predominantly direct or indirect.

However, it was evident that teachers who used very similar approaches used them with markedly different levels of skill. Classes operating by group methods could be models of purposeful, self-generated activity, or a place of confusion in which pupils sought—usually vainly—for guidance, while an overworked teacher sought to keep the show going somehow. Equally, teacher-centred classes could be stimulating places where virtually every pupil was eagerly engaged, or depressing ones characterised by rigidity, uniformity, and dullness. There were at least some grounds for thinking that what the teacher does may be less important than the way that he does it.

Another matter of which we became acutely aware was how misleading appearances could be. Pupils' sitting round tables was no proof of the use of group methods: those whose position at the table had them facing away from the teacher were often found with necks or chairs turned for many hours of the day while they engaged in whole class activities; some teachers who allowed their pupils to choose their next item of work in effect permitted their pupils to choose from work-cards that not only differed from one another in no significant way but had all to be done sooner or later. Thus grouping could be nominal or real; choosing could be nominal or real. It was indeed found to be the case that what amounted to group work occurred in some classes where pupils did not sit in groups at all, but rather in desks arranged in rows in the traditional fashion. Thus if one was to record the nature of class teaching one had to try to record what was 'really' happening rather than what was nominally happening.

A related issue was the context in which an act occurred. Take, for example, a sharp rebuke. The experience of receiving such a sharp rebuke from a teacher seemed to differ in accordance with the basic, lasting relationship between rebuking teacher and class or child. Thus a teacher who was generally recognised as being well-disposed could, without causing offence, speak bluntly or sharply, whereas another, viewed as generally hostile, could arouse hostility with speech not a whit more blunt. The need was to see events and actions as having meaning and significance in, and in relation to, the context in which they occurred. This implied, inter alia, *seeing things as a whole*.

Thus it was that we abandoned any idea of contrasting 'progressive' teachers with 'traditional' ones. The ill-defined nature of the terms could have been overcome by arriving at some arbitrary definitions to be applied within the context of the research, but there was no way in which so simplistic a dichotomisation of types of teacher could have been usefully pursued. We were faced with a direct choice between ending all investigation there and then, and, on the other hand, attempting to record, and to seek to understand, the complex patterns of activity that we saw in the primary classroom. We chose the latter.

CHAPTER 2

SEEKING A WAY

In seeking a way of accomplishing the task that we had set ourselves,we turned first to the many systems that had in comparatively recent years been devised to measure, with some accuracy, aspects of teacher behaviour and teacher-pupil interaction. These systems, typified in many respects by the work of Ned Flanders[1] in the USA, recorded behaviour in terms of predetermined categories and measured in terms of the frequency or duration of each category of behaviour for each teacher and/or pupil being observed. In this way, it was, for example, possible to determine to what extent in a particular class verbal interactions were initiated by the teacher and to what extent by the pupils, and also which pupils were initiators or participators in these interactions. In similar ways some researchers categorised the verbal utterances themselves. Quantity was typically established by recording at fixed—and usually frequent—intervals and by finding the total number of instances of each category or sub-category. Systems of this general type had, we realised, a number of key characteristics that determined both their usefulness and their limitations:

1. The behaviours recorded and counted were ones that could be unambiguously defined and recognised—and were therefore fairly simple ones.

2. The number of behaviours that could be categorised and recorded were, *at any one time*, quite small in number, and thus what was recorded was a very small sub-set of the total range of behaviours occurring.

3. The behaviours recorded had little meaning in themselves and it was therefore necessary to interpret the data collected after the action was over. (Although the recording itself may have been 'objective', subjectivity was involved in the subsequent interpretation of the data.)

4. When the interpretation was carried out, all behaviours placed in a category had to be treated as identical. Thus, for example, all initiations of verbal interactions were treated as identical events unless another simultaneous recording permitted some degree of sub-categorisation (eg, according to

[1] For example, see Flanders, N A (1970).

8

what was going on at the time), and even then was in practice limited by the amount of simultaneous recording practicable. [2]

As we surveyed the various observation systems available[3], we became increasingly aware that, whereas certain ones of them would very effectively quantify actions and other phenomena in which we were developing an interest—for example, whether a teacher's questions were directed to all or most of the pupils in the class, or were concentrated almost entirely on a minority—they would give us no means of recording the wide range of coincident behaviours and events that we saw as likely to be important. Moreover, by the very nature of the recording techniques used, these systems could never be used in conjunction to cover all the areas in which we had an interest, for the complete attention of an observer was needed to use each one of them.

Only two lines of approach were open to us, to endeavour to make for subsequent analysis a permanent record of the teaching we were interested in—by using (as some researchers had done) video recordings—or to devise an adequate technique of concurrent recording.

The first of these two options we rejected not only because we lacked the level of funding that would be necessary to obtain and operate the equipment but because we seriously doubted its value. To use it we should have had to

a) move equipment from room to room as required

or b) set equipment up in a single room in each school and move each class to be observed to this room

or c) bring all classes from their schools to a single, centrally located studio-classroom.

---

[2] Some researchers sought to overcome this difficulty by using video and sound recording and undertaking much more elaborate cross-classifications by using codings determined in the course of repeated replayings of the tapes. In doing so, they were hampered by the selectivity of what was recorded—for many behaviours require close-up pictures and the clear recording of words spoken, neither of which can be achieved on more than a sample basis—and by the distortion of the situation being recorded by the introduction of microphones and of film/video cameras.

[3] Critical accounts of observation systems then available may be found in Rosenshine, B (1971), Travers, R M W, (1973) and Dunkin, M J and Biddle, B J (1974). A valuable discussion of issues, also dating from that period, is found in Morrison, A. and McIntyre, D (1969). All these books are of undiminished interest today.

Course 'a' we believed to be disruptive of normal practice and in any case impracticable. Courses 'b' and 'c' would, apart from extreme difficulty of implementation, have divorced classes from their normal working environment and thus destroyed, at least in part, what we wished to observe.

This is not to say, however, that the alternative course we chose was an easy one, for not only did we have to devise our own system but we had to devise one likely to be wholly different from virtually every other classroom observation system currently in use and, therefore, one lacking many of the characteristics that our peers considered necessary to achieve a reasonable level of 'objectivity'. We accepted the implicit challenge and our System for the Classroom Observation of Teaching Strategies (the SCOTS schedule) was the eventual outcome.

Whatever are the merits or demerits of the SCOTS schedule, it is the central feature of the research described in this book. Thus it is essential for the reader gradually to become familiar with it. It is probably not possible to grasp all its subtleties without having both experience of its use and prolonged training. Nevertheless, in this book an endeavour will be made to help the reader to acquire sufficient understanding of it to be able to perceive the significance of the argument based on it. At this point the reader is advised to scan the schedule briefly. (It is to be found in Appendix A.) As he does so he will see that it is set out in a form reminiscent of a multiple choice test. For each item, one option can be ticked at the discretion of the observer. Five columns exist to permit the recording of five separate observations, each lasting for approximately one quarter of a school day. At this stage it is sufficient for the reader to acquire an approximate knowledge of the range of information the schedule seeks to record and to note the way in which the items are structured.

* * * * *

Now that the reader has perused the schedule but before any attempt is made to deepen the reader's understanding of the nature and significance of each of the 43 items constituting the schedule, it is necessary to explain the principles on which the schedule was constructed and indeed how these principles evolved in the course of the construction of the schedule.

It has already been mentioned that during the earliest of the observations carried out by Mabel Scrimgeour and the present writer the research tools were note-pad and pen. Extensive notes were taken of everything that occurred, and so far as possible things said by teacher or pupil were taken down verbatim. Since both observers were recording the same lessons, it was possible to discuss the lessons afterwards and note areas which seemed both to characterise particular classrooms and the teaching in them and to differentiate them from others.

Once any such area was noted, an endeavour was made to define on a five-point scale the range of variation that had been observed or was thought by the two observers—on the basis of their own previous experience as teachers—to be the range that would be found were more classes to be seen. The most common approach was to describe the two extremes (normally options 1 and 5) and then to fit in three intermediate points at what seemed subjectively to be approximately equal intervals.

To produce such a first draft was often not particularly difficult. What was difficult was to convert this draft into something that could stand up to use. It would normally fit well enough those teachers who were borne in mind at the time of composition, but when further teachers were observed difficulties were liable to arise. Occasionally the difficulty was simply that what was later observed had not been foreseen at all, but more often the difficulty arose from lack of unidimensionality. Thus, if in error the descriptors encompassed more than one variable and there was thus more than one dimension of variation, sooner or later the descriptors would point to different and conflicting codings for a single teacher. Often only the most rigorous intellectual analysis was enough to untangle two variables that, on account of some degree of co-variance, had initially been mistaken for only one. Although adequate records of cases where this occurred have not survived, it is possible to illustrate the point by referring to item 21 (see Appendix A). This item relates to the *type* of motivation observed. If there had been an attempt to take account also of the *degree* of motivation, the essential feature of unidimensionality would have been lost and observers would have been faced with sets of options in each of which were combined a particular type motivation with a particular degree of motivation. Although these particular combinations might commonly be found, they would not hold in every case, and it would therefore be impossible to code accurately any teacher whose type and degree of motivation did not match in this way. In short, each dimension of variation must be treated as a single item in the schedule.

It has already been said that the principles of construction themselves evolved. Initially the aim and practice was to define the five options in largely behavioural terms. The supposition was that if one described behaviours, it would be easy to see which teachers were alike in particular respects. The fallacy was in supposing that actions very similar in terms of behaviour were necessarily alike in their significance, and also in supposing that fundamentally very similar practices could not have quite diverse manifestations in purely behavioural terms. Thus it was that variation frequently came to be described in more abstract terms, while behavioural descriptions came increasingly to be used as exemplars rather than definitions. Two examples of the sort of change that was introduced over time may serve to clarify this important point.

a) The item relating to the transition from one activity to another was in the first (1974) version of the SCOTS schedule as follows:

1) Lengthy gaps between tasks, such that pupils engage in self-selected activities.

2) Although instructions for next task are given promptly on completion of existing task, teacher permits digressions that delay the commencement of new work. The change is possibly characterised by indecision.

3) Clear planning, but organisational difficulties cause delay on occasions (e.g., necessary materials not available, have to be borrowed, etc).

4) Pre-planning means no delay in selecting new task (though some minimal delay may occur when correction of one task is a prerequisite of commencing another).

5) As children are aware of range of tasks available and requisite materials are available, no delay is discernible and one task commences as another ends.

Option 3 demonstrates that experience in using items from the schedule had, even before the finalisation of the 1974 version, led to the use of a general statement fortified by an example. However, comparison of all these options with those in item 27 of the 1977 revision of the schedule (the version given in Appendix A) reveals that a need was later found to take the process a good deal further. It will be seen in particular that the 1977 version permits each single option to be matched to a range of behaviours that, while differing one from the other, are nonetheless 'equivalent' in terms of degree of time-lag involved.

b) A second example from the 1974 version, one relating to *the prevention/encouragement of inter-pupil co-operation*, demonstrates options that were too specific to be matched to conduct actually observed.

1) Teacher prevents co-operation amongst pupils; sustained insistence on working along.
2) Initially teacher seeks to prevent pupil co-operation but does not sustain a total ban.
3) Initially co-operation is not prevented, but subsequently is restricted by teacher.
4) Teacher encourages, either verbally or by the nature of the learning environment, co-operation amongst pupils but places limits on its extent or frequency.
5) Teacher encourages, either verbally or by the nature of the learning environment, co-operation amongst pupils whenever possible.
0) Not applicable (e.g., because of testing or work that would be invalidated by co-operation).

NOTE: For the purposes of this variable, minimal forms of pupil co-operation such as borrowing an eraser should be disregarded.

Again comparison with the 1977 version (Appendix A, item 34) shows the greater generality of the revised descriptors.

The central issue in the construction of the SCOTS schedule was, of course, the selection of teacher and classroom variables to be recorded. The initial choice of variables was, as has already been stated, made on a judgemental basis, factors that had struck us during our initial observations as potentially important being selected. We surveyed, however, a large number of other classroom observation instruments, using them as check-lists. In the case of every variable that we wished to adopt, we did, of course, have to satisfy ourselves that we could observe sufficiently well to be able to record it: there had to be adequate visible or audible evidence.

It follows from what has just been said that the variables finally selected were not ones chosen to reflect any particular theoretical perspective relative to teaching. Rather the approach was essentially eclectic, one drawing on variables associated with a variety of theoretical perspectives or none. The object was to include, so far as possible, all potentially relevant variables. It can, of course, be argued that the selection was biased by the prejudices of the schedule's two authors. And indeed this was probably so—at least to some extent. However, there was a conscious attempt to avoid bias: the use of check-lists was one of the means.

The next chapter is devoted to a detailed discussion of those variables which were selected and which survived subsequent trial. Before we reach this chapter, however, it is necessary to give a brief account of the steps followed in the development of the SCOTS schedule. The principal steps were:

1) Each item was drafted as described above, care being taken to ensure that there would be no difficulty in placing in one—and only one—of its categories each of the teachers that had been previously observed.

2) Groups of such items were tried out during observations of teachers not previously seen, and where coding difficulties were encountered, the draft was modified or specific interpretations of the existing wordings agreed.

3) When the complete schedule was ready, at the beginning of the school session 1974-75, the first team of observers (which was made up of three researchers, Mabel Scrimgeour, Christine Darroch, and James Calderhead) underwent a few weeks of training, which consisted of the discussion of schedule items, the carrying out of observations in a number of classes, and comparing and discussing attempts at coding. In this way the observers increased their understanding of the schedule and began to develop a good deal of the 'case law' that was in due time to find its way into an observers' manual. Although not a member of the team of observers, the present writer shared in these observations and discussions.

4) For the remainder of that school session, the schedule was put to the test of repeated use. 138 teachers in 30 schools in Edinburgh, Glasgow, the Lothians, Fife, Lanarkshire, Angus, Perthshire, and Roxburgh were each observed on five occasions, recordings being made on the schedule.

Though the schools involved in this fourth step did not constitute a random sample, it should be noted that an attempt was made in selecting them to represent a full range of Scottish primary schools in respect of school size, geographical areas, and social backgrounds of pupils. The prime objective was, however, to incorporate, so far as possible, a full range of teaching styles, and,

14

to achieve this, use was made of local advice, particularly in order to secure representation of teacher styles that pilot work had indicated might be represented inadequately simply because they were not, it appeared, widely employed. In this way, any representativeness that the sample might have had was, to a limited degree, deliberately distorted in order that even relatively uncommon styles could be adequately examined.

In each school, the observations were undertaken in classes P5, P6, and P7—though in some schools, mainly rural ones, mixed-aged classes (P4/5, P5/6, and P6/7) were included. In two-stream schools this policy normally yielded six classes; in one-stream schools, only two or three. In schools with three or more streams, no more than six classes were visited. Each class was visited five times, the minimum judged necessary. Each of the four quarters of the school day was included; the fifth observation was an additional morning one.

The object of this activity was two-fold. In the first place far more extensive experience of using the schedule was required in order to establish whether each teacher observed could be matched to one of the options of each variable and, if not, what needed to be done, either by modifying the schedule itself or by extending the 'case law' governing its application. The second objective was of even greater importance: to establish whether the three observers agreed in their codings, or, to put it another way, whether the set of codings produced was affected by which of the observers made it. To ascertain whether this was indeed so, approximately 20% of all the observations were conducted with two observers present, so that their independently made codings could be subsequently compared. In this way each observer was paired with each other observer on ten occasions, thus providing a total of 30 'reliability' observations undertaken in 11 schools.

The prime purpose of this exercise on this occasion was not to measure inter-observer reliability, but to discover sources of disagreement so that the schedule itself could be improved. Nonetheless it was reassuring that high levels of agreement were achieved in respect of many items in the schedule, and that, as the year progressed, such disagreements as did occur, diminished in frequency and extent.

In achieving this improvement in reliability, there was one important factor: as soon as the independently made codings had been recorded for the purpose of assessing reliability, the observers were asked to discuss such differences as had occurred. In this way, differences in the application of criteria became apparent and were rectified—where necessary after discussion with the third member of the observation team and the present writer.

Nevertheless it was necessary to drop 11 of the 54 items and to modify others. The principal reasonse for its being necessary to drop variables was insufficient evidence on which to base the codings: if relevant *observable* events seldom occurred, the level of inference became much higher; furthermore, if that seldom-occurring evidence was speech that was not equally audible to both observers, the difference in perceived evidence could account for differences in coding.

Where re-drafting of items was necessary, the task was often scarcely less demanding than in the initial drafting of items. Nevertheless, there were grounds for believing that the revised (1977) version of the schedule—ie, the one the reader has already perused in Appendix 1—was fit to be the central instrument of the research programme schedule for 1977/78. How far this confidence was justified, the reader may assess in the light of the data presented in Chapter 6. In the meantime, we must turn to other matters, and, in particular, first take a detailed look at the SCOTS schedule in its revised form so that the rationale of its individual items may be fully understood.

CHAPTER 3

THE SCOTS SCHEDULE:
An Analysis of Teaching and of Teaching Situations.

This is an important chapter, in that it reveals the multi-faceted view of teaching that arose from the initial observations and that constitutes the basis for the most important element of the data to which the later sections of this book relate. It is *not* therefore—despite its degree of detail—something that the busy reader can afford to skip if he wishes to follow with understanding the remainder of this book. *It should be noted that throughout the remainder of this chapter it will be assumed that the reader is making constant reference to the text of the schedule (Appendix A).*

It is a primary aim of the SCOTS schedule to allow the observer *freedom of inference within defined limits.* The observer has to be more than an efficient machine recording accurately what occurs: he has to make use of his understanding of what he sees occurring. In this lies his strength as well as some obvious dangers, unfettered subjectivity and bias. There can be no absolute protection against these dangers, but the SCOTS schedule seeks to minimise them. If the observer employing the SCOTS schedule uses subjective judgement, he does so on very narrow fronts. His recordings are the result of what might be regarded as a large number of small subjective judgements rather than a smaller number of single wide-ranging and possibly simplistic ones. His freedom is disciplined by procedures and defined requirements. He does moreover seek to record what happens rather than to fathom what the teacher intends should happen: something not only more practicable but also more relevant.

It is, of course, this need for the observer to interpret what he sees and hears that lays the use of this schedule most open to attack. The point to be borne in mind is, however, that all data, no matter how objectively gathered, have to be interpreted. The very decision of what to record in a machine-like way at fixed time intervals—as when, for example, using a Flanders-type schedule—itself involves subjectivity, and the decision as to how to use the frequency counts, even more. The essential difference between the SCOTS schedule, on the one hand, and one of the allegedly more objective schedules lies not in whether subjective judgement is employed but in *when* it is employed. In the former case, it is at the time of observation; in the latter, predominantly when the analysis is carried out or when the method of analysis is decided on. It is the contention of the present writer that subjective judgement, subject to well-thought-out rules of application, is much more soundly based when used 'live' at the time of observation, when the whole range of evidence is before the observer's eyes. And this advantage is over and above that of being able to record a great variety of factors simultaneously.[1]

This chapter, by describing each item in the SCOTS schedule and by giving the reader some information about how each item was operated in the field, gives the reader some insight into the particularities that have been referred to in terms of broad principle in the preceding paragraph. They cannot of course constitute a full training in the use of the schedule: training inevitably involves experience in the field and interaction between observers over the interpretation and application of principles in specific cases. In any case, each team of observers builds up its own 'case law', its own set of precedents; and to some extent the schedule is, therefore, something different for each team that uses it—a factor to be taken into account when comparing data collected by different teams.

Before we come to look at the schedule item by item, there are a few general points to be made. Firstly, although the schedule was designed first and foremost to be an observational instrument, it was recognised that some of the data needed could not be obtained by observation alone. Thus, for example, although an observer can see whether pupils are operating in groups, he may be unable to infer with any certainty the basis on which the groups were formed. The key events may have already occurred. It was, therefore, judged necessary to ask the teacher about certain matters and to use observation to check that there was no inconsistency between what the teacher said and what could be observed to be happening. (There are in fact five items that depend heavily on what the teachers say. These are the first five in the schedule.)

Asking the teacher is a practice not without disadvantage, for whereas it can in itself be a source of a variety of insights, it can also alert teachers to areas of their activity in which the researchers are interested—and thus it may cause them to modify their

[1] There is no intention here to suggest that the SCOTS schedule is 'superior' to, say, a Flanders-type schedule: each has its advantages. (On a very narrow front, the latter will certainly yield more accurate 'base' data.) The point is that both depend for their utility on the intelligent use of subjective judgement and that such weaknesses as arise from that do not lie exclusively with either type. For further discussion of the subjectivity/objectivity issue, see Powell, J L (1984).

behaviour in these areas in ways that they imagine would win the approval of the observers.[2] The timing of the asking of these questions was, therefore, a matter of importance. Except in the case of item 1, which was dealt with at the end of the first observation, the questions were all posed at the end of the fourth observation. (The letter 'T' at the head of the relevant column in the schedule in fact indicates this timing.) The reasons for choosing the end of the fourth observation in most cases was that

a) by then there had been plenty of time to observe what was observable before the teacher was alerted to the observer's interest, while, at the same time, there still remained one observation during which to pay attention to any special matter to which the teacher's remarks called attention, and

b) the observer could frame his questions indirectly by asking about specific relevant events that he had observed, instead of asking the question openly and bluntly. (In this way he was able to get the teacher to answer in respect of real instances rather than by a—possibly invalid—generalisation.)

The questioning for item 1 was seen to be sufficiently neutral for its early occurrence not to matter. It was also seen as an opportunity to establish a rapport with the teacher and for picking up miscellaneous but useful information.

It should be noted that in no case did the observer code the teacher's responses to questions in the presence of the teacher. Indeed, by seemingly engaging in a casual conversation about the class, the observers tried to disguise the fact that they were seeking answers to predetermined questions. A question about a particular pupil was often used as a means of initiating the enquiries and the essential questions were worked in as opportunity arose or was made. The codings recorded for the first five items of the schedule were therefore based both on teacher statements and on observation. In the case of all other items, the codings were based entirely on what was seen or heard during observations.

Codings were arrived at towards the end of each quarter-day observation. The matter of how the codings were combined after the end of the fifth observation will be returned to at the end of Chapter 4 but it should be noted at this point that for a small

[2] It was for this very reason, that whenever a teacher enquired what the observer was seeking to observe, the answer given was to the effect that we were interested in everything done—a statement that was, in any case, as true as any brief explanation could be.

minority of items it was necessary to have a second 'summative form' to provide means of arriving at the final coding (see Appendix B).

The reader will note from Appendix A that the 43 variables of the 1977 version of the SCOTS schedule were grouped under six headings:

Items   1- 5: Items requiring information from both teacher and observation.
        6- 7: Direction/control of work.
       10-17: Teaching/learning.
       18-26: Motivation, control, and discipline.
       27-36: Organisational variables.
       37-43: Teacher personality and relationships with pupils.

These headings were of some help to the observers in locating particular items, but they will not be used in this chapter. Instead the items will be grouped in accord with the way in which they were subsequently grouped in the course of the data analysis. (In this latter set of groups, the items in a group are linked not only by their relating to a common area but by the fact that these particular groupings proved a useful means of pointing to similarities and dissimilarities between 'clusters' of teachers.[3]) These groups of items relate to the following areas:

		Items
1)	Teaching Skills	4, 10-15
2)	Feedback and individual aid	16-17
3)	Pupil interest and motivation	18, 21, 22, 39
4)	Development of responsibility	6, 7, 9, 20, 34-36
5)	Level aimed at	5
6)	Grouping	2, 3, 31-33
7)	Efficiency of management	25, 27-30
8)	Authoritarianism and coercion	8, 24
9)	Class control	37, 42, 43
10)	Relationships with pupils	19, 40, 41

Items 1,23,26 and 38 were found to fit into none of these groupings. (The reasons for this are discussed on pp 44-46.) The ten groups themselves provide a structure for the following commentary.

[3] Each 'cluster' contains those teachers that, over all, were found to resemble one another most closely in respect of the 43 SCOTS variables.

COMMENTARY ON THE ITEMS OF THE SCHEDULE[4]

Although this commentary is written in a way helpful to those who wish to employ the SCOTS schedule themselves, its primary purpose is to assist the reader to study, and become familiar with, the schedule itself and with the frequently speculative ideas underlying its items. *It is, therefore, essential to read it in conjunction with the schedule itself (Appendices A and B).*

ITEMS RELATING TO TEACHING SKILLS

Item 4: Variation of Treatment According to Pupil Needs

This variable relates to the extent to which the teacher varies his treatment of pupils to meet what he perceives to be their individual instructional needs—eg, by varying type of explanation, amount of reinforcement, or type of materials used. Such variation of instruction does not necessarily involve the use of individualised or even group instruction. (Nor does the use of individualised or group work necessarily indicate that pupils are treated according to their needs, for such variation of treatment is not itself necessarily matched to needs.) The prerequisite of such matching is that the teacher be aware of children's differences.

It follows from this that, when the observer talks to the teacher after the fourth observation, the object is to discover whether any variation in treatment that has been observed to occur is based upon a perception of difference of individual need, of individual learning style, etc. The reason for observers' noting in the spaces provided in the schedule specific examples of difference of treatment is that these examples can be used as the basis of the discussion with the teacher: by enquiring why the differentiation is made the observer seeks to assess how far the teacher sees a need to differentiate amongst pupils in terms of their needs. Differentiation in terms of difficulty level only is *not* however to be regarded as differentiation for the purposes of this item.

Observational clues that may be useful include:

1) amount of time teacher gives to selected individuals/groups within the class

---

[4] Some clarification of certain terms used in relation to the schedule may be necessary. The schedule has 43 *items* each relating to a single *variable*. Since the variation is in most cases defined on a 5-point scale, the observer has usually five *options* to choose from when coding teacher or class in respect of that variable, each option constituting one of the *categories* or scale-points. In some contexts, the terms *item* and *variable* are virtually interchangeable, as are *option* and *category*.

2) whether level of concreteness or abstraction varies according to pupil ability or learning style

3) whether the type of questioning—eg, the extent to which it is open-ended—is varied according to perceived individual need.

For obvious reasons, the coding of this variable is very difficult until after the discussion with the teacher (ie, after the fourth observation). It is at the discretion of the observer whether to make any *provisional* coding(s) before this point. The final coding, made after the fifth observation, is based on a single evaluation of all the evidence available.

Item 10: Integration of Subject Matter

This variable is concerned with the compartmentalisation of knowledge and its opposite, seeing all knowledge as one and consequently trying to integrate learning from different subject areas to achieve the maximum cross-fertilisation. This integration will be achieved by either recalling for children (or encouraging them to recall) aspects of previous knowledge that will aid understanding of present work. Reference to individuals' private store of knowledge, such as particular hobbies, is likely to be encouraged by the teacher. The *relevance* of knowledge and its application to disparate parts of life (home, school, work, play etc) will almost certainly be stressed and the critical testing of relevance encouraged.

There is a critical distinction, of which the observer must be aware, between *superficial* and *meaningful* integration. Art and project-work are two areas where superficial integration is particularly likely to occur—eg, when a project, while perhaps unavoidably impinging on various subject areas, is *not* operated in such a way that clear links are established between elements of the project-work and the specific elements of the classwork, *or* when the project in effect involves simply doing more history.

This variable is one that gives rise to special difficulties for the observers, since even teachers whose work involves a quite high level of integration may on many occasions operate with none, at least overtly. In short, when observation is limited to only five quarter-day observations (as it was in the fieldwork in 1977/78), this variable does give rise to serious problems of sampling teachers' general practice.

It is in recognition of this difficulty that this item is not coded until all five observations are complete. (Only the summative form of the schedule (see Appendix B) contains the coding options. The classroom form (viz that in Appendix A) provides only provision for recording instances of integration when they occur.)

Item 11: Teaching for Memorisation/Understanding.

It appears to be almost universally accepted by teachers that pupils should be able to recall accurately at least some facts, ideas, etc. Where they tend to differ most obviously is in whether they see memorisation as necessarily the result of rote-learning, or as a product of acquiring understanding. Of course, many teachers do not regard these two ways of memorising as mutually exclusive, and many see a combination of the two as indeed desirable. Perhaps one of the more important issues is whether they see understanding as being of importance in its own right.

NOTE: After the completion of the 1977/78 observations it was found from the inter-observer reliability data that there was insufficient observer agreement in distinguishing categories 2 and 3 and therefore for the purpose of the subsequent analysis these two categories were amalgamated (see page 62). Thus all codings of 2 became 3 and all codings of 1 were renumbered as 2. [5]

Item 12: Encouragement/Prevention of Difference.

This variable relates, in essence, to whether the teacher encourages or indeed permits independence of thinking on the part of pupils. A teacher who, for instance, says to a pupil, 'Yes, that is the right answer, but that is *not* the way I told you to do it' is in effect inhibiting independent thinking and seeking a rigidly uniform performance in all his pupils. He is, moreover, encouraging convergent thinking at the expense of creativity and the depth of understanding that can come from thinking something out for oneself. It is important to distinguish such a teacher from another who might, for instance, say, 'That was clever of you to think out your own way of doing that, but can you see why it may lead you to go wrong?', for this latter teacher will be trying to help the pupil to discover for himself whether the method earlier demonstrated by the teacher was better or merely different.

NOTE: In 1977/78, inadequate agreement between observers in making the distinction between options 2 and 3 led to the combining of these two categories by recoding all 2's as 3's. 1's were

---

[5] In all cases where amalgamations of categories proved necessary these are shown in Appendix A in the left-hand margin.

exceptionally not recoded in order not to diminish what was seen as a major distinction.

Item 13: Teacher's Mode of Cognitive Questioning.

This variable specifically relates to questioning in the cognitive (but *not* the affective) domain. It is primarily concerned with whether the questioning is merely nominal—a means of the teacher's saying what he is determined to say no matter what answer is received (see option 1) or with whether questioning is used by the teacher such as to require thinking on the part of the pupils questioned (see options 4 and 5).

Allowance does of course have to be made for the fact that nearly all teachers make some use of questions that fall into categories 1 or 2. Accordingly, where high-level questioning occurs, high-level questioning is coded despite the fact that lower level questioning occurs as well.

Item 14: Clarity of Exposition of Basic Principles.

Clarity of exposition obviously depends on the teacher's own thorough understanding of what he has to teach as well as on his taking into account his pupils' existing state of knowledge. However, the observer's primary difficulty in respect of this variable is not so much making an assessment as obtaining enough evidence on which to base one.

NOTE: Teaching new work is not a frequent undertaking, and therefore when a teacher's teaching is sampled on a mere five occasions it is something readily missed.(In any case, many teachers probably saw teaching new work as something 'too risky' to undertake before an observer.) Accordingly, by the time the 1977/78 observations were undertaken, it was recognised that considerable reliance would have to be placed on a less infrequent activity, the re-teaching of individuals or groups that had not adequately understood earlier teaching. Even with this, however, there were problems: such instruction was not always audible from where the observer was placed, or, in some cases, even at short range. The result was that in some cases the observers were short of adequate evidence on which to base an assessment. For individual observations where no evidence was found, a coding of zero was used. In the last resort it was used also for the final assessment. Often such positive codings as were made were based on quite a small number of instances. The assumption that these instances

24

were typical of the teacher's general practice may not in all cases have been justified.

Item 15: Teacher Variety and Inventiveness of Explanation

This variable is complementary to the preceding one. (That it too has a 'zero' category points to the fact that it gives rise to the same problems of obtaining enough evidence to make a satisfactory coding.) Whereas item 14 concentrates on the *clarity* of the teacher's exposition, this one goes a step further by looking to see how skilled the teacher is in providing alternative explanations when an initial one—however good in itself—has failed in the case of at least some of the pupils. (It is a skill that is likely to depend both on an ability to perceive what a pupil's difficulties arise from and on a degree of inventiveness in finding alternative ways of explaining a point.)

NOTE: Because of inadequate inter-observer agreement in drawing the distinction between categories 2 and 3, these were combined, all 2's being recoded as 3's. 1's were then recoded as 2's.

ITEMS RELATING TO FEEDBACK AND INDIVIDUAL AID

Item 16: Nature of Teacher Contacts with Individual Pupils.

Two basic types of teacher-pupil interaction of an instructional nature are defined in the schedule as options 1 and 2. Since the first type occurs with virtually all teachers, the interest lies mainly not in its occurrence but in its relative frequency. In the case of the second option however there is an additional point of interest: whether it occurs at all.

It is for this reason that observers record (by using an appropriate number of ticks) the number of occurrences of each of the two sorts of instructional interaction. Only after the final (ie, fifth) observation is an overall coding made on a five-point scale. (This five-point scale is set out in Appendix B, p 207.)

The following excerpt from the guidelines used by the observers clarifies a number of important issues:

> The aim is to assess the extent to which the teacher uses individualised instruction as a teaching mode, taking account of the depth of this instruction.
>
> *Note:* Answering simple questions, giving instructions to individuals, making comments, classifying previously given instructions, and giving reminders of what was previously taught to the class (or group) are to be ignored for the purposes of

C   25

recording this variable since their occurrence is judged to be virtually universal.

Definition of "Quasi-individual instruction"

Quasi-individual instruction is deemed to occur when—

1) in a group situation the instruction is focussed solely on one individual pupil and his needs, and the remainder of the group is, therefore, little more than an audience; the special needs of the other group members are not being taken into account.

   OR

2) The needs of a very small group (of up to four pupils, or very exceptionally, five or six pupils) are so near to identical that the teacher may be regarded as conducting individual instruction simultaneously with each individual in the group.

Reading

The *hearing* of reading gives rise to special problems since it may be difficult to determine whether this even constitutes individual instruction. Where the reading aloud is simply heard and instruction is restricted to the correction of inaccuracies in the reading or to prompting, it should *not* be regarded as individualised instruction. Only when the questioning/instruction passes beyond this should it be regarded as individualised instruction.

Item 17: Feedback to Pupils.

The most common form of feedback to pupils is the marking or correction of work by the teacher, but pupils may obtain at least some feedback on their own if they have access to correct answers against which to check their own work.

Feedback may be provided at the time the work in question is being undertaken by the pupil. This is *concurrent* feedback. Other feedback comes later when, for example, the teacher has marked work overnight. This is *retrospective* feedback. (For purposes of recording only, the two are dealt with separately in items 17a and 17b. For their subsequent combination, see below.)

Concurrent and retrospective feedback complement each other, but for the purposes of observation it is necessary to distinguish the one from the other. Indeed much of the retrospective feedback can be seen by the observer only by examining jotters and exercise books that have been previously marked by the teacher, though it is sometimes possible to observe how this marked work is returned to the pupils and whether it is accompanied by instructional comments delivered to pupils either individually or collectively. Concurrent feedback, of course, is all directly observable.

Concurrent feedback has the obvious advantage of immediacy, of being provided just when the relevant ideas or problems are in the pupils' minds, and permits the immediate removal of misunderstandings. Moreover retrospective feedback may often suffer from the disadvantage that pupils make little real use of it (eg, when they look only at the mark awarded or the brief comment of approbation or disapprobation that may have been added to it.) It is therefore important for the observer to pay attention not only to the thoroughness and usefulness of the marking undertaken by the teacher but what steps are taken by the teacher to help or encourage the pupil to learn from the corrections/comments/instructions provided.

Concurrent feedback can, however, be provided not only with widely differing degrees of skill but with widely differing degrees of efficiency. If the system of feedback is not efficient, many pupils will get the feedback they need either too late or not at all.

Retrospective feedback provided after long delay is likely to be diminished in relevance and usefulness to pupils. It is therefore necessary when assessing quality of the feedback to take into account the length of time lapse before written work is returned to pupils, though, in so doing, allowance must be made for the nature of the marking being undertaken—eg, for the greater amount of time required to mark essays with care.

The SCOTS schedule makes provision for the combining of the assessments for concurrent and retrospective feedback after final overall assessments have been made for each of them separately after the fifth observation. The method of combining the two is shown in Appendix B (p 207). It does, it will be noted, allow for less of one type of feedback to be compensated for, to some extent, by more of the other, and it thus makes due allowance for the complementary nature of the two.

Note: The seven-point scale for the combined codings was, in 1977/78 reduced to an effective five-point scale by combining codings of 3 and 4 as 4, and codings of 1 and 2 as 3.

ITEMS RELATING TO PUPIL INTEREST AND MOTIVATION

Item 18: Teaching (or Teaching Situation) Stimulative or Dull.

Coding this item involves observing the pupils to judge their reactions to the teaching—or the teaching situation—in so far as it

27

is manifested in their behaviour, for observers have to avoid judging pupils' reactions by their own. (Of course, observers often do share the feelings of pupils, especially in the case of the most stimulating of teachers. Pupils appear to suffer dullness more gladly than observers!)

When the teaching is centred on the teacher, judging the responses of pupils is relatively straight-forward, in that overt responses from the pupils tend to follow closely on what the teacher says and does. When the learning involves pupils' studying alone, this is not the case (save in respect of interactions between teacher and individual pupils): consequently the general response to the learning situation set up by the teacher has to be judged more largely by reference to pupils' sustained reactions—keenness, lassitude etc—to the work undertaken.

Item 21: Extrinsic/Intrinsic Motivation

Extrinsic motivators—marks, points, rewards of one sort or another—are easily observable, and it is fairly easy to see whether they are employed by the teacher sufficiently actively to have any significant effect on pupils. Intrinsic motivation—that arising directly from undertaking the work in hand—is quite a different matter. In fact, it can only be inferred to exist when pupils are manifestly motivated in the absence of any source of extrinsic motivation. It follows from this that where intrinsic and extrinsic motivation are operating simultaneously, the former may not be identified by an observer.

It is to be noted that this variable is concerned with the *type* of motivation, not its degree (save in the case of the 'zero' category— which has to be available, since it is impossible to assess the type of motivation if the pupils appear unmotivated).

Item 22: Competition

This variable is concerned with whether the teacher deliberately employs competition as a motivator. (As the researchers have reason to know—see p 132—competition can arise that is pupil-initiated rather than teacher-initiated.) It seeks to measure the degree of teacher-initiated competition experienced by the pupils.

When the options for this variable were being devised, it was recognised that two distinct types of competition can occur. The first is *competition with others*, ie, competition where the relative success of one pupil implies the relative failure of another. (Such competition with others is referred to in the descriptors for this variable as 'cut-throat'—a term that implies the possibility of some pupils' being 'hurt'.) The second type of competition recognised is that sort where the competition is with oneself, the sort where one is seeking to do better than previously or even pursuing excellence. (Since this sort of competition involves attempting to achieve some specific level of performance, it was termed 'criterion-referenced'.)

It might appear from what has been said of this variable so far that it lacks unidimensionality in that it relates to both degree and kind. However, it was assumed when the schedule was constructed that in this case there is a direct relationship between degree and kind, that the type of competition determines its severity—in short that 'cut-throat' competition constitutes a potentially more stressful competitive situation for a pupil than does 'criterion-referenced'.

It is important, nonetheless, to realise that when observers are coding this variable they have to have clearly in mind that the line of variation that they are recording extends from severe (and possibly damaging) competition between pupils, through 'friendly' competition between pupils and thereafter 'criterion-referenced' competition, to a point where competition is trivial or non-existent.

It is perhaps worthwhile at this stage to make a point to which it will be necessary to return later, namely that the variables of the SCOTS schedule are essentially descriptive despite the fact that it is possible to see them as extending from 'good' to 'bad'. It is important to remember that an extreme that may be seen by one person as 'good' may be seen by another as 'bad', and that the midpoint may be seen by a third as the optimum. Every reader may place his own value judgements: the descriptive options in the schedule are themselves neutral.

Item 39: Negative/Positive Approach.

This variable may at first seem to be the odd one out in this group, for it seems to be focussed on how the teacher acts, whereas the others have been centred on the interest and motivation aroused in pupils. Nonetheless this variable is in fact one relating closely to the level of pupil motivation. It is, of course, built on an assumption, namely that there is a relationship between, on the one hand, laying emphasis either on error and failure or on success, and, on the other, the level of motivation. It was indeed the assumption of the authors of the schedule that constant criticism is for most pupils demotivating and that praise judiciously used is supportive of confidence and motivating. They remained neutral, however, on what might be the optimum position on this continuum from the negativeness of constant criticism to the positiveness of never-ending reinforcement. The options provided are in any case purely descriptive and do not in themselves impose any value judgement. The reader may place his own value judgements where he will; it was one of the tasks of the researchers to find, if possible, relationships with outcomes.

ITEMS RELATING TO THE DEVELOPMENT OF RESPONSIBILITY

It has often been seen as an important aim of education to develop in pupils both a desire to act responsibly and skill in doing so. Hence this group of items seeks to record elements in teachers' practice that, intentionally or unintentionally, have a bearing on this development.

Item 6: Directness of Teacher Control of Learning Activities

Most teachers see it as their duty to control pupils' activities so that they are enabled to learn effectively. Not all of them, however, seek to do so by direct means such as the issuing of instructions.

This variable is therefore concerned with whether teachers seek to control/influence pupils' work activities *directly*, by use of instructions, or *indirectly*, by training pupils to depend on their own judgement and initiative in working and maintaining a work flow. It thus relates not to the teacher's control of what work is covered but to *how* this control is achieved.

It is particularly important to note that this variable in no way provides a measure of effectiveness of control. The fact that a teacher controls directly is no guarantee of his controlling effectively. On the other hand, the fact of pupils' being self-supporting and pursuing work even in the absence of the teacher can be used by observers as evidence of indirect control having been established.

Clearly the extent to which a teacher seeks to control directly may reflect not only his wish so to do but also his success in training and/or inducing pupils to work without being dependent on constant direction: a teacher who fails to train and/or motivate pupils adequately may therefore be forced to control more directly than he would wish.

Item 7: Pupil Responsibility for Managing Own Work.

This item needs to be carefully distinguished from the preceding one. It seeks to measure the degree of responsibility given to pupils in managing the work allocated to them, and thus how far they are responsible for how long they spend on each sub-unit of work and the order in which they undertake tasks allocated.

It is of course possible to conceive of schools where work is not allocated by teachers at all, and in such schools it would be impracticable to code classes on this variable. This was, however, a difficulty not encountered in any of the classes visited during both main phases of this research.

Item 9: Teacher Pressure on Pupils to Secure Work

This item is intended to measure the amount of pressure exerted on pupils by the teacher, *not* the amount of work secured. Thus, for example, a teacher whose constant pressure is ineffectual is nonetheless coded as 1, and a teacher coded as 5 on account of his exercising no pressure may have an industrious class with high work standards.

It is of course the case that only *overt* pressure can be recorded. Where there is little or no overt pressure to record, two fundamentally different situations may exist, namely the situation where there is genuinely no pressure on pupils and the situation where, although the teacher is doing almost nothing to exert pressure, there is a pervading pressure operating—perhaps the result of some action taken by the teacher before the arrival of the observer, perhaps the result of a psychological relationship established earlier. It is clear that, under these circumstances, a glance from the teacher may exert more real pressure than overt pressure great enough to justify a coding of 1. Unfortunately there is no way in which, in specific cases, the observer can be sure enough that such covert pressure is operating to justify taking it into account in the coding arrived at. This item has therefore an inherent limitation.

There may, of course, be some need to justify including this item in a group of items relating to the development of responsible conduct in pupils. The reason for its inclusion is that if a teacher secures application of work from his pupils solely by the exercise of pressure, he is not helping them to become people capable of making demands on themselves.[6]

[6] Perhaps too much should not be made of this point. Even the most conscientious of us may from time to time need some pressure to overcome lassitude, whether this pressure be personal or (as when a situation itself demands a response from us) impersonal. Moreover some experience in accommodating external pressure may be necessary.

Item 20: Fostering a Sense of Responsibility

Giving pupils duties to perform—giving out jotters, running a class library, etc—may, obviously, serve either or both of two functions: to save the teacher some work and to give pupils experience and training in the exercise of responsibility.

As almost all teachers have at least some of their pupils carry out such duties, the observer's task is to concentrate on finding answers to the following questions (on the basis of which answers he can arrive at a coding):

Do all pupils have duties to perform at least intermittently?

On what basis are pupils selected and duties allocated?

Is the teacher more concerned about getting the duties performed satisfactorily than about helping pupils to perform them responsibly, or is the opposite the case?

Although some teachers are probably inhibited by their own feelings of insecurity relative to maintaining good order in class from allocating responsibility to pupils, the majority seem to act as if they held one of the following beliefs:

a) Pupils are incapable of behaving really responsibly. Training them for responsibility is, therefore, useless and close supervision of their undertaking any duties is essential. (These teachers fall into category 1 or 2.)

b) It is important for jobs to be done efficiently, and responsibility should therefore be given only to those who are likely to be both interested and efficient. (These teachers fall into category 3.)

c) All pupils can act responsibly and it is the duty of teachers to see that all pupils are given some responsibility, even at the cost of some loss of efficiency and of some additional burden on the teacher. (These teachers fall into category 4 or 5.)

Although this item is not one where asking the teacher for information is prescribed, it is one where in some cases evidence derived from observation may need to be supplemented by the teacher's responses to questions—probably after the fourth observation—about his policy in allocating responsibilities.

It is to be noted that observers can obtain much of the evidence needed for coding this variable by noting the words used by the teacher when allocating duties. (This is, of course, very frequently the case with other variables also.) Wall charts, if any, relating to the allocation of duties are another important source of evidence: these may well be the object of some questions directed to the teachers.

Item 34: Encouragement/Prevention of Inter-Pupil Co-operation.

Clearly this variable is not unrelated to item 25 (Competition), which has already been dealt with under 'Interest and Motivation'. The type of competition that has been defined as 'cut-throat' is likely to be, in most instances, incompatible with promotion of inter-pupil co-operation. 'Criterion-referenced' competition, on the other hand, is not incompatible with such co-operation. It is important to bear in mind, nonetheless, that neither the use of 'criterion-referenced' competition nor the absence of any form of competition guarantees the presence of inter-pupil co-operation.

Clearly co-operative learning is a context in which pupil responsibility can be developed. However, co-operation may be encouraged by some teachers not for this reason but because they believe it to be a good way for children to learn, at least some of the time, and, similarly, some teachers who see co-operative learning as possibly a good thing in itself may reject it because they feel that it may give rise to disorder or because they believe that some pupils will use the situation as a shield for laziness and non-application. It might, therefore, be questioned whether there are adequate grounds for classifying this item with others relating to the development of pupil responsibility. The reason for its being so classified is that those who sought in other ways to develop responsibility were found to be more likely than others to permit (though not necessarily encourage) co-operation. Developing responsibility in children implies trusting them.

Those who do not trust children are unlikely to see inter-pupil co-operation as an acceptable risk, but neither are they likely to see as an acceptable risk giving children the freedom of action (in other contexts) that it is necessary for them to have if they are to be able to exercise responsibility to a significant degree.

Item 35: Constraint on Pupil Movement

The extent of the need for pupils to move about the classroom at their own volition obviously varies in accordance with other factors, such as whether inter-pupil co-operation is permitted. Nonetheless, in all classrooms there are occasions when, most teachers would agree, there is justification for pupils to leave their seats. Whether these necessary movements are permitted without specific authorisation by the teacher in every instance is therefore very much a matter of whether the teacher trusts the pupils to move only for good reason. Those who see it as desirable to promote pupil responsibility have therefore an opportunity to use pupil movement as a context in which to do so. The options have been, for this reason, drafted in such a way that the movement permitted is measured not only by the range of purposes for which movement is permitted but in terms of the level of trust involved.

Item 36: Freedom of Access to Resources.

This is yet another case where level of responsibility and of trust go hand in hand. There is, however, one complication: teachers are themselves responsible for ensuring that materials are not wasted and frequently also, where provision is less than adequate, to make a little go a long way. In short, they have to reconcile their personal responsibility with any wish they may have to delegate responsibility to pupils. The observer therefore has to ask himself whether restrictions are limited—and to what extent—with the object of permitting pupils to exercise responsibility.

NOTE: On account of inadequate inter-observer agreement in 1977/78, it proved necessary to amalgamate categories 3 and 4. 4's were recoded as 3's, and thereafter 5's as 4's.

LEVEL AIMED AT

For this area, there is but one schedule item.

Item 5: Teacher Philosophy (relating to cognitive outcomes).

Coding this variable depends to an unusually high degree on what the teachers say of their objectives. Observation can be used only to check whether practice is consistent with what has been stated.

Note: The fact that it was found feasible to have no more than three categories had the inevitable result of giving this variable a very low weighting in the cluster analysis described in Chapter 7.

GROUPING

Some general comments on grouping have already been made (see pp 6-7).

Items 2 and 3: Number of Work Difficulty Levels

Since teachers' practice is likely to vary from one subject area to another, the two subject areas to which most class-time is known to be devoted (Arithmetic/Maths and English) are covered.

It is important to recognise that, while different work difficulty levels *may* correspond to segments of a class operating as groups, they do not necessarily do so. Indeed having differing difficulty levels for different pupils is entirely compatible with operating a complete class as a single instructional unit. Difference in difficulty level may relate only to the difficulty of the examples worked at by the pupils—eg, easier and more difficult multiplication sums for different members of the class. Those working at a particular difficulty level—either permanently or temporarily—do not necessarily form a group in terms of any other criterion and they are not treated as 'groups' for the purposes of the SCOTS schedule. (Teaching groups are dealt with in items 31 and 32—see below.)

Observers are, of course, faced with practical difficulties (in so far as observation contributes to the coding of this item) when the class is operated on a group basis and the groups work at any one time in different subjects areas, for to establish the number of work difficulty levels the work of the class *within a subject area* has to be viewed as a whole despite its not occurring simultaneously. (There is, for example, the possibility that like work at the same difficulty level will be undertaken by different groups at different times within a period of two or three days.)

In so far as teachers' practice in respect of the number of difficulty levels for a particular subject varies from time to time, the final code arrived at after the fifth observation has to be that number most commonly occurring. Since teachers have to be questioned on this matter, the codings arrived at are heavily dependent on what they say.

Items 31 and 32: Size of Teaching Groups

As in the case of Number of Work Difficulty Levels, some variation was expected in different subject areas, and the same two subject areas were taken for investigation. In this case, however, each was given only half weight in the subsequent cluster analysis (see p 251).

Framing the options for this item gave rise to problems relating to whether to define categories in terms of number of groups or of group size. The former clearly relates the better to the teacher's organisational problems, whereas the latter has more to do with the type of learning experience pupils in the class typically have. The choice made was in fact one constrained by the need to cope with differing class size. If number of groups were to be the basis of classification, the size of group within each category would vary considerably according to class size; if the size of groups were the basis, the number of groups would vary considerably within each category, again according to class size. In the event, the latter course was chosen—as can readily be seen from the definitions of categories 3-5. The definitions of categories 1 and 2 may seem at variance with this principle. However, it will be realised that it is in fact impracticable to define a group size for category 1 if all five categories are to be possible codings for all classes irrespective of their size. By defining category 1 as relating to classes taught as a whole, one is identifying a) teaching a large group (large even in a relatively small class) and b) approximately uniform instruction for all pupils. Similarly by defining category 2 as relating to classes taught in two groups, one is in fact covering the case of fairly large groups and only limited differentiation. In short, it is believed that by defining these categories in these two ways one is in fact securing as consistent a basis as possible for the differentiation of all five categories.

The notes appended to these two items make it clear that groupings of a temporary nature (eg, separate instruction for a pupil who has been absent) or ones of an exceptional nature (eg, individual instruction for exceptionally backward pupils—or for those presenting behaviour difficulties—in classes otherwise run on a large group basis) should *not* be taken into account when calculating the average size of instructional group. It is regrettable —but inevitable—that classes with most unequal group sizes and others with approximate equal ones are classified together if their average size falls within the same range.

Item 33: Variety of Activities

This item is concerned with the degree of differentiation of activities *at any one time* when grouping is employed. Thus, if the class always operates as a single group, one should expect there to be no such differentiation. If a class operates as a number of groups there *may* be different activities going on simultaneously, but not necessarily.

A class operating with a number of simultaneous activities might, for example, have one group engaged in arithmetic, one in English, one in reading, and one in working on a project. In such a case, coding the number of activities presents no problem, but obviously cases can arise when it may be difficult to determine whether the work of two particular groups does or does not

36

constitute two activities. Thus, for example, when two groups are working at any one time in the same subject area, a decision has to be made as to whether the work is sufficiently different to justify regarding the groups as having different activities. Difference in difficulty level alone is specifically excluded as a basis for such differentiation, but one group working on, say, percentages would be deemed to be engaged in a different activity from one of working on the use of brackets in arithmetic expressions.

The justification for incorporating this variable in the schedule is that a) it highlights the extent of the organisational problem with which the teacher is coping, or attempting to cope, and b) it is an indicator of the extent of the operational independence of the groups, since a number of activities cannot be supervised as closely as one.

Of course the number of simultaneous activities in a class is liable to vary over time: even classes with a large number of activities at one time may operate as a single group at another. During the 1977/78 observations the resulting coding difficulty was resolved as follows:

a) where variation occurred in the course of a single observation, the coding *for that observation* was based on that number of simultaneous activities that was predominant during the observation

b) for purposes of providing a summative coding, the codings for each of the five observations were treated as points (category 1 = 1 point, category 2 = 2 points, etc) and the points for the five observations were totalled. Appendix B (p 208) shows the number of points required for each 'summative' category and a statement of what the number of points indicates in each case. In the case of a summative coding of 5, it will be noted, at least one initial coding of 5 is a pre-requisite.

ITEMS RELATING TO EFFICIENCY OF MANAGEMENT

The first four of the five items in this group in effect define the teacher's efficiency in management in terms of how well pupils use, or are able to use, their time.

Item 25: Application to Work / Work Avoidance

This item is concerned with whether the teacher operates his class such as to prevent or effectively discourage work avoidance by pupils and with whether he is successful in inducing pupils to be industrious.

The 'isolated exceptions' referred to in option 5 should be taken to include: a) occasional deviations from the patterns of behaviour that have been observed to be normal and b) individual pupils that are clearly special cases (eg, pupils of very low ability or ones that are markedly disturbed). The 'distinctive minority' referred to in option 4 should be taken to refer to a group apparently differing from the rest of the class only in respect of the deviance of its behaviour.

Item 27: Unemployment and Underemployment of Pupils

This item is concerned with whether the teacher operates his class in such a way that the pupils cannot avoid being unoccupied at times and/or underoccupied at others.

Loss of time covered in Item 28 is to be ignored for the purposes of this item.

Item 28: Time-lag Between Activities

Even in a class that displays neither work avoidance nor unemployment/underemployment in other respects, changing from one work activity to another—whether by the whole class or groups within the class—can give rise to unnecessary loss of time and even imperil teacher control.

The avoidance of time-lags between activities may depend directly on the actions taken by the teacher or on the pupils' having had previous training in self-management. Having materials readily available when they are needed is likely to be a factor in all cases.

In coding this variable, observers have to make allowance for factors beyond the teacher's control—eg, another teacher's having failed to make a piece of equipment available at a previously agreed time.

Item 29: Mode of Performing Administrative Functions

There is a wide variation in the ways in which teachers perform routine administrative functions, such as checking attendance, collecting lunch money, and class dismissal. Collecting lunch money, for instance, may, at one extreme, be undertaken while teaching is proceeding, pupils coming out with their money in response perhaps to a tiny nod or even (in a prescribed order) without any signal at all. At the other extreme, the whole operation may be ritualised, take a considerable time, and preclude any other useful activity.

The former of these two extremes obviously requires that the teacher should be able to perform efficiently at least two tasks simultaneously, and that early in the school year he should have given instruction to pupils in how the system is to operate. It probably also depends on class control functioning without effort. Reasons for ritualisation may well be various, but a likely one is securing class control, for the emphasis is on doing things in the way the teacher prescribes. Ritualisation is, however, usually a time-consuming procedure.

Whether, for example, lining-up at the door before dismissal should be taken into account in coding this item depends on whether it is done at the teacher's instigation or is a school rule. It is to be noted, however, that teachers who ritualise one administrative function are very likely to ritualise others also.

It would be unwise to underestimate the amount of time that can be absorbed in ritualisation, particularly of frequently repeated functions such as the distribution and collection of books and materials. Moreover, although ritualisation can be used as a means of underlining the teacher's authority, it has to be recognised that the delays can provide opportunities for misconduct to start.

What has been said so far may suggest that ritualisation is most likely to occur when the teacher's control is direct rather than indirect. However, it is compatible with 'indirect' control and/or 'pupil-centredness'. In the latter case, however, its manifestations are likely to be different. In particular, it may show itself in pupils' being required to perform certain operations in an elaborated and time-consuming way even though they may do so in their own time rather than at a given moment.

Item 30: Extent of Teacher Attention to Class

In the first four items in this group of variables there has been some tendency to equate administrative efficiency with the avoidance of time-wasting and thus to imply that a 'high' coding (a 4 or a 5) is better than a lower one. There is no such tendency in this item, for, while most would regard it as desirable for a teacher to be well aware of what is going on in his class, some—or perhaps many—would see the teacher who appears 'never to miss a thing' to be oppressive.

It may, of course, be a good thing for a teacher to be aware of more than he reveals, and particularly so in the context of this item, which relates to awareness of pupils' progress with work as well as of their behaviour.

The fact that some teachers do not reveal that they have noticed as much as they in fact have is, of course, a problem for observers seeking to code this item. They do therefore have to be alert for signs of the teacher's having been aware of things to which he has not reacted at the time. Talking with the teacher may, it should be noted, reveal occasions when a blind eye has been turned.

ITEMS RELATING TO AUTHORITARIANISM AND COERCION

The two items in this group operate in two distinct contexts—choice of work and class control—but both reflect a single view of what the relationship between teacher and pupil should be.

Item 8: Authoritarian/Democratic Practices

It seems to be the case that most teachers have a reasonably clear idea of what work they wish their classes to cover. Nevertheless they differ in respect of whether they impose their will on the class overtly. Some, of course, do see it as important that pupils should make choices—though most are likely, at the least, to monitor these choices and endeavour to secure by one means or other that these choices are 'wise' ones. In view of this, this item is more concerned with whether the pupils have the impression that they are making effective choices than with whether these choices are in fact influenced by the teacher. It might be said to be concerned with whether the class has an authoritarian or a democratic atmosphere.

That only one category—5—should record that the pupils' choices are 'more than nominal' in respect of what is to be studied reflects the fact that earlier work in this project revealed that few, if any, teachers allowed choice at this level and that it was therefore better to try to distinguish variation in practice at a lower level of freedom. (It is necessary, however, to stress that more than a small minority of teachers had been found willing to accept pupil choice where the programme of work was not affected, eg, choices about whether this story or that should be read, or about whether task A should precede task B, or vice versa.)

Item 24: Teachers' Mode of Exercising Control

This item is concerned *not* with whether the teacher secures a satisfactory level of disciplinary control but with the means he employs to secure it. The line of variation recorded extends from deterrence to persuasion and, ultimately, to self-control. Thus, as well as relating to means of control, it highlights a co-variant: the type of relationship between teacher and pupil. The descriptors used endeavour to cope with the problem presented by the fact that some teachers seek to control parts of their classes in substantially different ways.

ITEMS RELATING TO CLASS CONTROL

Item 37: Teacher Overt Anxiety/Calmness

This variable is concerned with the atmosphere in which pupils work. It is *not* concerned, for instance, with deep personal anxieties which might underlie, say, a teacher's very calm exterior. A tendency to over-react to error, minor mishaps, or minor breaches of discipline are common signs of teacher anxiety—signs of which pupils are aware.

The decision to record *overt* anxiety in this way was based on the plausible supposition that some, if not all, pupils would learn better under calm and predictable conditions.[7]

Note: Lack of adequate inter-observer agreement led to the amalgamation of categories 3 and 4 (as 3) and to the renumbering of 5 as 4.

Item 42: Teacher Hostility

A teacher's speaking to pupils in a hostile way is, in almost every case, a response to what the teacher perceives as a threat to his control. The response is not necessarily a *direct* reaction, since it is sometimes pre-emptive, an attempt to prevent the recurrence of conduct previously perceived as a threat to good order and control. Since this teacher hostility typically is manifested by those whose control is—or is felt to be—insecure, it is not suprising that it seldom achieves more than a short term disciplinary effect. Indeed it appears often to induce a hostile reaction or attitude from pupils, and thus to worsen the teacher's disciplinary control.

Pupil hostility is, of course, by no means always provoked by teacher hostility, but, whereas some teachers do react to it with hostility, others, with varying degrees of skill, seek to dissipate it or disarm it.

Since hostility either by or towards teachers implies that teachers and pupils are not 'pulling together', it appears very likely that a

---

[7] This decision was in accord with the essentially eclectic approach adopted in the selection of variables: any variable, irrespective of what body of theory it is related to, was selected if it might plausibly be related to pupil performance.

teacher's failure to control hostile feelings either in himself or in pupils will have a detrimental affect on his teaching.

If no sign of hostility appears on the part of either teacher or pupil, one cannot be sure whether this is due to absence of any threat from pupils or from teacher skill in avoiding any hostility arising. However, since interest lies primarily in whether teacher and pupils are at one or in conflict, there appears to be no disadvantage in both situations being covered by a single option (4).

Item 43: Degree of Teacher Control Achieved.

The extreme situations covered by options 1 and 2 are very rare. Indeed, since, during the observations in 1977/78, no teacher was placed in either category, there are good grounds for amalgamating categories 1 and 2—though it should be noted that one teacher who was observed during the initial preparation of the schedule did provide an empirical basis for the definition of category 1. There is, of course, a total lack of evidence on inter-observer reliability in respect of these two options, since they were not used by any observer while reliability was being measured.

It has to be noted that, during the 1977/78 observations, this variable was, with the exception of the special case of item 10, alone in being coded only after the five observations on a teacher had been completed. At the time it was thought that the assessment was so general that records in respect of each observation were unnecessary. This *may* have been in error in so far as it *may* have led to less use of categories 3 and 4 than would have otherwise have been the case.

It will be noted from perusal of the options that considerable emphasis is laid on whether any difficulties in maintaining control appear to have any adverse effect on the execution of the teacher's programme. Of course there are difficulties for observers in judging this matter, for, whereas one may be able to see failures to achieve what is attempted, one may not be able to take into account what is not even attempted because the teacher thinks himself unable to bring it off.

VARIABLES RELATING TO RELATIONSHIPS WITH PUPILS

Item 19: Teacher Sensitivity to Pupils' Self-confidence and/or Self-esteem

It is widely held that self-confidence—which is likely to be based on one's self-image and one's perception of the view(s) held of one by those others one judges to be significant people—is a state of mind that (provided it does not amount to over-confidence) is much to be desired both for one's own happiness and for its contribution to competence in learning and to performance in general. Yet teachers clearly differ widely in respect of whether they build up pupils' self-confidence or undermine it.

It was appreciated that those who do undermine the self-confidence of some or all of their pupils may do so inadvertently—simply through lack of sensitivity for the feelings of others.

Teachers' level of sensitivity may of course vary considerably in respect of different pupils in the class. The problem is, however, resolved by laying emphasis on the fact of insensitivity being displayed at all (save where the insensitivity relates to only a very small minority).

The following detailed points should be noted:

1) Whereas category 1 implies insensitivity to the degree of callousness, category 2 implies a lack of awareness only.

2) The phrase, 'of short duration' (category 3) implies that the effect on the pupil quickly declines (perhaps because of the over-all relationship between teacher and pupil) or that the teacher, having noticed a strong effect on the child, subsequently takes steps to compensate for it.

3) Category 5 does not imply that no criticism is offered but that any criticism that there is is offered with sensitivity and with due allowance for the individual pupil's current ability to accept constructive criticism.

Item 40: Pupil-Teacher Social Relationship

There is, inevitably, some sort of social (as distinct from instructional) relationship between the teacher and each pupil. It can vary from being very distant and formal to being informal and friendly.[x] Extreme distance is seen as best evidenced by pupils' avoiding any form of interaction with a teacher that they can avoid (option 1). At the level of option 2, interaction is not inhibited, but takes place in a formal, teacher-defined manner. Options 4 and 5 are characterised by the pupils' being keen to talk with the teacher about anything that interests or concerns them and by the teacher's showing pleasure in, or at least readily accepting, these approaches. The distinction between options 4 and 5 relates to whether the

[x] The two varying elements—formality and distance/friendliness—seem to co-vary closely enough for this item to operate unidimensionally.

43

teacher maintains a social inequality in the relationship, *not* with how friendly the relationship is. There is no implication intended that social distance is necessarily bad or that a coding of 5 is necessarily better than one of 4.

Item 41: Apparent Teacher Attitude to Class

If the teacher's 'real' attitude is different from his apparent one, it is a matter of no relevance for this item: what his attitude appears to be is, after all, what the pupil experiences. Although the observers in 1977/78 had therefore to interpret behaviour, there was in fact no problem relative to inter-observer reliability. This may result from the fact that these category definitions are only one step removed from being direct behavioural descriptors.

NOTE: It might be thought that item 24 (Coercion/Persuasion) would be best included in this group, for it has an obvious bearing on teacher-pupil relationships. However, the 1977/78 data gave greater support for linking it with Item 8 under the general heading of Authoritarianism and Coercion.

MISCELLANEOUS VARIABLES

Of the four remaining variables, two (26 and 38) were ambivalent in their significance, and, probably in consequence, showed little relationship to clusters—ie, there was no sign of any cluster 'norms'.[9] To some degree this was also the case with Item 1. Item 23, following an enforced amalgamation of two of its four categories, lost much of its utility through low variance.

All these reasons we shall explore more fully in the following paragraphs.

Item 26: Pupil Talk

This item was, when it was first devised, seen as a measure of teacher tolerance of noise. However, it is clear that whereas in some classes the noise level may be the result of a teacher's deliberate policy (in respect of whether he sees talking as associated with beneficial inter-pupil cooperation), in other cases it may represent the teacher's inability to maintain more than intermittent control of pupils' talking. Moreover, talking may be judged, even by the same teacher, as beneficial or harmful according to the circumstances

---

[9] Within-cluster variation was characteristic of most items, but, in all items but these two, there proved to be for many clusters a level shared by many, *though not all,* of its members.

and according to whether it is or is not work-related—and, in either case, by whether it promotes or endangers the success of the work itself. It is in this essential ambivalence that this item's weakness lies. It is also necessary to recall that the matter of inter-pupil co-operation is already itself covered by item 34.

Item 38: Noisy/Quiet Teacher

Much of the difficulty to which this item gives rise is probably related to the variance covered in this item having no uniform effect. The teacher who speaks very quietly may either be inaudible or may cause pupils to listen more carefully in order to hear. The noisy teacher may disturb pupil concentration, but does not necessarily do so. During the observations, pupils in general appeared able to shut out or ignore what they did not need to heed, but appeared also to be able to pick up at a peripheral or subliminal level clues as to when they should listen. Perhaps whether a teacher's speech is audible to those who do not need to hear it matters less than whether the message precedes or follows the indication of to whom it is addressed, for, if the former, the pupils have either to listen to everything or run the risk of missing what is intended for them. Whatever the validity of these speculations, there certainly appeared to be no consistent effect that could be related to the level of loudness of the teacher's speech, and that may well explain the lack of relationship with cluster membership or with any of the subsets of variables.

Item 23: The Use of Rational Argument

Some teachers give no reasons for their instructions or requests, some give a semblance of justification by giving explanations that are too vague or too general to carry conviction ('useful when you grow up' etc), and some put forward the best case that they can argue. This item therefore seems to belong to the group of items relating to authoritarianism and coercion.

Unfortunately categories 2 and 3 had to be amalgamated after the 1977/78 observations on account of inadequate inter-observer agreement, and this in turn led to very low variance, the vast majority of cases falling into the combined category. Thus unless this item can be improved, it serves little useful purpose in the schedule.

Item 1: Visible Differentiation by Ability/Achievement

Although this item was at first designed to describe seating arrangements, it was adapted over time to relate primarily to pupils' knowledge of their individual status in the eyes of the teacher. It was also found to constitute a neutral topic that could be discussed with the teacher, and thus a means of establishing a relationship with the teacher as early as the end of the first observation.

What has already been said about how poor a guide seating arrangements are to how a class operates explains the abandonment of the original purpose. However it was recognised in many instances that a pupil's awareness of his status in class depends at least partly on seating arrangements or on the way in which they are operated. Although cases covered by option 1 (pupils seated in 'order of merit', with changes according to progress) are the most obvious ones, it would be wholly wrong to assume them to be the only ones where knowledge of status is gained. Grouping by ability is likely to reveal status—although to what degree may depend on such factors as whether there are changes in group membership that either overtly or implicitly constitute 'promotion' or 'demotion', or whether the teacher makes pejoritive reference to particular groups and/or contrasts them with other more successful groups.

This variable does, however, suffer from a disadvantage inherent in those that have no intrinsic importance *and* have no *uniform* effect on all or most pupils. For it can be argued with some plausibility

a) that it does not matter what knowledge pupils have of their status unless this knowledge affects their self-confidence, motivation, and attainment

and b) that the effect, if any, is probably favourable on those that have high status and adverse on those that have low.

The fact that there proved to be no sign of any relationship between codings on this variable with those on any of the other variables covered by the schedule is certainly consistent with the effects' differing according to what the status was. However there is another possible explanation: a pupil may have good knowledge of his status no matter what the teacher does, and, if so, what is recorded in this item will clearly make no difference.

There is thus cause for thinking that this item lacks value either on the ground of its lack of relevance or on that of its having an equivocal role in any explanatory structure.

CHAPTER 4

USING THE SCOTS SCHEDULE

Many matters relating to the use of the SCOTS schedule have been referred to in the course of the preceding chapter, but there remains a need to deal with these and other related issues systematically. It is the function of this chapter to do so.

OBSERVING CLASSROOMS

Ob. erving in a classroom inevitably alters to some degree what or: wishes to observe. To minimise such alterations was, not surprisingly, a prime concern of the researchers engaged in the Teaching Strategies project.

The first decision made was that the observers would be non-participant: children who addressed them directly were to be responded to pleasantly, but not in such a way as to encourage further approaches. The observers would sit quietly and unobtrusively and not intervene even if pupils misbehaved in the absence of the teacher.

So far as children were concerned, the problem of observers' affecting the situation was not a great one. There was inevitably some curiosity during first observations, but it was the experience of the observers that they came very quickly to be regarded by the children as both unthreatening and unimportant.

Teachers were quite a different matter: they were apprehensive about being observed. A first step on the first visit to a school was, therefore, invariably a meeting with the teachers, who had—usually, at least—been forewarned by their headteacher. The researchers were represented by the present writer and those of the research team who were to work in the school as observers. The teachers were immediately assured that everything observed would be treated as confidential, that nothing that happened would be communicated in a way that would enable the teacher concerned to be identified by anyone outside the research team (not even to the headteacher). Secondly the researchers endeavoured to demonstrate themselves to be understanding, non-threatening individuals. The fact that all the observers—except for one in the 1974/75 observations—were themselves experienced teachers was emphasised.

In no case, to the best of the writer's knowledge, did any teacher in a participating school refuse to take part, though a few were known to do so reluctantly. It has to be said, however, that in any school where there were more teachers with classes at the desired level (Primary 5-7) than were required for observation, those who were omitted may have been those who most strongly objected, and also that, in some schools, the 'expectations' of the headteacher may have constituted considerable pressure to participate.

Throughout the time the observations were being undertaken (usually 1-2 weeks) the observers endeavoured to develop and maintain an easy and informal relationship with teachers. To this end, they did, for example, take coffee or tea in staffrooms along with the teachers they were observing whenever this was possible. (In some schools, where it was the wish of the headmaster, they did however do so in his room.)

There is no doubt that many of the teachers found being observed a strain and only a few indicated that they had, while busy, forgotten about the presence of the observer.

At the initial meetings with the observers, the teachers were asked *not* to prepare special lessons, but to undertake whatever they would have done had there been no observation. Teachers frequently knew at what time the observations would take place, for, although the observers did not routinely say when they would come, they never refused to do so when questioned—as was commonly the case. It is impossible to say how far the teachers did in fact follow exactly the programme they would otherwise have done, though in some cases it was apparent that they were adopting 'defensive' policies, avoiding things—eg, teaching new work—that they saw as 'risky'. However, only a very few adopted policies so defensive as to impede seriously the effectiveness of the observations.

Teachers were, of course, anxious to appear well, but it was the impression of the observers that attempts by teachers to hide particular characteristics were, when they occurred, largely unsuccessful. Inaudibility was, however, in some cases a serious problem to observers.

NUMBER AND DURATION OF OBSERVATIONS

The two halves of the morning and the two halves of the afternoon—both usually separated by a timetabled interval—provided 'natural' units for observation and avoided the disruption of an observer's arriving during a period of teaching. It was found particularly important for the observers to be present from the very outset of a period of teaching, since the instructions given to pupils at that time typically provided a context that was important in the interpretation of subsequent events.

Obviously, the more observations undertaken, the more that can be learned, but experience showed that there was a rapid fall-off in the amount of useful new information obtained after a fifth observation. Accordingly the number of observations was fixed at five—three morning ones and two afternoon ones. To prevent any bias arising from various types of work being undertaken at particular times of day, each of the four quarters of the day was observed at least once. (Because the high level of concentration necessary when observing, observer fatigue may be considerable, and observers were therefore rarely asked to observe more than three times in a day.)

THE OBSERVER IN THE CLASSROOM

In any classroom it was of course desirable for the observer to be placed where he could both hear and see well, while not being more in the teacher's line of vision than could be helped. Optimum positions differed according to pupil seating patterns and class-organisation, but in any case the observers always observed any teacher request concerning where they should sit. Observers did not change position during an observation save occasionally in classrooms where there was much movement by pupils and where, therefore, it was possible to do so unobtrusively.

The problem of observer placement was of course accentuated when there were two observers present, as was necessary when inter-observer reliability was being tested—ie, in approximately 20% of all the sets of observations, and sometimes during observations when the present writer was there. (The present writer alone among the researchers was not a regular member of the observation team, but, save in a few instances where other commitments prevented his doing so, he in fact observed every teacher once in order to be able to discuss observers' problems on a basis of first-hand knowledge. On no occasion did more than two observers observe simultaneously. (In cases where a class was a 'reliability' one, the present writer always observed on another—ie, a sixth—occasion.)

THE TECHNIQUE OF OBSERVING

The SCOTS schedule requires its own observation techniques, since every action, gesture, or speech unit is potentially a source of evidence germane to the coding of one or more of the 43 schedule items. Since there is no means of foretelling the order in which units of evidence will present themselves, it is necessary for observers to have a note-pad on which to record events sequentially. Since *actual words used* may constitute important clues, they have to be noted selectively. (Knowledge of the schedule, of course, aids the choice of phrases to note.) Sometimes it is helpful also to note tone of voice, gestures, etc.

Normal practice is to record the codings for a particular observation shortly before the end of that observation, for accurate recall of what has occurred is seriously impaired by undertaking an observation of another class before recording codings. On the other hand, it is both practicable and desirable to use the notes taken during an observation to undertake a subsequent review of codings, particularly to ensure that account is taken of any fact or incident that has been noted but that has been forgotten at the time of coding.

Completing the record for an observation consists primarily of ticking the category judged most appropriate for each item, but when uncertainties exist, question marks may be used instead, or alternatively ticks may be placed on the boundary between two categories.

The items of the schedule cover two broad groups of variables, those relating to characteristics that tend to remain constant across all observations and those that differ from one to another. In the former case, the observer has to find what the one 'right' coding is, and this is something he typically moves towards with increasing assurance as one observation follows another. The 'right' coding is then also the final 'summative' record of the whole set of the five observations. However, in the case of items where the coding varies from one observation to another on account of actual variation in teacher practice, the final assessment has to take account of the extent of variation as well as of the average level. In many of these cases, this process is aided by there being a special summative form of the item (see Appendix B).

CHAPTER 5

THE CONDUCT OF OBSERVATIONS

The limiting of observations to class Primary 5 and above (ie, ages 9-ll inclusive) was not the result of there being any difficulty in using the SCOTS schedule with the younger classes, but of our wish to test classes before and after the 1977/78 observations using test instruments requiring at least some degree of reading ability.

The choice of schools from which to draw these classes was influenced principally by the desire to include as wide a range of teaching styles as could be achieved. It was decided to include in the sample

a) schools in areas served by a number of colleges of education [1]

b) schools with catchment areas which, taken together, included pupils of every social background from the most disadvantaged to the most advantaged (though not necessarily in the same relative proportions as in the population at large),

c) schools which, on the basis of local advice, were thought to include teachers whose styles might otherwise be inadequately represented. (In 1974/75, such action had proved necessary because of the scarcity of teachers whose teaching style had features commonly regarded as 'progressive'.)

Within the selected schools, the teachers chosen were the ones that happened to be teaching classes P5, 6 and 7 in the session when the observations were undertaken. It must be emphasised that a sample drawn in this way is in no way representative and it cannot therefore afford evidence of the proportion of teachers of any particular type. On the other hand, it has a reasonable chance of including a full range of extant styles.

The schools involved were largely the same in both 1974/75 and 1977/78, though the teachers were not necessarily the same. In neither case was any school included that had been involved during the construction of the SCOTS schedule or the training of the observers. Two of the 30 schools that had participated in the

---

[1] The teachers observed in fact included some from each of the nine Scottish colleges of education then offering professional courses for primary school teachers, despite the fact that none of the schools visited was in the hinterland of two of them, Craigie College of Education (Ayr) and Aberdeen College of Education.

1974/75 observations decided not to do so in 1977/78, and two others were replaced, in one case because the school was threatened with closure and in the other because it had recently moved into a new open-plan building that was, at that time, being used substantially in excess of its designed capacity and that, it was thought, would give observers unacceptable difficulties in hearing accurately on account of the close proximity of other classes. The schools used as replacements were drawn from the same over-all geographical areas. The arrangements made were expected to yield a sample of approximately 130 teachers. In the event 128 were observed.

The arrangements for 1977/78 were very similar to those already described for 1974/75 (see pp 14-15). Because none of the original team of researchers/observers was any longer available to work on the project, a new group of three, who joined the project in January 1977, had to undergo a period of training in the use of the SCOTS schedule just as their predecessors had done, and this occupied most of September 1977. Pre-testing of the pupils in the classes concerned, using the test instruments designed for the purpose (see Chapters 9 and 10), had taken place in the preceding May/June, and, since post-testing had to take place in the following May/June, the time available for observations extended from early October 1977 to Easter 1978.

The most usual situation encountered was that where a school was large enough to provide a group of 6 teachers who taught classes in the P5 to P7 range. This justified deploying all three observers in the school for approximately one week. However, in one single instance, seven teachers in one school were observed, and in another, eight. In five schools it was possible to observe only five teachers instead of the expected six.

When the schools involved were smaller ones yielding two or three teachers each, they were normally grouped together to provide six teachers (either two teachers from each of three schools or three teachers from each of two) to be covered over the same period. Since this sometimes necessitated an observer's operating in more than one school at a time, it was so arranged that the schools involved were in reasonable proximity to one another. On one occasion the exigencies of scheduling observers' time made it necessary for the same observer to cover all six teachers in a single school.

All five observations of a particular teacher were, of course, carried out by the same observer (or by the same pair of observers if

52

inter-observer reliability was being tested). The time spent in a school was, of course, increased when 'reliabilities' were undertaken. So far as possible only one observation of a teacher was carried out on any one day.

The necessity of deploying observers over a period of 6-7 months to undertake the observations inevitably resulted in some teachers' being seen fairly early in the school session, and some after teaching the class for up to two terms. (A minority had in fact taught some or all of the pupils in their class during the preceding year.) The minimum time any teacher had spent with a class before being observed was approximately 6-7 weeks. All had thus had time to establish some sort of working relationship with the class. None were seen during the initial stages of establishing that relationship.

It will be seen that when in due time the data were analysed that it had to be assumed that the style of teaching observed at the time when a teacher was visited was that operating throughout the school year up to the time of the post-testing. This may not of course always have been the case, and, in particular, the relationship between some teachers and their respective classes may have changed over the period. [2]

The initial meeting with the teachers (see p 47) very often occurred at the morning interval on the first day of the observations, before any observation had been undertaken. The present writer, who had always met with the headteacher some time previously to discuss arrangements and indeed the very participation of the school, was almost always present at these initial meetings.

Relationships between observers and teachers appeared to be almost uniformly excellent, though the degree of strain experienced by the teachers clearly varied greatly. (Special steps were taken to ease the sense of 'threat' in the case of young and inexperienced teachers by allocating one of the younger observers; similarly, when a teacher of long experience appeared to resent the idea of being observed—or 'judged'—by a relatively young observer, the most experienced of the observers was, if possible, allocated.) Reference has already been made to the fact some teachers adopted

[2] Earlier, after the ending of the 1974/75 observations, in order to make some assessment of whether such change occurred, a few teachers that had been observed in October 1974 were re-observed just after Easter 1975. There were some signs of difference, but since in the latter of the two occasions it had been possible to observe only two or three times (instead of five), the observers did not feel sufficiently sure of their second set of codings to draw any firm conclusions about whether changes had in fact occurred.

'safety-first' policies in apparently avoiding during observations any activity they saw as risky. This did cause some difficulty to observers, particularly in relation to the coding of some of the 'teacher-skill' variables, but it appeared to be very difficult for a teacher over any sustained period to 'disguise' normal behaviour. A very few teachers did adopt extremely defensive tactics, in that they did little more than give pupils written work during the observations. In these cases the accuracy of the codings may have been more severely affected.

As soon as possible after each observation, and particularly at the time when final, 'summative' codings were being determined, the observers reviewed their notes taken while observing in order to take cognisance of any piece of relevant information that might not have been taken into account already. (When making their notes, the observers were of course aware of what sort of information was likely to be of relevance for arriving at particular codings.)

Once final codings had been arrived at, unless the observation was a 'reliability' one, it remained only to record on a punched card the 43 codings together with a code number to identify the class (and thus a teacher) and some coded biographical data derived from a brief questionnaire completed by all the teachers (see Appendix C).

In the case of 'reliabilities' however, the first step after each observer had *independently* finalised 43 codings was to record on punched card his codings for the purpose of comparing codings with those of this partner and thus of assessing reliability. After this, in order to discover why differences had occurred, the observers discussed all instances where they had not agreed, and, where necessary, consulted with the third observer and the present writer on any issue that seemed to call for the establishment of a further item of 'case law'.

For each observer pairing, the two observers were each, on alternative occasions, designated the 'senior' observer—ie, the one whose codings would be used for the research programme. If, after the discussions referred to above, the 'senior' observer thought any of his codings ought to be revised, he had the right entirely on the basis of his own judgement to change his original 'final' codings *for the purposes of the research programme.* (Change in the records used to assess reliability were *not* permitted.)

Before 'final' codings were recorded as data for the research programme, both in the case of ordinary observations and 'reliability' ones, there was, if necessary, discussion—involving all

54

three observers and the present writer—of any coding problem(s) that had arisen. Such problems usually related to the coding of any variable where what was observed did not seem to 'fit' any of the categories as defined in the schedule. In such cases, a judgement had to be made as to how the actions, events, etc, described by the observer(s)—and possibly also by the present writer if his own single observation provided more relevant information—should be related to the continuum of variation underlying the categories as defined in the schedule. *In this way, a point on the scale was, by agreement, assessed as being equivalent, even though there was no close match to the descriptors.* (In so far as this was necessary, it probably indicated that the abstractness of the category definitions, which had tended to increase during the evolution of the schedule—see pages 11-13—was still not sufficient.)

The decisions reached in these discussions added to the 'case-law' which the observers took into account in subsequent observations.

On the completion of a set of observations of a class, and before any such discussions as those described in the last three paragraphs, the observer (and in the case of 'reliabilities' both the 'senior' and the 'junior' observer) had one further duty—to record a short note relating to his over-all impression of the class and, in particular, any teacher practice or characteristic that seemed to contribute disproportionately to the sort of experience pupils had in being in that class. (The present writer made a similar note on the basis of his single observation, though not if he felt he had discovered too little to do so.) These notes were made in the belief that, though the schedule data were likely to have reflected these matters, they were unlikely to have given the variables concerned their due weight—a weight that these same variables would not have merited in respect of other teachers.

CHAPTER 6

THE MEASUREMENT OF INTER-OBSERVER RELIABILITY

Of the 128 sets of five observations undertaken in 1977/78, 24 (ie, just under 20%) were used to test inter-observer reliability— eight for each of the three possible pairings of the three observers. Each sub-set of eight was spread over the whole period in which the observations were conducted. They were undertaken in 11 of the 28 schools involved, in no case more than three being undertaken in a single school, and in no case more than one of these three for each pairing.[1]

Table 1 shows the data arising from each of the eight 'reliabilities' for each of the three pairings of observers. These codings represent those arrived at *before* any discussion between the observers (see page 62) and, of course, represent the categories of the 1977 version of the SCOTS schedule *before* any renumbering following the amalgamation of certain categories arising from the reliability data. (See below and Table 2). Table 3 shows the extent of agreement and disagreement for each pair *after* these amalgamations had been carried out. A striking feature of this table is the reduction in the extent of disagreement between observers as time passed and as discussion of earlier disagreements helped to unify the criteria being employed.[2] The levels of agreement attained in the second three months of the observations demonstrates just how good are the levels attainable using this schedule. The somewhat poorer levels attained in the first three months point to the need for observer training that extends for more than the three to four weeks that was the most that a tight timetable allowed in 1977/78. (That the researchers required training in use of the schedule arose, of course, from the unavoidable change in personnel engaged on the project that had occurred in the early months of 1977—see p 52.)

Although any disagreement between observers is regrettable, it is important not to attach greater weight than is merited to that which occurred. In the first place, it must be noted from

---

[1] To have three 'reliabilities', one for each pairing of observers, in a single school where in all six teachers were being observed was found to permit an economical employment of observer time.

[2] The same phenomenon had been observed in 1974/75 observations.

TABLE 1

SCOTS SCHEDULE: INTER-OBSERVER RELIABILITY CODINGS FOR EIGHT JOINT OBSERVATIONS BY EACH OF THREE PAIRINGS OF THREE OBSERVERS (1977/78)

SCOTS VARIABLES 1-43

OBSERVATION NO.

OBSERVERS 1 AND 2

Obs.						
1	23341422	31435445	54453533	42443311	23333343	445
	33321322	31333334	44444423	42443311	22334344	446
2	43322322	42434445	43533434	42443311	22335343	446
	43321422	41434435	44443434	52554411	22344343	446
3	43222232	42333334	43432523	43333221	22334334	344
	43222222	42324334	33342523	42333321	22333343	344
4	51122311	31223233	53332522	51553411	21225333	446
	51122211	31323233	43333522	51553411	11224333	446
5	22232223	51233224	42343522	24222133	22333333	343
	32232122	51423234	42343512	24322133	22333333	344
6	22212211	31112113	33322422	42333311	11225123	346
	22222311	31112213	33322422	41443311	11225233	346
7	25331422	53435445	64443534	51554433	31335344	446
	23331522	43434445	64443523	51554433	31335244	446
8	22222232	41132113	32332523	34224222	32333434	344
	22222222	51232212	33342523	34223222	34345434	444

Obs						
1	11222111	21112222	12131311	42342311	21111131	225
	11123111	22112224	32221222	41241411	21115222	325
2	42322222	42232233	42443524	33733212	22353344	345
	41322321	42232223	32335522	33323213	22334333	345
3	42232421	51233334	53434525	42444413	21345434	446
	42332321	41324324	64433434	52443323	21434344	446
4	52223111	31112224	42230512	31343411	21213433	345
	52222111	21123224	32333523	41442411	21322533	345
5	32211311	51525334	43323513	43443321	22253333	346
	32221211	51324324	43323513	32343222	22325333	346
6	42222312	31122224	32342511	41433311	22243332	346
	42212312	31224324	42343512	41443411	21224333	346
7	33421433	41333335	44544524	51554333	32355354	446
	33321433	41343325	43554534	42543333	32345344	446
8	52223233	51233222	33333523	33322211	34345334	446
	52222222	51233223	42333523	33433211	33335334	446

58

1	22122311	42353234	43433423	42323321	22334333	345
	23122211	41225224	42433524	42323321	22325232	345
2	22222322	22223224	43332422	42544311	11324333	344
	32222322	32333223	53332332	42533311	11323333	345
3	11112211	31122114	52342423	42333311	11224433	345
	22122211	31123214	53443434	42443321	12344433	345
4	23112312	42343332	54445534	42443321	22334334	446
	33112312	42434322	54443434	51543421	22334344	446
5	43321332	31434334	54445534	52443443	23334334	446
	43321322	31434424	53344524	42443443	22334333	346
6	43122211	21213223	43231712	41443321	21223322	336
	43122311	21323223	43232332	41443421	21334323	336
7	23341321	41324225	43443533	42443444	31325334	346
	23321322	41334225	43443533	42443344	32335334	346
8	22221211	51233113	44234522	42322311	23334435	446
	22221212	51333213	44335523	42422311	23434335	446

59

TABLE 2

AMALGAMATIONS OF SCOTS SCHEDULE CATEGORIES IN THE LIGHT OF
THE 1977/78 INTER-OBSERVER RELIABILITY DATA

ITEM/VARIABLE	ORIGINAL CATEGORIES AMALGAMATED	CODING CHANGES IMPLEMENTING AMALGAMATIONS (including consequential recodings of neighbouring categories)	RESULTING RANGE OF CATEGORIES
11	2 & 3	2→3, 1→2	2-5
12	2 & 3	2→3	1-5*
15	2 & 3	2→3, 1→2	2-5
17 (Summative)	1 & 2, 3 & 4	3→4, 1 & 2→3	3-7
23	2 & 3	2→3, 1→2	2-4
37	3 & 4	4→5, 5→4	1-4

* with no category 2

TABLE 3

SCOTS SCHEDULE, 1977/78 RELIABILITY DATA: AGREEMENTS/DISAGREEMENTS FOR 43 ITEMS

(The figures for agreements etc. represent the situation *after* the amalgamations of categories in Table 2 had been implemented)

Observers:	Agreements			Disagreements by 1 Category			Disagreement by 2 Categories		
	1 and 2	2 and 3	1 and 3	1 and 2	2 and 3	1 and 3	1 and 2	2 and 3	1 and 3
1st Observation	28	23	34	13	18	9	2	2	0
2nd ,,	29	31	35	14	11	8	0	1	0
3rd ,,	35	25	28	8	18	14	0	0	1
4th ,,	38	28	33	5	14*	10	0	0	0
5th ,,	36	33	34	7	9	9	0	1	0
6th ,,	35	33	35	8	9	8	0	1	0
7th ,,	37	32	38	6	11	4	0	0	1
8th ,,	31	33	35	11	10	8	1	0	0
Mean	33.63	29.75	34.00	9.00	12.50	8.75	0.37	0.63	0.25

* There was one further disagreement where one observer used a zero coding and one attempted a positive coding.

61

Table 3 that disagreements to the extent of two categories were very few in number (only 10 in the course of 24 observations, for each of which 43 codings had been made.)

The more numerous disagreements to the extent of one category did in many cases represent only marginal differences of judgement, for it must be appreciated that the categories were points on a continuum and that therefore it was possible for two observers to agree that, for a particular variable, the correct coding was close to the borderline between two categories and yet, in some cases, code on opposite sides of that borderline.

It has already been explained that after reliability data had been recorded, the observers discussed their differences and that the 'senior' observer for that observation (ie, the one whose data was to be used for the main research) had the option, if he thought fit, to revise in the light of the discussion his initial coding, though not in respect of the reliability data. In the event, in six out of the 10 cases of disagreement by two categories, the senior observer varied his coding to the extent of reducing the disagreement from two categories to one. The number of disagreements by even one category was also substantially reduced. (There was, of course, no means of similarly revising codings in the non-reliability observations.) It is likely that the number of remaining disagreements by either one or two categories would have been further reduced by the 'junior' observer's being willing to amend his codings, but this was not recorded since the junior observer's data were not to be used.

The schedule items where the ten disagreements by two categories occurred were:

(once each): 11, 16, 24, 34, 36, 37

(twice each): 4, 13.

Amalgamation of Categories

Where the reliability data suggested that observers could not agree adequately in making discriminations between the categories in question, certain pairs of categories for a limited number of variables were amalgamated.[3] These amalgamations are shown in Table 2. It will be observed from this table that implementing these amalgamations involved the recoding of not only the variables

[3] Table 1 constitutes the data on which the decisions to make these amalgamations were based. However, in order to make the relevent facts more readily observable, cross-tabulations for each of 43 variables for each set of eight 'reliabilities' were produced for each pair of observers.

immediately involved but neighbouring ones also. Thus, for example, if categories 2 and 3 were amalgamated, all 2's were recoded as 3's and all 1's as 2's. This closing up was necessary since the numerical difference between categories was subsequently used as a 'distance' measure in the cluster analysis (see Chapter 7).[4]

The reader is reminded that the codings given in Table 1 are those *before* these amalgamations were carried out, whereas the inter-observer differences recorded in Table 3 are those remaining *after* these amalgamations.

Conclusions

In summary it can be said that very high levels of inter-observer agreement can be obtained using the SCOTS schedule and, although these levels were not fully attained in the earlier observations when the observers were less experienced and the criteria they were applying less uniform, the data used in the cluster analysis were, over all, reliable to an acceptable degree.

[4] There was one exception to this: item 12, where it was judged that those coded 1 were sufficiently different from those originally coded 2 or 3 to justify a 'distance' of two units.

CHAPTER 7

TEACHER CLUSTERS

The 43 items of the SCOTS schedule provide a profile of how an individual teacher conducts his class, but in itself it gives no indication of whether that teacher is similar to many others or highly idiosyncratic. For this reason—and for a number of others that will become apparent—it was necessary to divide into groups the 128 teachers observed in 1977/78, such that each group contained those with most in common in the way they taught—ie, those that might be said to share a teaching strategy or style of teaching.

It appeared likely from the outset that such groups would vary greatly in size, but it was unknown how many groups (or clusters) would have to be formed if the requirement that each be reasonably homogeneous was to be satisfied.

The Formation of the Clusters

The readers of this book will be likely to include many who are uninterested in the technicalities of research. Nevertheless, in this chapter, an attempt will be made to describe simply—so far as possible in non-technical terms—how the grouping or clustering was carried out, for it is important to understand the basis—and the limitations—of the groupings that were established. However, the reader impatient to learn the results of the clusterings should proceed straight to Chapter 8 (p 70).

Obviously the starting point of clustering has to be some measure of similarity or dissimilarity—in this case, one based on teachers' codings on the SCOTS schedule.

How similar two teachers are in respect of just one of the 43 SCOTS variables can readily be seen: they may be the same (ie, have the same coding) or they may differ by one or more categories (up to 4, in the case of a 5-point scale). This difference in terms of number of categories may be described as the *distance* between them.

Even at this early stage of the argument, the reader may have detected a problem: distance is normally measured in terms of a fixed unit such as inches, but no such unit exists to measure the distance between one category and another. There is therefore no way of determining whether the distance from category 1 to category 2 is equal to that from category 2 to category 3 or of

64

equating the distance between categories 1 and 2 of one variable with that between categories 1 and 2 of another. *It is, therefore, the case that in using difference in category as a measure of 'distance' one is using as a constant unit of measurement something that cannot be demonstrated to be constant.*

There are only two arguments that can be put forward in defence of using such a measure. One is that there is no other better one available for this sort of data and the other is that it appeared to the constructors of the SCOTS schedule that a) the points on the continuum to which each item related were, as judged subjectively, reasonably evenly spaced and b) the distance between, say, categories 1 and 5 of one item and that of another seemed to them to be of similar degree of magnitude in terms of educational significance.

There is then a case for dismissing these distance measures and everything based upon them as invalid. It is the present writer's view, however, that this should not be done: an imperfect measure can be a great improvement on having no measure at all, and there is, moreover, a case for saying that the categories do form the basis of a valid measure, albeit a rough one. Nonetheless, the limitations of the measure must constantly be borne in mind.

From this point on we shall disregard this difficulty and concentrate on another issue, that of combining many separate distance measures into one over-all measure.

If our concern were the differences between teachers on only two variables, we could plot each teacher on a graph using his scores on the two variables as a means of placing him in respect of the two axes and we should be able to see which teachers were most alike because they would appear in the same area of the graph. The more dense the collection of plotted points, the more similar the teachers as a group.

Even three variables would cause us only slightly more trouble, for we could plot each teacher at a point in a three dimensional model, for there would still be one axis for each variable. Moreover, similar teachers would still appear in groups. We might compare them to stars in space, and a dense group or cluster of them to a galaxy. Of course the shape of the cluster would vary according to the degree of difference found within the group in respect of each variable. Thus, for instance, if there were less similarity in respect of one variable, the cluster would tend to be more spread out in the direction of the axis for that variable.

Our problem is, however, that we have to deal with many more than three variables and therefore with many more dimensions of space. Since we cannot picture more than three dimensions, we have to proceed more abstractly and depend more on mathematical procedures.

One way of measuring the distance apart of two teachers plotted in three-dimensional space is to total their distance apart along each of the three axes—and this is something that can readily be done no matter how many dimensions, and therefore axes, are involved. The greater this total of differences is, the greater is the dissimilarity between the two teachers.

Once we have clear in our minds that, with a large set of teachers, the aggregate distances between them in respect of all the variables combined in this way are likely to vary from small to large, it is not so difficult to continue to think in terms of densities, in terms of stars that are relatively close together forming clusters, and of clusters or individual stars that are far apart. Just as all stars in a galaxy have a *relatively* short distance between themselves and all other stars in the galaxy, so do teachers in a cluster all have *relatively* short distances from every other teacher in the cluster. *For this to happen, they must have very similar ratings on a large proportion of the variables.*

The reader may be relieved to know that we do not have to extend our conceptualisation any further and that it is sufficient for us to concentrate on certain concepts that we have met with in the course of the last few paragraphs, namely

i) *relatively* greater densities are the basis of clusters,

ii) greater densities imply relatively short distances between all pairs of cluster members,

iii) these distances are calculated by summing distances apart in respect of each variable.

Various ways of measuring the distance between cases on individual variables for the purpose of clustering have been advocated. The one adopted for this research was 'squared Euclidean distance'. This is most readily understood by means of an example: if two teachers are coded as 3 and 5 respectively on a particular item in the SCOTS schedule, their simple distance apart—2—is squared to give a distance of 4. Simple distances of 1,2,3, and 4 thus become 1,4,9, and 16 respectively. This is useful in that it gives little weight to minor and perhaps borderline differences, but lays increasing emphasis on larger ones. A teacher differing from another teacher by 2, 4, 0, 1 and 2 categories respectively on five variables respectively would, *in respect of just those five variables*, have an aggregate distance from that other teacher of 25 $(4+16+0+1+4)$. The large contribution of the second of these differences—where the two teachers are at opposite ends of a five-point scale—is obvious.

We must now turn to the process of forming clusters. *It is of the utmost importance to realise that clusters are not entities that we have simply to recognise. Where one cluster ends and another begins is to some degree arbitrary*, for it is the criteria we lay down that decide cluster membership. These criteria determine both the *shape* and the *size* of the clusters.

There are two fundamental types of cluster with which it is necessary to become familiar. The first is based on linking 'nearest neighbours'. In such a cluster, the distance between any two cases within it is never greater than a prescribed figure, but there is no limit on the distances to other members of the cluster. If cases are distributed as in Figure 1[1], long chain-like clusters will be formed and the cases at the extreme points will be far apart. Such clusters may well represent where the densities lie, but their membership lacks homogeneity. The second fundamental type of cluster is based on 'minimum-variance'. Minimum variance ensures a high level of homogeneity within the clusters—ie, all the members of each cluster are at least reasonably close to *all* other members—but the clusters themselves may cut across the distributions identified by 'nearest neighbour' type clusters. Thus there may be excluded from a cluster some cases that are far nearer neighbours of *some* of its members than are *some* of the cases included in it (see Figure 2).

Since it was desired to be able to identify groups of teachers that had a lot in common, the type of cluster analysis—for such is the name given to the type of grouping procedure we have been discussing—undertaken in this research was one producing clusters of the minimum-variance type and the disadvantage mentioned in the previous paragraph was accepted. Such minimum variance clusters can usefully be pictured as approximately spherical in shape, though of course, since the number of dimensions exceeds three, they are properly 'hyper-spherical'.

The Clustering Procedures

We have already seen an example of how an aggregate squared Euclidean distance can be calculated in respect of variables

---

[1] Both Figures 1 and 2 represent hypothetical distributions, and, of course, represent only two-dimensional clusters.

FIGURE 1

HYPOTHETICAL (2-DIMENSIONAL) 'NEAREST NEIGHBOUR' CLUSTERS

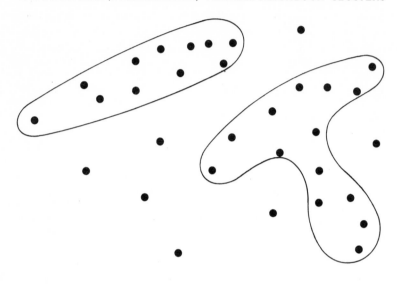

FIGURE 2

HYPOTHETICAL (2-DIMENSIONAL) MINIMUM-VARIANCE CLUSTERS
FOR SAME DISTRIBUTION AS FIGURE 1

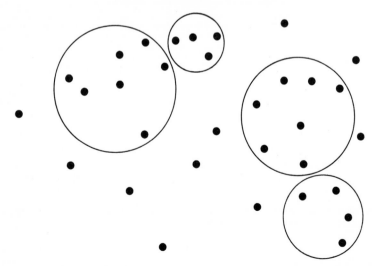

of the type occurring in the SCOTS schedule. In the event, the distances were calculated in respect of all but one of the 43 variables in the SCOTS schedule, though with two of these variables half-weighted (see page 251). A separate aggregate distance was calculated for the difference between each teacher and every other teacher. For the 128 teachers, this produced 8,128 inter-teacher distances. (The matrix containing them is therefore too large to reproduce in this book.) The greatest inter-teacher distance found was 307, and the smallest, 11.

How the Cluster Analysis was Performed

Since the account of this analysis necessarily includes much of a technical nature and is thus outside the interest of the majority of readers, it has been placed in an appendix (Appendix K, p 249).

CHAPTER 8

THE CLUSTERS OF TEACHERS

Those reading this chapter alone in order to come straight to the findings of the research should note that many of the ideas that form the basis of these findings were first presented in Chapter 3. A careful reading of that chapter in conjunction with Appendix A will greatly assist the understanding of what follows here; the reading of page 20 of that chapter, where the way the SCOTS variables have been grouped is presented in tabulated form, is, however, even more necessary if the text of this chapter is not to be misunderstood. It should be noted also that the reading of Chapter 7 will assist the reader to understand the nature and the limitations of the procedures used to produce the clusters described in this chapter.

The full set of codings for the 128 teachers during the observations carried out between October 1977 and April 1978 are given in Appendix D. The codings shown incorporate all necessary emendations arising from the amalgamation of certain categories for certain items of the schedule (see Table 2, page 60). Each teacher is identified by a number in the range 1 to 128. The sequence of these numbers does *not* represent the order in which the observations were carried out. The teacher number therefore affords no clue to the identity of the teacher or the school.

Since the basic data as presented in Appendix D are of little value to the reader save for reference concerning individual cases or for undertaking further analyses, it is the function of this chapter to present in a meaningful way data derived from them. The data given in Appendix D were in fact those used to calculate the inter-teacher distances and these were in turn used in the cluster analysis, details of which are given in Appendix K. The 17-cluster (minimum-variance) solution finally adopted is given in Table 4. (The case numbers used in Table 4, and elsewhere in this chapter, to identify the teachers are the same as in Appendix D.)

For reasons given in Appendix K, the price of obtaining clusters of homogeneous membership was, in some instances, the placing of two teachers in two different (though adjacent) clusters despite the fact that they were more similar to each other than they were to *some* of the teachers included in their respective clusters. This was particularly likely to happen in respect of the large 'middle-of-the-road' clusters whose members were classified in respect of many variables at levels that were modal (ie, at levels with the highest frequencies for all clusters taken together).

It cannot be emphasised too strongly that the clusters do not so much represent distinct groups of teachers as a 'carving up' into convenient groups of teachers that may be conceived of as being scattered through a multi-dimensional space. The reason for having

TABLE 4

SCOTS SCHEDULE: 17 TEACHER CLUSTERS

Cluster	No. in Cluster	Teacher Case Numbers
A	2	21, 106
B	6	17, 39, 63, 66, 67, 117
C	4	38, 41, 45, 122
D	2	2, 46
E	9	16, 18, 19, 29, 40, 51, 57, 118, 121
F	10	6, 10, 25, 61, 99, 109, 112, 119, 123, 128
G	6	28, 30, 52, 65, 68, 85
H	12	3, 23, 35, 36, 43, 62, 69, 74, 78, 79, 87, 116
I	7	12, 24, 89, 90, 100, 102, 115
J	5	48, 81, 82, 86, 111
K	7	1, 26, 27, 56, 76, 105, 108
L	16	7, 11, 13, 20, 34, 50, 54, 60, 64, 72, 80, 83, 84, 88, 98, 114
M	10	8, 22, 47, 53, 70, 71, 103, 104, 107, 110
N	9	4, 5, 14, 32, 37, 49, 96, 113, 120
O	10	31, 33, 55, 73, 91, 92, 93, 94, 95, 125
P	7	9, 15, 75, 101, 124, 126, 127
Q	6	42, 44, 58, 59, 77, 97
	128	

Note: The letters in parenthesis indicate the order in which these clusters are described in Chapter 8.

as many as 17 groups or clusters is that teachers resemble, and differ from, one another in very many different ways. There are not types of teachers; rather there is an infinite and continuous variation amongst them.[1]

[1] The relatively small number of dense cluster nuclei (5 or 6) identified by the DENSITY analyses—see Appendix K—together with the fact that the cases in each of their nuclei are typically found in two or three different maximum-variance clusters, leads general support to this view of the data.

Clusters simply gather together those that are sufficiently similar for it to be convenient to talk about them as a group. (As explained in the preceding chapter, the more alike two teachers are, the shorter the 'distance' between them. Dense clusters are therefore those where teachers are, relatively speaking, close together and therefore like each other. Dense clusters are homogeneous; less dense clusters, more heterogeneous.) Teachers who show many unusual characteristics are not only less numerous but tend to differ more amongst themselves. 'Out-lying' clusters thus tend to be small and only moderately homogeneous.

Note: The Labelling of Clusters

An alphabetic identifier (running from A to Q) has been attached to each cluster. This corresponds to the order of presentation in this chapter (and in Table 6). *It is important to note that this order does NOT arise from the cluster analysis and that it is therefore arbitrary.* Although it tends to keep adjacent to one another clusters with features in common, the pattern of similarities and dissimilarities is, as Table 6 shows, complex, and the sequence of presentation and the associated alphabetic labels should not therefore be seen as anything other than a matter of convenience. (The sequence of clusters as output by the cluster analysis was different, but was also random.)

THE PURPOSES OF THE CLUSTER DESCRIPTION AND HOW TO USE THEM

Those who have expected to find the clusters ordered so as to stand approximately in a line from 'progressive' to 'traditional' will find their expectations unfulfilled. The variation was far too complex for such an ordering to be possible. Nor do there appear to be grounds for equating 'progressive' with 'good' and 'traditional' with 'bad', or for the reverse. Indeed those that the present writer would judge to have been outstandingly skilful teachers differed very much one from another in respect of characteristics commonly associated with these terms. Many of these teachers had characteristics that might be classified as broadly 'traditional', others ones that might be classified as broadly 'progressive', and still others some of each. In short, there appeared to be very many ways of being a 'good' teacher, ways that made nonsense of any 'traditional-progressive' dichotomy.

Of course, there are great dangers in describing one teacher as 'good' and another as 'not so good', for value judgements of many kinds are involved. On the other hand, descriptions devoid of value judgements may be less than helpful. It is, accordingly, the aim of this chapter to make some value judgements but at the same time to distinguish them clearly from descriptive data. It is likely that many readers will share with the writer a substantial number of the value judgements made or implied, but it should also be possible for the reader to dissociate himself from any conclusion based on a value judgement he does not accept.

In this chapter an attempt will be made to relate teaching objectives—objectives that are probably very widely shared—to what teachers do in attempting to achieve them. It is indeed the author's contention, based upon his observations and the data presented here, that even very different teachers commonly have many objectives in common, that they seek to achieve these objectives in a variety of ways, and that their success in achieving their objectives may often depend less on the means they adopt than on the skill with which they employ them.

In the cluster descriptions given later in this chapter the order in which they are presented may give rise to one false impression, namely that of progressively moving from the 'best' to the 'worst' clusters. It is true that the first clusters presented do include many of the teachers whom the writer regards as being amongst the most skilled, and the last two presented many of those he judges to have been amongst the weakest, but the clusters cannot by any scale of values be placed in a simple order of merit. Table 5 shows the inter-cluster distances, ie, the average distances between the members of each cluster and those of each of the others. (Those that differ least have the lowest distances in this table, but these differences are usually not in respect of the same characteristics.[2]) The cluster characteristics that give rise to these distances are shown—in greatly simplified form—in Table 6 (pp 80-81).

The reader is likely to need to make regular reference to Table 6 in order to avoid the loss of the broader picture in a mass of detail. Those columns of the table that are shaded in relatively strong colours show (by means of a uniform colour sequence) a trend from 'strong' to 'weak' in a number of areas (eg, 'teaching skill'). *They do of course represent the writer's value judgements. The reader will have in the course of this chapter an opportunity to examine the basis of these value judgements and thus to decide whether to*

---

[2] In no way can these differences be plotted on a single plane, let alone on a line.

TABLE 5
INTER-CLUSTER MEAN DISTANCES

	A	B	C	D	E	F	G	H	I	J	K	L	M	N	O	P	Q
A	–	44	56	63	55	67	81	100	92	98	106	106	122	71	128	192	166
B	44	–	55	50	39	49	58	70	73	79	82	82	102	61	102	169	148
C	56	55	–	51	39	45	60	54	48	46	85	68	73	57	76	128	143
D	63	50	51	–	55	64	55	70	73	88	93	83	99	85	87	163	155
E	55	39	39	55	–	29	44	43	47	48	59	53	63	37	63	115	112
F	67	49	45	64	29	–	38	35	45	41	43	38	46	33	49	87	89
G	81	58	60	55	44	38	–	41	56	43	48	44	53	49	46	96	87
H	100	70	54	70	43	35	41	–	47	42	43	33	40	40	39	70	78
I	92	73	48	73	47	45	56	47	–	43	79	60	53	57	56	99	125
J	98	79	46	88	48	41	58	42	43	–	71	46	39	45	48	72	107
K	106	82	85	93	59	43	48	43	79	71	–	37	57	44	53	73	51
L	106	82	68	83	53	38	44	33	60	46	37	–	38	39	36	56	54
M	122	102	73	99	63	46	53	40	53	39	57	38	–	47	34	51	79
N	71	61	57	85	37	33	49	40	57	45	44	39	47	–	51	77	75
O	128	102	76	87	63	49	46	39	56	48	53	36	34	51	–	52	72
P	192	169	128	163	115	87	96	70	99	72	73	56	51	77	52	–	68
Q	166	148	143	155	112	89	87	78	125	107	51	54	79	75	72	68	–

accept or reject them. Even if some or all of the value judgements are rejected, the colour sequence will probably still be useful in showing trends and their inter-relationships. Those columns where the colouration is lighter relate to areas of variation that are *instrumental* and that can be judged 'good' or 'bad' only in terms of their effects, whatever these may be. For example, whereas having a high level of interest or motivation or developing pupil responsibility may perhaps be seen as good in themselves, a high level of feedback and individual aid is essentially *instrumental*, 'good' only in so far as it helps to produce desired results. *Thus, although, to avoid confusion, the same colour sequence is used, there are NO value judgements implied in the columns where the colours are lighter.* A further example may help: a low level of coercion may be beneficial, for example in promoting the development of pupil responsibility, but it is by no means self-evident that it is so, and indeed *any* particular level of coercion may possibly be optimal, or, perhaps more plausibly, what is the optimal level may depend on the context in which it occurs or the manner in which whatever degree of coercion there is is applied.

The reader must be cautious also in interpreting the column headings in Table 6. They are essentially 'short-hand' and meaningful only in terms of the sets of SCOTS variables to which they relate. Appendix E provides a link between Table 6 and the SCOTS schedule. In the first place it provides, in its own 'short-hand',[3] information on how each cluster stands in respect of each variable contributing to the summary classifications in Table 6, and secondly it gives the distribution of codings for each variable. Between them, Table 6 and Appendix E contain an enormous amount of information. Some perusal of Appendix E is a prerequisite of understanding Table 6 at all accurately, though the depth and extent of this perusal can be varied by individual readers in accordance with need and interest. It should be noted that each section of Appendix E relates to a single column of Table 6. The final column of Table 6 gives the number of teachers in each cluster.

THE CLUSTERS DESCRIBED

In the following descriptions, three sources of information are drawn upon:

[3] The cluster characteristics named in the second column of Appendix E each relate to the items in the SCOTS schedule indicated in column 1. Accordingly what is meant by terms such as 'Exposition' or 'Feedback' can be fully understood only by reference to the relevant descriptions in the SCOTS Schedule.

i) the codings for each item of the SCOTS schedule (see Appendix D)

ii) the short general comment on the outstanding features of each teacher and class made by the observer(s) on completion of five observations, and the present writer's comment (if any) after the completion of the single observation he undertook of most classes.

iii) a tape-recorded and selectively transcribed discussion—by the three observers and the present writer—of the clusters produced by the cluster analysis.

The length of the descriptions that follow differ considerably. The reason for this lies in the purpose of the descriptions, which is to highlight issues of general importance that particular clusters happen to illustrate. The clusters have no importance in their own right: they are, as has been previously emphasised, merely useful, but to some degree arbitrary, groupings of teachers whose ways of teaching have quite a number of features in common.

Cluster A

This is one of the two smallest of the 17 clusters. In the two classes involved, the use of group methods proved to be a key feature of the teaching strategies (which, as we shall see, is by no means always the case when such methods are utilised).

Probably the greatest dangers when group methods are employed are of pupils' drifting through lack of clear understanding of how to proceed, of their lacking stimulation, and of their waiting for long periods for attention from an over-extended teacher. These dangers were manifestly avoided in the two classes under discussion.

In the first place, both teachers, while clearly in command of what was happening in general, secured from individual pupils independent and responsible activity, activity often involving co-operation with other pupils. The pupils were taught, but had also clearly been taught how to work and learn. Teacher 106, for example, spent much of his time teaching groups, but the groups he was not teaching worked actively together. Thus on one occasion, when he had been discussing a passage with a group, he told them, on leaving them to go to another group, to ask each other questions about it. The remarkable thing was that this was exactly what they did: they had learned how to ask questions. It was also notable that individual pupils often, apparently spontaneously, took over the running of their respective groups, operating in a teacher-like way. However, he did not depend wholly on group-instruction: part of the instruction was undertaken with the class as a single unit. It is probably the case that by so doing he avoided having pupils left to work on their own in groups for longer periods than they could sustain. Moreover, by devoting part of the day to project-type work, he was able to require pupils to find out things for themselves and to provide individual help at a time when he himself was less committed than when he was involved in group instruction. In all, he enabled his class to maintain a high level of activity and, at the same time, matched work to the needs of individual pupils by means of a high degree of differentiation in what was taught and in what work was set. The work was, moreover, typically thought-provoking. The sort of operation described in the preceding paragraph is unlikely to be successfully maintained without a considerable amount of preparatory work. (Materials and resources have to be available when pupils need them—Teacher 106's were all clearly labelled—and the teacher's heavy involvement in group instruction leaves little opportunity to make up for any lack of prior preparation.) Its success depends also on the establishment of an appropriate relationship between teacher and class. What exactly that relationship is inevitably varies with the personality of the teacher as well as with the teaching strategy being employed. In the case of teacher 106, any inappropriate pupil behaviour evoked blunt rebuke—'Frank, that's a disgrace: everybody else keeps books in order, so why can't you?'—but the underlying positive relationship between him and class meant that he could speak sharply without souring relationships. Indeed he seemed to be building up the social and academic confidence of a class whose social background was far from being privileged.

Despite the very substantial similarities between the two teachers in this cluster, there were substantial differences. Teacher 21 was coded differently, for example, on items 19 and 39: she was distinctly more *overtly* sensitive and sympathetic than teacher 106 and, in the words of the observer, there was 'an accepting and supportive atmosphere where sharp remarks were more than balanced by kind ones'. Moreover, her class organisation was characterised by its extreme flexibility. Thus, although pupil seating positions within groups tended to remain constant throughout the day, pupils were free to move, to work at a communal table, or to take back personal assignments to their own seats. They were able to co-operate with one another in a way that was more self-initiated, and the teacher was probably more available to pupils at times of *their* choosing. Her enthusiasm, lively questioning, and thoughtful and versatile explaining made it a lively class to be in, though the observer wondered whether the class—an able one—might not have benefited even more from greater challenge, such as would have been provided by one of the teachers in cluster C. It is also to be noted, however, that when she was working with a group, she controlled what was to be learned far more rigidly than did Teacher 106. She was looking for specific responses; teacher 106 was inclined to require the pupils to think out what sort of response should be made and he was prepared, within the limits of reason, to accept their decisions:

'If you come back and tell me why you want to do it, I'll listen.'

'Good, I like that (a mobile). Think of some way of hanging it up. If you want it supported in two places, all right by me'

(Teacher 21 would have probably used questions to lead the pupils to adopt *her* method, while understanding the reasons for doing so).

'Awful long sentence: could you break it up a little bit?'

(Teacher 21 would have been likely to question with a view to having the sentence split up in a way that *she* saw as good).

It is to be noted that teacher 106 was nonetheless concerned that the solution adopted by a pupil for any problem was satisfactory: he sought to achieve this through meticulous correction of work—corrections that were accompanied by careful explanations.

Cluster B

This cluster and cluster A are nearer to each other than either is to any other and skilled use of group methods is a notable feature of their similarity. Nonetheless the differences between them are substantial. As a glance at Table 6 will reveal, the principal area in which these differences occur is that relating to 'efficiency of management': whereas cluster A is described as being 'high', cluster B is 'very high'. In the course of the discussion amongst the researchers (the third 'source' referred to on page 76), the following conclusion was reached:

'It is notable that [cluster] B has a greater variety of activities than [cluster] A, but in a way the children in B are less free than those in A. This is probably what makes the organisation in B slightly better: it is a little bit better controlled. They less often waste time, for instance, but they lose, relative to A, in respect of this freedom, freedom of letting the children go off and really do things for themselves – and think for themselves.'

The marginally lower degree of 'efficiency of management' in cluster A thus, perhaps, represented no more than the price of a freedom that was valuable in itself. Where cluster B had its advantage was in its somewhat greater control of the pupils' learning experience. Nevertheless, it should be noted that four out of the six teachers in cluster B were coded on item 6 as controlling class work indirectly – ie, once basic instructions as to what to do had been given out, the pupils knew how to operate the system and repeated consultation with the teacher was unnecessary. Teacher 117, for instance, gave out a whole week's programme at a single time, and, although she indicated when particular activities should be undertaken by each group, strongly encouraged individual thinking and initiative and secured a high level of enthusiasm. The independence of the pupils' work was, in fact, enhanced by her imaginative suggestions – e.g. about the use of materials.

Guidance and organisation are thus not necessarily incompatible with the pursuit of independent learning. The provision by some teachers in this cluster of folders for pupils to keep particular sets of work encouraged orderliness of working and facilitated the monitoring of work by these teachers, but, in itself, in no way limited pupils' opportunities to undertake independent work. Nor did the frequent interactions many of these teachers had with their pupils in themselves limit pupil initiative, for, in general, those teachers acted as a guide to resources, rather than the source of answers, and accordingly pupils had to obtain information and/or ideas for themselves. (They were, in fact, usually keen to communicate to their teacher what they had found).

A further glance at Table 6 reveals that the areas in which the two clusters are very similar are classified very favourably, given acceptance of the writer's value judgements. (Appendix E, used in conjunction with Appendices A, B, and D, gives the reader the opportunity to question or confirm those value judgements.) These classifications do, of course, obscure some fine differences besides those already described in the preceding paragraph. The reader painstaking enough to study Appendix D closely for himself can see what these were, both for individual clusters and individual teachers—for example, in respect of different degrees of stress on

TABLE 6

DIAGRAMMATIC PRESENTATION OF GENERAL CHARACTERISTICS OF 17 CLUSTE

CLUSTER	TEACHING SKILLS	FEEDBACK AND INDIVIDUAL AID	INTEREST AND MOTIVATION	DEVELOPMENT OF PUPIL RESPONSIBILITY	LEVEL AIM
C 13 (A)	VERY STRONG	VERY HIGH LEVEL	VERY HIGH LEVEL	STRONG EMPHASIS	HIGH
C 12 (B)	VERY STRONG	VERY HIGH LEVEL	VERY HIGH LEVEL	STRONG EMPHASIS	HIGH
C 15 (C)	VERY STRONG	HIGH LEVEL	VERY HIGH LEVEL	MODERATE EMPHASIS	HIGH MID
C 2 (D)	VERY STRONG	VERY HIGH LEVEL	VERY HIGH LEVEL	STRONG EMPHASIS	MIDDLE H
C 11 (E)	QUITE STRONG	HIGH LEVEL	HIGH, LEVEL	FAIRLY STRONG EMPHASIS	HIGH
C 5 (F)	QUITE STRONG	MODERATE LEVEL	HIGH LEVEL	FAIRLY STRONG EMPHASIS	HIGH
C 3 (G)	QUITE STRONG	MODERATE LEVEL	VERY HIGH LEVEL	STRONG EMPHASIS	MIDDL
C 10 (H)	QUITE STRONG	MODERATE LEVEL	HIGH LEVEL	MODERATE EMPHASIS	MIDDL
C 9 (I)	QUITE STRONG	HIGH LEVEL	HIGH LEVEL	MODERATE EMPHASIS	HIGH MID
C 17 (J)	SOMEWHAT LIMITED	HIGH LEVEL	VERY HIGH LEVEL	WEAK EMPHASIS	MIDDL
C 1 (K)	SOMEWHAT LIMITED	FAIRLY LOW LEVEL	MODERATE LEVEL	MODERATE EMPHASIS	MIDDL
C 6 (L)	SOMEWHAT LIMITED	MODERATE LEVEL	MODERATE LEVEL	WEAK EMPHASIS	MIDDL
C 7 (M)	SOMEWHAT LIMITED	FAIRLY LOW LEVEL	MODERATE LEVEL	WEAK EMPHASIS	MIDDL
C 4 (N)	SOMEWHAT LIMITED	MODERATE LEVEL	MODERATE LEVEL	MODERATE EMPHASIS	HIGH
C 14 (O)	SOMEWHAT LIMITED	MODERATE LEVEL	MODERATE LEVEL	WEAK EMPHASIS	MIDDL
C 8 (P)	WEAK	FAIRLY LOW LEVEL	LOW LEVEL	NO EMPHASIS	MIDDL
C 16 (Q)	WEAK	FAIRLY LOW LEVEL	LOW LEVEL	WEAK EMPHASIS	MIDDLE L

GROUPING	EFFICIENCY OF MANAGEMENT	AUTHORITARIANISM AND COERCION	CLASS CONTROL	RELATIONSHIPS WITH PUPILS	N
VERY ᴏMINENT ᴇATURE	HIGH	VERY LOW	GOOD AND EASY	VERY GOOD	2
VERY ᴏMINENT ᴇATURE	VERY HIGH	VERY LOW	GOOD AND EASY	VERY GOOD	6
ᴏMINENT ᴇATURE	VERY HIGH	LOW	GOOD AND EASY	VERY GOOD	4
ᴎONE	VERY HIGH	VERY LOW	GOOD AND EASY	VERY GOOD	2
ᴏMINENT ᴇATURE	VERY HIGH	MODERATE	GOOD AND EASY	VERY GOOD	9
ᴍITED ᴇATURE	HIGH	MODERATE	GOOD AND EASY	VERY GOOD	10
ᴍITED ᴇATURE	HIGH	LOW	GOOD AND EASY	VERY GOOD	6
VERY ᴍITED ᴇATURE	HIGH	MODERATE	INSECURE FOR SOME	GOOD	12
VERY ᴍITED ᴇATURE	VERY HIGH	HIGH	GOOD AND EASY	GOOD	7
ᴍITED ᴇATURE	VERY HIGH	HIGH	GOOD AND EASY	FAIRLY GOOD	5
VERY ᴍITED ᴇATURE	MODERATE	LOW	INSECURE FOR SOME	GOOD	7
VERY ᴍITED ᴇATURE	MODERATE	MODERATE	SOMEWHAT INSECURE	GOOD	16
VERY ᴍITED ᴇATURE	HIGH	HIGH	SOMEWHAT INSECURE	FAIRLY GOOD	10
ᴏMINENT ᴇATURE	HIGH	MODERATE	INSECURE FOR SOME	GOOD	9
VERY ᴍITED ᴇATURE	HIGH	VERY HIGH	INSECURE FOR SOME	GOOD	10
ᴎONE	MODERATE	VERY HIGH	SOMEWHAT INSECURE	POOR	7
VERY ᴍITED ᴇATURE	LOW	HIGH	INSECURE	FAIRLY GOOD	6

grasping concepts and on rote memorisation. (The general bias of cluster B was in the direction of an emphasis on concepts.)

That the writer sees the teachers in both these clusters as highly skilled is in no way related to the fact that they both laid some emphasis on pupils' working individually or in groups: the point is that they seemed to be very successful in how this operated group or individualised learning. (They may thus be contrasted with those in cluster N, whose use of group methods, while no less central to their approach, seems to have been far less successful.) It is perhaps worth noting that in respect of 'feedback and individual aid' only cluster D is classified as highly in Table 6.

Perhaps at this point a cautionary note is justified: despite all their similarities, teachers in this cluster, just as in cluster A, differed very greatly in personality, and this is something picked up relatively little in the schedule codings. In one instance, where the school was situated in a city area well known for its social disadvantage, the teacher's speech was very similar in terms of accent, lexis, and structure to that of his pupils, and even included what in terms of 'standard' usage might be termed 'errors' (eg, a past participle replaced by the past tense): this similarity of speech may well have helped him in working with these particular pupils. In another instance, the teacher was friendly and laughed a lot as she spoke, but the pupils typically did not laugh with her: although there was no obvious dissimilarity in terms of social background between her and her class—a background much more favourable than that of the preceding instance—there was clearly some sort of basic difference of outlook. The way a teacher's personality and social background affects his relationship with a particular class is obviously both subtle and complex.

A second cautionary note arises from the first. There were very big differences in the classes taught and in their attainment at the time they were first taught by the teachers with whom we are concerned. The researchers made no attempt to measure pupils' social background, and it is by no means clear that they could have done so well enough to have found it useful, though the more extreme instances of advantage and disadvantage were obvious to see. Part of a teacher's task is to adjust the type of teaching to the needs of the particular class—as the teachers in clusters A and B probably did—*but doing so is unlikely to produce equal results with all pupils/classes*: the effects of social and educational disadvantage are unlikely to be eliminated even by the most skilful teaching. In this may lie one of the causes of difficulty in linking cluster membership to particular measured outcomes, something to which we shall return in the later chapters of this book.

Cluster C

The four teachers in this cluster also were very highly skilled. Their approach was, however, far more teacher-centred. This is reflected not only in their tendency to teach somewhat larger groups, or even in one case the class as a whole, but in the far lower emphasis they placed on developing pupil responsibility (see Table 6). Although it would be fundamentally wrong to say they did not in fact develop responsibility in pupils, they did give less scope for the free exercise of it[4]. Their greater teacher-centredness simply precluded it.

What the observers were impressed by was the fact that these teachers seemed to echo many of the achievements of clusters A and B *by markedly different means*. Thus, for instance, although they did not have pupils in small groups and controlled their pupils' learning far more, they knew the needs and characteristics of every individual pupil well and modified their questions, responses, approaches etc to each pupil in the light of this knowledge, so that they in fact produced a differentiated learning experience for each pupil, one apparently well adjusted to need. That their teaching skill was of a particularly high order was nowhere more strongly demonstrated than in the skill and variety of their questioning. Teacher 122, for instance, was extremely challenging in her questioning and required thought-out responses from all her pupils. What was so striking about her pupils was that they were manifestly thinking as they framed their answers. Moreover the teacher typically did not say an answer was wrong, but instead, if she thought it was not altogether right, would respond non-committally in a tone that suggested to the pupil that he should go on thinking about what he had just said. In this way pupils were led to find faults in their own responses and to amend them.

The tasks faced by these teachers in this particular cluster did, however, differ a great deal, for whereas teacher 122 had a class that obviously included some able children and teacher 45 had pupils from, in almost all cases, a socially privileged background, the other two taught pupils from a deprived city area. Teacher 38 moreover had a class that, to the first-hand knowledge of the researchers, had been badly out of control while taught by another

[4] One of them was an exception and was coded 5 on item 20.

teacher in the preceding year. She had had, therefore, not merely to 'tame' them but to teach them fundamental learning skills and assist them to develop better attitudes. This she did, but she clearly did have to make allowance for the difficulty they experienced in maintaining concentration on a task over more than a short period. The result was that the time she spent working with any individual or group had to be substantially limited. She was, however, highly adept at exploiting chance occurrences as a means of capturing pupils' interest and pursuing what were possibly planned objectives, in ways that could not possibly have been planned. Teacher 122 was adept in this way also. (It should be noted that the choice of teaching style may often be made in the light of knowledge of the characteristics of the children to be taught.)

The reader who is astonished to find a teacher in this cluster (in fact, teacher 122) coded as 1 on item 1 has, in fact, discovered for himself how misleading seating practices can be as an indicator of the teaching situation. A situation where pupils are seated in rows and regularly promoted or demoted in their seating positions seems, on the face of it, positively Victorian. The practice belied this. Promotions and demotions were handled with a lightness of touch, and promotions could be gained for greater effort or a greater amount of work as readily as for superior performance. All could be promoted, and all appeared in fact to be so reasonably often. The practice did not underline failure; it constantly emphasised a possibility of progress and improvement. This, together with the constant challenge and the constant pursuit of interesting topics—pursued at quite an elevated level for pupils of their age—seemed to produce an active and happy class. The ways of being an effective teacher do indeed appear to be extremely varied.

Cluster D

Like cluster A, this is a very small cluster, having in it only two teachers. The cluster clearly had many things in common with the three already discussed, the most obvious difference being in respect of grouping. The two teachers in this cluster used whole-class teaching almost exclusively, and were strongly teachers-centred, though, like those in cluster C, they compensated strongly for this by their intimate knowledge of their pupils and the differentiation of their treatment of individuals. Both were highly skilled teachers and their questioning was of a particularly high order. Teacher 46 was particularly penetrating in her questions, which laid much stress on pupils' thinking out for themselves the difference between apparently similar ideas or phrases (eg, the distinction between 'moving away' and 'going away'), and when questioning was going on she kept all children involved in the thinking process by asking them whether they agreed or disagreed with answers given and why they did so. The stress on language work was, however, at the expense of time spent on arithmetic. Her relatively high coding for concept (item 11) in fact represented high concept in English but not in arithmetic.

Both teachers were possessed of highly individual personalities which may well have had an effect over and above their recorded characteristics. The positive reinforcement provided by teacher 46 was, of course, recorded by the coding of 5 for item 39, but even that could hardly take adequate account of so all-pervading a phenomenon. Whereas repeated praise can easily degenerate into something which, like a babbling brook, is after a while simply not noticed, her constant warm approval seemed to create an atmosphere in which the pupils would think well of themselves and see most things as lying within their scope. (After observations, like warm approval was bestowed on the observers: one 'felt good' even though one was conscious of the technique inducing the feeling!)

Teacher 2 too provided much reinforcement of effort, though more selectively. He did much to foster interests and aptitudes and explained the purposes of whatever he was doing even to excess. Perhaps what was most notable was the fact that pupils were given responsibilities that were notably 'real'—such as being entrusted to ring up the education office to make an enquiry of an adviser! The individuality of both these teachers serves to explain the relatively large distance of this cluster from even its nearest neighbour (see Table 5).

Cluster E

Table 6 shows this cluster to be nearer to clusters B and C than to clusters A or D. Table 6, however, immediately calls attention to one feature that distinguishes it from all four of these clusters — a greater use of coercion.

Two of its members (teachers 16 and 51) are particularly near to teacher 41 in cluster C, and another of its members (teacher 29) to teacher 17 in cluster B. This well illustrates a factor already referred to, that where the clusters lie in close proximity, a case in one cluster may be nearer to one in the other than to some cases in its own. The relatively low within-cluster distances do, however, show cluster E to be a strongly coherent unit.

It is not unreasonable to regard cluster E as a borderline one between, on the one hand, the in-many-ways outstanding clusters we have surveyed so far and, on the other, a number of middle-of-the-road ones. The observers certainly saw the teachers in this cluster as being considerably more *formal* than the former, but nonetheless as very competent teachers. If they were 'ordinary', they were certainly very good at it: they typically provided 'something extra'. Thus, while many of them did not favour pupils' working together, the majority of them were positive and supportive in their approach, enthusiastic about teaching, and highly expert in the way they fostered the development of pupil responsibility. (Teacher 118, for instance, gave pupils the real responsibility of checking the dinner money—though she avoided possible problems, by keeping lunch tickets safely for pupils once they had put their names on them.) The majority of them did not exert significant pressure, but their efficiency of management ranked with the best. Their pupils were generally industrious and enthusiastic, and the fact that most of these teachers were alert most of the time—but not constantly—suggests that they had no need to be more alert than they were. Their skill in teaching was considerable, though their explanations tended to be stereotyped rather than varied and inventive. There was little integration between subject areas, and, although concepts figured in the teaching, almost half of them laid greater stress on memorisation.

It has been already pointed out that they differed from teachers in clusters A, B, C, and D most strongly in being more authoritarian in respect of choice of work, but it is important to see this difference in terms of a wider perspective. Virtually all teachers—so the author believes—wish to control in general, if not in detail, what their classes do. Where they differ is in respect of whether they achieve this control directly—in ways that are completely obvious to the pupils—or indirectly. Indirect control seems to be the province of a minority whose control is so subtle that the pupils are less aware of being controlled at all and may even gain the impression that they are following their own bents even when in fact they are being manipulated by their teachers. The teachers in cluster E belonged to the majority who do not, for the most part, disguise the fact that they are in control of what is to be done. On the other hand they were not notably coercive. Indeed while six of them were coded on item 39 as being neither notably coercive nor notably persuasive, the remaining three were coded as depending predominantly on persuasion. It is, therefore, perhaps notable that, whereas they were typically highly expert in giving pupils management responsibilities well matched to their needs and interests, most of them allowed their pupils little freedom in managing their work programme even when the programme of work was announced in advance for, say, a period of three days, and more than half of them imposed some restriction on pupils' freedom of movement and access to resources.

Giving responsibility while limiting intellectual freedom can be illustrated in the case of teacher 16, who ran an interesting project on weather. The pupils did have real responsibility in respect of collecting data and making records, for they learned to use conventional instruments and modes of recording. What was introduced at no stage was any opportunity to devise their own means of measuring and recording. Had they done so as a first step, they might, it could be argued, have acquired a greater understanding of the advantages of the established methods their teacher wished them to learn about.

Perhaps observers' general comments noted at the end of the observations may be helpful in giving an impression of three of the teachers and their classes:

Teacher 18:
Very efficient experienced teacher who demands and usually achieves very high work standards. Although teacher might regard herself as traditional, in fact in work of class teacher was concerned with progress of each individual rather than seeing class as a whole. She had tried many different Maths syllabuses and was concerned to get the best. Very good rapport with class. (Observer)

Teacher 57:
Very efficiently run, quiet class. A weekly programme of work for English worked out on the basis of the previous weeks' work. Classroom characterised by its orderliness, quietness, extremely efficient feedback system, and the constant awareness and vigilance of the teacher. (Observer)

Teacher 118:
Children encouraged to co-operate in groups for project activities including, for one group, devising dialogue for a play.

This group was however taken to the blackboard for some instruction *re* setting out the text of the play. The teacher appears to relate well with the pupils. (Present writer)

A subtle blend of reinforcement and cajoling—the latter tempered by a teasing manner. The atmosphere is relaxed and friendly but class works well and with obvious interest. An integrated day type of approach is combined with a motivating type of supervision. This seems to combine the stimulation of good class teaching with tailoring of work and work rate to individual needs. Pressure is steady but not driving or oppressive. (Observer)

Cluster F

Although Table 6 shows this cluster to be particularly near to cluster E, it is somewhat further from the other clusters previously described than is cluster E itself.[5] It is however a notably homogeneous cluster.

Specific areas where notable differences were found between this cluster and those already described can be readily seen by perusing Table 6. In particular it should be noted that they combined poorer 'feedback' with generally poorer 'efficiency of management'. These are probably more significant differences than those in respect of 'grouping' *per se*—seven out of ten of the teachers gave instruction to the whole class or to large groups and only three to small or medium-sized groups—for these teachers differentiated amongst pupils in respect of work difficulty level rather than in other respects, and even those who taught smaller groups differed markedly from those in earlier clusters in how they taught. Thus it was that in one of the classes where smaller groups were taught (teacher 119), some of the problems we shall find in respect of group-methods in an otherwise very different cluster (cluster N) revealed themselves:

Very conscientious teacher who tends to overload herself with work but does not reflect this onto pupils, with whom she has a close relationship. Teacher finds it necessary to use a fair number of groups in order that she can cater for all the pupils whom she sees as being of diverse ability (composite class). Teacher teaches these groups individually and so this cuts down the time which she has available for concurrent feedback. Further, teacher does

[5] Teacher 99 is notably close to five of the nine teachers in cluster E, and four teachers (10, 119, 123, and 128) are each very near to at least two teachers in cluster E. Teachers 123 and 128 are indeed also near to one teacher in cluster B.

all correction of pupil work and so finds this very time-consuming (though much done in evenings). This is not due to a lack of trust but because she sees it as a better way of maintaining control over pupil work and also because pupils are not so skilled at marking. (Observer's note)

The observers revealed in the discussion of the clusters that they found the teachers in cluster F to be very serious and dedicated teachers with a very considerable degree of competence. It is only when they are compared with the teachers so far discussed that they appear somewhat less than inspired. From discussions with them, they appeared to be teachers who gave much thought to how best to teach what they had to. On the other hand, they were probably inclined to think of what they had to teach as being fixed or predetermined. Teacher 112, for instance, depended heavily on the arithmetic textbook in use—one prescribed by the headteacher—and whenever pupils had difficulties he referred them to the appropriate explanation within that book. That these teachers were coded for questioning (item 13) as 4 (or, in two cases, 3) rather than 5 is probably significant, for it points to persistence in seeking from each pupil *a particular answer* rather than the more open questioning of the teachers we have already discussed, who were prepared to let pupils' thinking lead wherever it might and to capitalise on whatever might come forth. The teachers in cluster F were, it seems, likely 'to cover the course' very competently, but not to open many windows beyond it.[6]

It would be wrong, however, to imply that these were dull classes. Most of the teachers had a high level of rapport with their classes—though the means by which they achieved it varied according to their strongly contrasted personalities. Thus, for instance, teacher 128 was notable for his brusque, challenging approach (which the pupils appeared to enjoy despite the fact that it involved his hurling abuse at them), whereas teacher 6 conducted her class in a relaxed but orderly manner.

[6] The observers did, in their subsequent discussions, have some doubts about the rightness of including teacher 25 in this cluster. She was notoriously difficult to code on many variables, and her placement in this cluster may well have been the result of 'coding for safety'—ie, using a midle-of-the-range coding when in doubt. She was a highly complex teacher who had been observed also in 1974/75. Both then and in 1977/78 she was the subject of a set of joint ('reliability') observations and on both occasions she gave rise to more disagreements of a major nature than any other teacher. Apart from her complexity, an undoubted factor in causing these disagreements was difficulty in hearing what she said while working with individual pupils.

It would also be wrong to assume that, because this is a notably homogenous cluster as assessed by the codings of its members on the SCOTS schedule, there were no individual differences of which these codings had taken inadequate cognisance. Two examples may suffice:

a) teacher 61 conducted some very challenging thought-provoking work, which involved the P7 pupils in finding out things for themselves—issues discussed included: which jobs should be highly and which lowly paid, and why—and yet also conducted what the observer described as 'some very humdrum work in maths and English'. Moreover, she 'was able to run her class very adequately without being particularly efficient (eg, she would change her mind regularly without causing disorder)'.

b) although teacher 3 was not, at the time of observation, teaching her class in small groups, she was apparently in the process of moving in that direction a class that had been accustomed to whole-class teaching.

Cluster G

Although this somewhat less homogeneous cluster lies nearest to clusters E and F (see Table 5), Table 6 shows it to be more like than they to the other four clusters already discussed in respect of some areas, notably 'interest and motivation', 'development of pupil responsibility', and, to a lesser degree, 'authoritarianism and coercion'. On the other hand, it resembles them (E and F) more in the areas of 'teaching skill', 'feedback and individual aid', and 'grouping'. Indeed, most of them displayed some weakness in 'teaching skills', though in some cases this weakness related only to the teaching of arithmetic.

Closer examination of the data, together with the observers' comments, makes it clear that these teachers were particularly skilful in their relationships with pupils and in winning their willing co-operation. All six of them were recorded as being sensitive to pupil needs, and three as extremely so. (One of them, teacher 65, had a most motherly relationship with her primary 4/5 class and was observed to be very gently supportive of a boy who stood out from the rest of the class as being socially and economically deprived. There was, however, some evidence that *some* of the pupils disliked her protectiveness). Three teachers (teachers 28, 52 and 85) however were quite weak in their questioning—they were coded 2 on item 13—*and* as weak or very weak in their exposition. In particular, the teaching of arithmetic by teachers 52, 68 and 85 was especially mechanical. Teacher 85, it is true, was quite clear in her explanations of how to perform computational processes mechanically and did make an attempt to teach concepts, but her presentation of concepts was thought by the observer to be wholly confusing. (The observers felt that the pupils in these three classes were heavily dependent on what they had learned in arithmetic in the previous year. They noted, however, that the pupils did struggle on with their arithmetic. The excellent relationship between them and their respective teachers seemingly encouraged them to do so—and their efforts to learn, possibly aided by assistance at home, may have enabled them to learn almost as well as if they had been better taught.)

These teachers taught other subjects much better, the observers thought—a fact that may have resulted in their being coded a category higher in respect of exposition (item 14) than would have been the case had they been coded only in respect of their teaching of arithmetic. It has to be noted also that the other three teachers in the cluster were coded more highly in respect of both exposition and questioning, teacher 65 particularly so (see Appendix D).

It has already been seen that good teacher-pupil relationships were apparently a factor of great importance in this cluster. Yet the pupils operated in a moderately restrictive situation—eg, in respect of movement about the classroom or access to resources—and they had little freedom in work management. Where these teachers seemed to have particular strength was in a quality of personality that made children like them, accept their objectives, and enjoy working with them. The pupils were not under pressure, but they were interested and motivated, and worked willingly in an uncompetitive and basically unstimulating situation.

Cluster H

Like cluster G, this large cluster is only moderately dense. Indeed the fact that homogeneity of the cluster is somewhat limited makes the description of the cluster difficult, for although Table 6, in conjunction with Appendix E, does give a good general picture, most members of the cluster differ from that picture in a few respects.[7] (Thus even a 17-cluster solution does not in every case achieve quite the level of cluster homogeneity that might be desired.)

[7] See also Appendix D.

Save for the highly exceptional case of cluster D, this is the first cluster we have come to discuss where, for the majority of teachers in it, the normal practice was the teaching of the whole class[8] together or the teaching of two large groups. Moreover, save for teachers 69 and 116, even the number of work-difficulty levels did not normally exceed two.

It would probably be fair to describe those in this cluster as, in general, middle-of-the-road teachers of considerable, but not outstanding, competence. This is not to say that they necessarily lacked some notable skills. Teacher 79, for instance, controlled with very great skill a potentially difficult class of pupils from an area of notable social disadvantage: she detected signs of trouble very early and defused the situations with great verbal skill. And though she maintained a considerable distance from her pupils, she bestowed favours judiciously: she made it seem an honour to be given her attention, and this the pupils accepted. (On the other hand, the work undertaken was notably formal and the pattern of operating appeared to be a well-established routine.) The style of her teaching was obviously influenced considerably by the problems presented by the pupils she had to teach.

A number of teachers in this cluster not only took great care to give credit to pupils for success or improvement but were able to make their public approval something valued by pupils. Others, however, were simply business-like in approach and were less likely to be approached by pupils on purely social grounds. Teacher 23, who was an example of this latter approach, was in fact most notable for the excellence of her questioning and the clarity of her exposition; indeed, 8 of the 12 teachers in the cluster explained ideas well or very well and only teacher 116 was weak in respect of questioning. For half of these teachers the feedback provided to pupils was rather limited. Save in the case of teacher 62, sustained individual instruction was not common.

All the teachers seemed to maintain the interest of their classes though only three of them to the extent of arousing enthusiasm. Two of these three, and one other, were positive in their manner, seeking to reinforce what was good rather than criticise what was bad. Most of them were neither notably positive nor notably negative, though two (teachers 3 and 74) tended to be critical. In the case of teacher 3, however, it must be said that she made clear her high expectations of her pupils and thought it right that they

[8] Only teacher 43 and 78 taught two large groups in both English and arithmetic. Teacher 116 had 3-4 groups for arithmetic.

92

should be in no doubt about when they had failed to live up to them.

With the exception of teacher 116, these teachers were particularly well prepared and well organised in the work they undertook. On the other hand, the course of their day's work was something much more predictable than was the case with many of the teachers in clusters A, B, C, and D, for the latter were much more likely to respond to pupils' initiatives or exploit spontaneously a situation or interest that had chanced to arise. The majority of them also laid more stress on memorisation than on the grasping of concepts.

Cluster I

With the possible exception of cluster P, this is, in general, the least dense (ie, least homogeneous) of all the 17 clusters. Yet despite some high distances between teachers within the cluster, they had a large number of important characteristics in common, and the result is that substantial differences in respect of some variables appear much less important than the same ones would in most other clusters—for these differences do, for the most part, represent different ways of being similar. They were all teachers of strong and independent judgement who thought out their own ways of doing things, and this very independence was an important characteristic in its own right, one that almost certainly had an impact on their classes. They were teachers their pupils were likely to remember.

They can perhaps best be described as being very able, traditional teachers—and particularly so because they believed they knew what their pupils should know and think, and set about ensuring that they did know these things and did think these thoughts *with understanding*. They thus were primarily teachers who sought to pass on the knowledge, concepts, and understanding already achieved by man, but they also wished their pupils to grasp these ideas, to think logically about them, and make them their own.[9] They were strongly intellectual teachers.

Of course such an approach is open to the criticism that it does not permit pupils to discover for themselves, that it stresses convergence and inhibits divergence of thought, and that it gives pupils no opportunity to learn how to be independent learners. There is little doubt that, if challenged by such criticisms, they

[9] Unlike the teachers in cluster F, they did not see what was to be taught as predetermined: they themselves were the arbiters of what should be taught.

would have defended their standpoint strongly and been critical of teaching that lacked the rigour they clearly saw as important. However, the way in which they individually approached the problems of teaching makes it clear that they were each aware of the need to compensate for at least some of the weaknesses that might be inherent in their basic approach. It is clearly worthwhile to spend some effort in examining what these teachers did.

Ironically, it was teacher 90 that the observers were surprised to find in this cluster, for he is one of its most central members. The reason for their surprise is clear: the atmosphere in his class was quite different. Indeed quite frequently he permitted talking to occur. The other classes were characterised by total silence: the proverbial pin could be heard to drop.[10] Control by the teacher was absolute and unchallenged. No pupil argued or treated the teacher other than with respect. Work was treated seriously by teacher and class alike, and was undertaken by the class industriously and indeed enthusiastically. The work was interesting and the pupils were involved in it, albeit on the teacher's terms.

In respect of giving instruction, the skill of these teachers was very high. What they had to teach was carefully and soundly thought out and clearly presented, and most were aware of what difficulties pupils experienced in following what they were taught. More than half of them displayed considerable ingenuity in finding alternative explanations to help surmount them. With one exception, their questioning was of a high order, and pupils had to think in order to respond. All but two laid at least some stress on acquiring concepts, and none ignored this altogether. Perhaps surprisingly, only one (teacher 89) sought to integrate knowledge to any extent, and only teacher 90 gave any encouragement to pupils who sought to do things differently.

The high quality of the feedback they provided reflected the fact that, with the possible exception of teacher 90, they were extremely well organised. The amount of sustained individual instruction given was, however, with one exception not large.

Although work was treated very seriously, these were far from dull classes. Indeed, on the contrary, a high level of interest was sustained. Some extrinsic incentives were used, but the general view transmitted to their classes by these teachers seemed to be that, while work was generally interesting, if it was not, it still had to be done. (Presumably this is why they considered some use of extrinsic

[10] It is interesting that a variable, pupil talk (item 26), found generally of little value, should be so strong a marker of this cluster.

incentives—such as grades, stars, etc.—worthwhile.) In respect of the use of competition, they differed widely, though where it was used, it tended to relate to bettering one's own performance, to competing against oneself rather than others. In the one case where inter-pupil competition was prominent (teacher 89), the pupils appeared to enjoy it.

Again with one exception, these teachers did not go out of their way to praise, but neither were they unnecessarily critical and negative. (Teacher 90 was very critical of the able—those he reckoned to be able to stand up to criticism—but supportive of the weak.)

It would be fair to say that 'the development of pupil responsibility' was not amongst the highest priorities of these teachers, though four of them did spread classroom duties widely amongst pupils. There is little doubt that their prime aim was that the work of the class should proceed efficiently. This did not necessarily mean that control was direct or that pupils necessarily had no responsibility for organising the conduct of their work. Their policy in respect of these matters was essentially instrumental, for it was not a matter of *whether* the teacher should control but of *how* he should control. Teacher 24, for instance, controlled work indirectly (see item 6) and gave pupils much responsibility for managing the programme of work allocated to them (see item 7), whereas teacher 102 did neither. (The pupils in all the classes operated competently—ie, were *not* unduly teacher-dependent—no matter what the mode of control.) All the teachers were, however, at one in allowing no co-operation between pupils: each pupil had individual responsibility to do his own work for himself. Movement of pupils within the classroom tended to be restricted and, in the case of teacher 12, permitted at all only when he gave specific permission. (Teacher 102 did allow greater freedom of movement—and choice of activity; *after formal work was completed* informal chats with teacher and other pupils were also permitted.)

The issue of pressure on pupils to work (item 9) is an interesting one in respect of this cluster, for observers' codings for different teachers in this cluster varied widely, despite the fact that it is virtually certain that all the pupils involved were in fact under a good deal of pressure. The point is that the observers were correctly coding only overt pressure whereas only in some cases was the pressure exercised overtly. The pressure exerted by teacher 12, for instance, required no action on his part. His all-pervading, silent presence constituted extreme pressure—a pressure totally unchallenged! In the case of teacher 115, however, the pressure arose from the system operated: work for a day or a week was allocated and there was no question but that it was going to be completed by the time required, whether in class or at home. ('Leisure' activities for those finished early were used as an incentive.) The pressure that was exerted in one way or another was not, it should be noted, necessarily a strain on the pupils, for the certainty and predictability of events, in some respects at least, made their lives simple.

In this cluster, the issues of pressure and of coercion are closely linked. However, whereas pressure was recorded only if overt, the observers attempted to assess whether the pupils were being coerced, irrespective of whether any specific coercive actions were seen. Where, as with teacher 12, retribution was implicitly so certain in the event of transgression, transgression—and therefore retribution—must indeed have been a rare thing, but that the effect was coercive there can be no doubt.

A generally higher level of 'authoritarianism and coercion' than in the other clusters so far discussed is certainly a major marker of this cluster—though teacher 100 used persuasion rather than coercion.

Although the teachers in this cluster tended to teach either the whole class or large groups, their general approach did not necessitate this. In fact, teacher 100 taught medium sized groups for both English and Arithmetic, and teacher 102 for arithmetic only. Moreover the number of work difficulty levels for pupils differed widely in these classes. This is not in fact surprising, for it has to be remembered that even when a class is taught as a single unit, the work subsequently set can still vary in difficulty. Moreover, when an 'integrated day' type of working is adopted—as it was by teacher 115—it is possible for there to be a number of different activities going on at any one time, even though the pupils are not operating in groups. Another distinction also needs to be drawn: *there is a very clear difference between pupils' working on their own as individuals—as was done in some classes in this cluster—and individualised or small group instruction such as found in cluster A.*

Reference has already been made to the generally high efficiency with which classes in this cluster were conducted. In view of this and of the strong control exercised, it is hardly surprising to find that the industry of the pupils was great, that the transitions from one activity to another were smooth, and that the teachers were highly alert. On the other hand, it may be surprising that in the classes taught by teachers 90 and 102 respectively there was some under-employment. Just as in classes very different from these it is possible for the teacher to be over-involved, so it is in these: queuing for the teacher's attention can waste a great deal of time. However, most of the teachers in this cluster avoided this trouble, for example by having systems organised which permitted pupils to correct their own work.

Whatever one's view of the type of teaching exemplified in this cluster, there is no doubt that it highlights many issues in teaching that all teachers have a need to face and consider.

Since the diversity as well as the similarity of members of this cluster has been very much before us in the preceding paragraphs, the following quotations from the observers' general comments made on completion of their observations are included: they may help the reader to form a clearer picture of some of the classrooms concerned.

Teacher 12:

Characterised by the sheer precision with which everything took place with a minimum of direction from the teacher. A very high level of expectation on the part of the teacher to which the children responded. Very careful and well thought out introduction to new work etc. plus quite a lot of individual teaching. Teacher a very good judge of his own strengths and weaknesses. A lot of stimulating oral work. The meticulous organisation should be stressed, as should requiring the pupils to be "adult". (Note by observer).

Pupils encouraged to bring material: comments on work at fairly high level—pupils treated seriously. Plenty of reference books available. Dismissal orderly and speedy, but without rigidity. Class did not budge when lesson passed bell. (Note by present writer).

Teacher 24:

Outstandingly well organised system of individual records of pupils' work. (Each pupil had a record card which was brought to the teacher along with work and appropriate entries were made.) Teacher kept very close check on individual progress and this permitted pupils to be following their own programmes. They appear to be given real responsibility for doing things—eg.

adjusting the distance of a microphone—and pupils were given a role in checking other pupils' work such as checking the drawing of angles using a protractor). (Note by present writer).

Teacher 89:

Extremely competent well organised teacher who is very systematic in her teaching. She creates a challenging atmosphere in the classroom but one in which the poorer children can participate. She has great concern with the competence of *all* the children. Makes substantial demands on the childrens' commonsense and competence. Very well established system of feedback for *all* the children. Great stress on rote learning *and* understanding, rather than one at the expense of the other. (Note by observer).

Teacher 90:

A confident teacher with an open and informal class atmosphere. All pupils are encouraged to ask questions, which he answers at length, and the whole class is frequently thrown back on its own resources by 'puzzles' with which he gives minimal instructions. . .(Note by observer).

Teacher 102:

She said she tried to give weak pupils the same work where possible, to keep them feeling part of the class, but gave separate work and individual attention when classwork was too difficult for them. (Note by present writer).

Cluster J

As Table 5 shows, this cluster stands relatively near to clusters F and I. Unlike cluster I, however, its five teachers constitute a markedly homogeneous group. It appears also to occupy a central position amongst clusters, having nearly equal mean distances from clusters C, E, F, H, I, L, M, N, and O—see Table 5, page 74.

Reference to Table 6 reveals a characteristic that it shares with cluster I but that it does not with any other cluster we have so far discussed, namely a rating of 'high' for 'authoritarianism and coercion'. However, detailed reference to the data (see Appendix D) reveals that, whereas, on average, they were somewhat less coercive than the teachers in cluster I, they were even less given to being influenced by pupil wishes in respect of choice of work.

In general, in fact, there are very considerable similarities between clusters I and J but also some particularly significant differences, for whereas both could be described as being made up of competent teachers in the traditional mould, those in cluster J lacked the notable individuality that we have observed in cluster I — hence the greater homogeneity in cluster J. They lacked the strongly intellectual bias of those in cluster I and hence their work was more 'ordinary', more unremarkable. Moreover, although their class control was fully effective, it was something more obviously in the minds of these teachers: they were typically making sure that they kept a grip of their classes and did not do anything that might permit disorder to arise. (In three of these cases, the classes are known to have been troublesome in the preceding year — with different teachers — and these teachers were determined to avoid any recurrence. One of these three teachers, who had been observed with another class in 1974/75, had had a much more relaxed relationship with the class she had had at that time, and it is possible that, as she hoped, she did in fact become more relaxed with her current class later in the session.[11]) Good class control and good organisation were things visibly achieved rather than ones that occurred apparently effortlessly — as was the case in cluster I. Interestingly, pressure was recorded as being greater than in cluster I, whereas in fact it was merely of a more overt kind.

As in cluster I, the pupils in cluster J were certainly industrious — more perhaps than might have been expected in view of the generally lower level of intellectual challenge. (They undertook rather 'ordinary' work and effected it competently but unexcitingly.) Standards were not low, but there was no sign of minds being stretched and two of the teachers seemingly did not even tolerate, let alone encourage, any independent way of working devised by any pupil. Like the teachers in cluster I, these teachers knew what the pupils should know and what they ought to think, but in the pursuit of these things there was little sign of the intellectual rigour so characteristic of the teaching in cluster I.

The view that pupils should work alone and not co-operate was one shared with cluster I. Thus, although in contrast to cluster I 'working in groups' (medium to large in size) was practised by most of them, it implied no more than a degree of differentiation of programme and/or difficulty level for various groups of pupils. It is not, therefore, surprising that this group stands so far from cluster A (see Table 5).

[11] She was observed quite early in the school session.

Although three of the teachers in this cluster ensured that duties were widely spread in the class, none of them showed any sign of a real concern to give pupils a wider measure of responsibility. Control of work by the teacher tended to be direct and hence what happened depended on the continued presence and activity of the teacher: as the observers explained, these pupils had not been trained to operate any system; they simply knew what to expect of their teacher.

Cluster K

Table 6 reveals that this cluster is more strongly differentiated from those that we have so far discussed than any of them from one another: not only is 'teaching skill' 'somewhat limited', but 'feedback and individual aid' is at a 'fairly low level'; and, moreover, 'interest and motivation' and 'efficiency of management' are both only 'moderate'. We are, in short, now coming to clusters where the teachers are not merely different but might be judged to have some clear weaknesses.

Cluster K is, on the whole, reasonably homogeneous but for one case—teacher 105. Teacher 105 was, however, probably the most skilled of the teachers in the cluster. All but he expounded new work with emphasis on the 'mechanical' and lay greater emphasis on rote memorisation than on the acquisition of understanding. None showed much, if any, inventiveness in overcoming pupil difficulties, knowledge was typically not integrated, and pupils' inventiveness in finding different ways of doing things was no more than tolerated. Sustained contact with pupils for the giving of individual aid was almost totally lacking and feedback was only 'moderate'. (Surprisingly teacher 105 provided the poorest feedback.)

With the exception of teachers 27 and 76, whose pupils showed interest only occasionally, these teachers generally maintained the interest of pupils, but only teacher 26 aroused any enthusiasm. (Teacher 26 was, in fact, potentially a better teacher than any other in the cluster, but his performance, and his attitude to the class, were erratic. In particular, he tended to lose interest in the less able.) However, pupils were often lacking in industry and frequently underemployed (though this was not so in the case of teacher 105). The reasons for this situation were varied. In some cases where the instructional contacts between teacher and pupil were not only brief but infrequent, the pupils were aware that low application to work would go undetected. The less able pupils in the class taught by teacher 26 knew that he would be impatient with them if they consulted him but that they would be left in peace if they kept quiet and did little. In other classes, pupils were neither trained to cope with minor problems nor encouraged to do so, with the result that the teachers concerned were overwhelmed with trivial enquiries and pupils spent large amounts of time waiting for often unnecessary attention. A further result was that the teachers had inadequate time to devote to more serious pupil difficulties. Even teacher 105 had some difficulties: he made great efforts to get pupils to organise themselves but was less than successful in his efforts—something to which rather weak class control may have contributed.

All the teachers in the cluster except teacher 105 were seen by the observers as being casual in their approach. (Teacher 1, for instance, was described as being 'disorganised, pleasant, and ineffective': he was very sensitive and the children clearly liked him, but the work lacked coherent direction and there was never enough work to put any sort of pressure on the pupils.) Instruction was typically given to the class as a whole or separately to each of two large groups—though teacher 1 had medium-sized groups for instruction in arithmetic. The majority had work in both English and arithmetic at no more than two levels of difficulty. Clearly the problems of providing adequate feedback arose from factors other than having to cope with many different groups.

Save in the case of teacher 76, relationships between these teachers and their pupils were friendly and the pupils typically conversed with them socially. Teacher 26 indeed maintained almost no social distance, allowing the pupils—particularly the more able ones—to relate to him on a basis of virtual equality, though, when it came to control, he was coercive. The other teachers were not particularly coercive and three of them indeed controlled largely through persuasion.

Whatever the means, be they direct or indirect, there is, as the cluster amply demonstrates, a need for teachers to know where they—and the class—are going, and how they will get there; to have means of monitoring and ensuring progress; and to have a system that enables them to apply their own time and energy to best advantage. It is interesting to contrast the lack of pressure on pupils by these teachers with the corresponding lack by those in clusters such as A, B, and I: the latter three did not need to exercise pressure either because the work system provided its own pressure or because the high level of motivation established caused pupils to

101

make demands on themselves. In the cluster K classes, there was virtually no pressure from any source.

Cluster L

This cluster is, with 16 members, the largest of all the 17 clusters, but, despite that, it is remarkably homogeneous for its size. Indeed, only one teacher—teacher 50—fits in it less than easily. It lies nearest to cluster H, but since the differences between them, as Table 6 shows, are concentrated in the areas of 'teaching skills', 'interest and motivation', and 'efficiency of management'—in respect of all of which cluster H stands higher—the educational significance of these combined differences is probably high. This cluster also stands near to two other clusters we have studied, namely clusters F and K.

The comparison between this cluster and cluster K is perhaps particularly instructive. Table 6 shows the similarities between them to be considerable in many important areas, but also shows cluster L itself to be different from cluster K in having rather better 'feedback and individual aid', in laying still less emphasis on the 'development of pupil responsibility', and in being somewhat more coercive. In terms of 'teaching skill', the differences between the two clusters are slight, save that in the case of cluster L a far larger proportion did, in their exposition, tend to give mechanical and superficial explanations rather than present basic principles, and thus they gave their pupils little aid in seeing the application of what was taught to anything but the immediate context. However, like teachers in cluster K, they treated rote learning as important.

The somewhat higher level of 'feedback and individual aid' already referred to in fact applied to individual aid rather than feedback, for the teachers in cluster L, with only two exceptions, gave pupils some (though not a lot of) sustained individual aid or instruction. However, the fact that the level of feedback was found to be very similar to that in cluster K possibly indicates that the quality of this aid and instruction was not, in general, such as to contribute greatly to the quality of the concurrent feedback provided.

In respect of 'development of resonsibility', the differences between the two clusters were considerable, and especially so in areas where giving responsibility implies trust on the part of the teacher. Thus only a quarter of the teachers in cluster L spread duties in the class widely (item 20 of the schedule), the remainder confining these responsibilities to those who were likely to perform them well and responsibly. Similarly, they at most tolerated limited inter-pupil co-operation, and in three cases prevented it altogether. Pupil movement and access to resources tended also to be more controlled. All these differences may well be associated with the less than fully secure class control that was found to exist in all but three of the classes. (In the case of teacher 84, considerable amounts of time were taken up in securing order and the work programme was to a degree adversely affected.) Whether the less secure control was a cause of their giving pupils less responsibility cannot of course be established from the data.

Another factor that may have contributed to control difficulties was rather weak organisation. Certainly only two of the teachers—11 and 80—were recorded as securing consistant industry and enthusiastic application to work. In most cases, the class was taught as a whole, though in others, in two large groups. Work difficulty levels were typically restricted to one or two, as was the maximum number of coincident activities.

In general, the observers felt that the teachers in this cluster lacked any outstanding characteristics and that their whole approach to teaching was stereotyped: they could not 'get out of their normal run-of-the-mill way and re-think their problems very easily: they would just repeat the same thing again'.[12] With few exceptions, motivation was not built up by these teachers. With only two exceptions (teachers 50 and 80), there was, for instance, no form of competition within these classes and no extrinsic incentives. (Of course, many other clusters that we have surveyed lacked such incentives, but in most of these they were not required: clusters A, B, C, D, and I, for instance, provided work that was in itself so interesting as to be motivating.) Differentiation of work or approach to meet the needs of different pupils was, for the most part, lacking. (This was not simply the product of whole-class or large-group instruction, for we have already come across many cases where differentiation was achieved when instruction was so organised.) The pupils were given little opportunity to 'feel involved', to be active, positive participants in the learning process. It might indeed be thought that the fact that most—but not all—of them applied themselves to their work for most of the time was more a tribute to them than to the teaching they received.

These generalisations do, however, require some qualification. Despite the considerable measure of homogeneity in this cluster, some of the teachers in it did display some marked, though

[12] Excerpt from observers' discussion of clusters.

localised, individuality. Thus, for example, teacher 11 'showed a competence in exposition, explanation, and questioning in her maths that was not matched in her English' (observer's note), whereas teacher 80, whose teaching of arithmetic was mechanical and in many respects poor, operated at a high conceptual level in his English teaching, mature concepts such as 'truth' and 'proof' being effectively discussed by at least some pupils in the class. (Teacher 80 was in fact difficult to code on a number of variables because of such lack of consistency in his practice: he showed concern for some and demanded much of them; others he bothered little about and treated with disdain. His organisation was decribed by one of the observers as 'chaotic' and 'off-the-cuff', but, despite periods of time when he appeared simply not to bother, a 'seemingly high degree of motivation was achieved'. There is a likelihood that the experience of being in his class was quite different for some pupils from what it was for others.)

Even teachers who were similar in, for example, having poor class organisation, were sometimes so for quite different reasons. Thus, for example, whereas the poor organisation that has already been referred to in the case of teacher 80 was the product of neglect, that recorded in the case of teacher 88 arose probably from that teacher's inexperience and certainly from his indecisiveness while operating a system that involved whole-class teaching followed by prolonged, individualised correction/instruction: pupils in his class spent large amounts of time queueing for attention. In another instance, that of teacher 13, time wasting arose directly from failure to have adequate differentiation of work: pupils who had mastered a particular task were obliged to sit through prolonged explanations of the work that were needed only by some members of the class. What none of these teachers had apparently done was to stand back and look at the effects of what they were doing and think about new approaches.[13] In this lay their greatest weakness.

Cluster M

This cluster is almost equidistant from its two nearest neighbours, clusters L and J. Perusal of Table 6 shows the similarities to cluster L very clearly, but such differences as there are are important ones: the teachers in cluster M are higher in 'efficiency of management' and display a higher level of 'authoritarianism and coercion', but their 'relationships with pupils'

[13] In some, but not all instances, this was possibly due to over-involvement in simply keeping things going.

are only 'fairly good'. However, the comparison with cluster J is probably, on the whole, the more instructive of the two.[14]

There is little doubt that to the casual observer the teachers in both clusters M and J would have appeared to have greater teaching skill than those in cluster L, but this would have been due to greater administrative efficiency (and, in the case of cluster J, to the teachers' greater motivation of pupils), for close examination of the data relating to all three clusters shows great similarities in respect of those variables subsumed under 'teaching skills'. Most notably they were alike in the rigidity of their approach to teaching, in their lack of inventiveness, and in their propensity to require rote learning. (Nonetheless, even by these standards, teacher 103 stood out in respect of rote learning: her drilling in respect of spelling was unlike that of any other teacher observed and indeed reminiscent of practices usually associated with the last century!)

The fact that cluster M had lower levels of 'feedback and individual aid' probably reflected a belief on the part of these teachers that anything other than very simple feedback is unnecessary, for, if all a pupil has to do is to find out whether he has memorised correctly or followed a procedure correctly, all that he needs to know is whether his answers are right or wrong. *In terms of their own very narrow objectives*, they may have been effective teachers. Most of them appear, moreover, to have taught the whole class (or two large groups) not because they were able to differentiate amongst pupils while they were so doing, but because they simply saw no need for differentiation. Even those few of them who saw some need for it—most notably teacher 22 in respect of arithmetic—saw it only in terms of work difficulty level: the 'less able' or 'less successful' could be given easier tasks. That different pupils might have different learning styles or different types of difficulty in acquiring understanding appeared not so much as to have entered their minds.

Their simple—perhaps simplistic—view of learning accorded with their tendency to see the work to be undertaken by pupils as merely a job, something that might be interesting but that had in any case to be done. That seven out of ten of them treated competition (of one sort or another) as important seems fully in keeping with this view, as does the coerciveness characteristic of some of them. Most of them were business-like in manner, not

---

[14] In making these comparisons, it is necessary to take into account that although cluster M is, on the whole, reasonably homogeneous, it has two members that fit into it less easily, teachers 22 and 70.

particularly approachable (though there was variation in respect of this), and, in some cases, far from sensitive to pupils' feelings. (In respect of the less sensitive ones, the observers commented on the marked difference in their attitudes to different pupils—something that gave rise to difficulties in coding items such as 8, 19, 24, 40 and 42.)

Reference has already been made to teacher 22 as being a relative 'outlier' in this cluster. Particularly notable was her having a large number of difficulty levels for work in arithmetic (though only one in English) and her seeing it as necessary to keep all the work of the class within the range of weaker pupils. She indeed monitored pupils' work extremely thoroughly, checking it at quite short intervals, though at the cost of pupils' spending much time in queueing. That she employed tests at the end of every week did, however, show her approach to learning to be fully consistent with that of the other members of the cluster. However, although she was among the more extreme in the cluster in respect of maintaining very strong pressure on pupils to work and in being in direct control of every aspect of pupils' activities, she was one of the few in the cluster who treated work as something of intrinsic interest. Here once more, then, we have an instance of the complexity of the variation to be found amongst generally quite similar teachers.

It is interesting to compare the teacher-centredness of this cluster with that of cluster I. Control from the centre was equally strong in both cases: what was lacking in cluster M was the very high level of intellectual challenge characteristic of cluster I. Although, on the whole, the teachers in cluster M were themselves probably academically more able than those in cluster L, they were certainly no match for the cluster I teachers. The more able of them provided some quite interesting work, but it was what *they* saw as interesting. They certainly showed very little inclination to follow the interests of their classes: the classes had to attune themselves to them. They tended also to see themselves as the source of all knowledge required by their classes. This was particularly unfortunate in certain cases. In respect of one (teacher 110), the observer noted: 'The teacher is the sole source of information and so will give the wrong answer rather than consult a book'; and in another case (teacher 71) the observer noted that the pupils 'might be wary of how they reply to questions as she is likely to ridicule them—this seems all the more extreme when she has her facts wrong.'

106

These teachers in cluster M used types of questions that were, in most cases, clearly indicative of their standpoint, for the questions were, as the observers noted, typically designed to reinforce what they had already said or were about to say. In the present writer's view, *this sort of teacher-centredness where everything emanates from and is controlled by the teacher is a factor far more significant than is teaching a class as a single unit, for, whereas the latter is compatible with pupils' having roles ranging from that of responder to that of initiator, the former allows pupils to be responsive only.*

Cluster N

Table 6 again serves to give us guidance as to those areas in which the cluster to which we now turn differs from those with which we have most recently been dealing — and these differences are ones of considerable importance, for, although Table 5 shows it to stand quite near to its nearest neighbours, clusters E and F, this is indeed the first cluster we have come across since cluster E where teaching pupils in groups is a general characteristic of the cluster. Thus in cluster N teaching in groups seems not to have been a mere tool in the pursuit of a wider aim — as has been the case with some individual teachers in clusters we have been surveying — but a fundamental feature of their approach to teaching.

With the exception of teacher 5 — the one who fits least well into this cluster — the teachers in cluster N stand, moreover, quite high in respect of 'efficiency of management', something that reveals itself in their coping with the needs of different groups. Significantly, however, they are classified as having 'teaching skills' that are 'somewhat limited', as evoking only a 'moderate level' of 'interest and motivation', and as laying only 'moderate emphasis' on the 'development of pupil responsibility'. It is in respect of these characteristics that it is most similar to cluster L and it is these that explain its lying at a relatively low mean distance from it.

The fact that only two of the teachers 'sometimes encouraged' co-operation and that the rest either at the most tolerated it or (in two cases) prevented it, makes it clear that this cluster's group work stands in very strong contrast with that found in clusters A, B, and D (where most teachers encouraged co-operation amongst pupils). This difference between, on the one hand, seeing learning as something to be achieved alone or perhaps with the assistance of the teacher, and, on the other, seeing it as, at least in part, being helped by interaction with other learners is clearly a major one. The teachers in cluster N had overcome the problem of differentiating work for individual pupils, especially in terms of varying the difficulty levels both for instruction and individual work and of keeping work flowing at least fairly smoothly, but they had *not* changed the nature of the learning process. Indeed, they probably had less interaction between pupils than did many teachers who, while employing teacher-centred instruction of large groups or even complete classes, involved their pupils in a great deal of quite high-level discussion. What they did give training in was working alone. Teacher 37, for instance, was doing much to get quite young pupils (primary 5) of markedly deprived social background to adjust themselves to pursuing their task alone for more than a few brief moments: they were learning to concentrate on tasks. How important such experience is for particular classes is obviously very varied, and some teachers may choose not to provide it simply because their pupils do not need it.

Even those teachers who believe pupil responsibility should be developed may, of course, differ as to how it may be effected. Thus some teachers may see responsibility as developed only by exercising it, while others may see a need to allow it in strictly controlled amounts until they are satisfied that their pupils have, under guidance, learned to be responsible. The practice of teachers in cluster N suggests that most of them tended to be fairly cautious in respect of giving responsibilities other than for recognised duties.

It is interesting that the observer should have recorded of teacher 96 that she would often 'intervene where it is not necessary in supporting pupil work simply in order to get a response from the class'. Could it be that she was seeking to compensate for a lack of stimulation to her pupils while they were engaged in fairly lengthy periods of what was in effect solitary work? Group work—and particularly, though not necessarily exclusively, group work that involves solitary rather than co-operative activity—may be as much, if not more, prone to leaving pupils without regular stimulation than is the type of teacher-centred work where the whole class works as individuals over a sustained period. The teacher who seeks differentiation of work for individuals and groups can give to individuals (or even small groups), on average at least, only quite short periods of direct attention and unless some form of compensation is found, under-stimulation, and thus under-motivation, can arise. Intermittent interaction with the class as a whole—or with an individual in a way that redirects the attention of the whole class—is just one possible form of compensation. If it is used, good judgement as to when to provide it is probably important. For instance, as the observer noted, teacher 37's class was much dependent on her being able to produce new tasks at the right moment.

It has already been noted that teacher 5 was the least well-fitting member of this cluster. She was notable for the very large number of separate activities occurring simultaneously in her class, for her responsiveness to pupils' interests, for her efforts to allow each child to work at his own level, for her working with individuals for substantial periods of time, for her encouragement of co-operation at least at times, for her skilled matching of responsibilities to pupil needs, and for the very marked informality of her relationships with her pupils, but her 'efficiency of management' was below that of other teachers in this cluster. In attempting to achieve her ends, she tried to be everywhere at once. The result was considerable under-employment of pupils and a lack of application on the part of some of them. In view of the unrealistic demands that she placed on herself, it is not surprising that the observer noted that she was 'sometimes irritated' by the demands the class made on her. The level of demand made by pupils is the product of the teacher's system of management.

Despite her informality, teacher 5 was slightly coercive in her control of her class, though less so than other teachers in this cluster. The observers noted, however, that, despite a lack of positive reinforcement from their teachers, the classes in this cluster in general worked well, if without obvious enthusiasm. In general they were kept interested, but were seldom made aware of the 'excitement of learning'. It could be argued that these teachers were giving their pupils instruction matched to their needs and training them to be self-dependent in a working situation—and thus providing a good basis for further development. Perhaps much depends on the pupils' needs, on whether, as in the case of teacher 37's pupils, giving experience in concentration on *any* task for more than a few minutes is a basic requirement.

Cluster O

Although Table 6 shows a number of areas in which this cluster resembles cluster N, the areas in which difference occurs are the more significant. Most significant of all is the difference in 'grouping', for underlying this difference in practice were clear differences of objective. (In fact the cluster most like cluster O is cluster M).

For teachers in cluster O, the emphasis was on *the performance of the class as a class*. The emphasis was therefore not on individualisation (as in cluster N) but on everyone's 'getting the right answer'. Hence mechanical means of getting the right answer were emphasised at the expense of understanding, and testing was prominent. (For some of the teachers this practice may have been a response to a school policy of weekly testing of arithmetic.) Explanations were correspondingly stereotyped. Rote learning was characteristic, though less dominant than in at least some teachers in cluster M.

In view of the emphasis on class performance, it is not surprising that instruction was given to the classes as a whole and that there was a single difficulty level—or, at the most, two—for all pupils. Weaker pupils simply had to try to keep up by learning, by 'rule of thumb', to get the right answer. Moreover, the work to be done was so clear-cut that the idea of acceding to pupil requests to choose what to do, even at the most superficial level, seemed unlikely to be considered. Class control was coercive, though to varying degrees, and control of work activities was notably direct. The development of pupil responsibility was clearly a matter of low priority, and in only four of the classes did the pupils appear to be able to sustain work activities without direction being constantly given or available. Administrative efficiency was generally good, though the type of class operation minimised administrative difficulties, for, for the most part, everyone was doing much the same thing at the same time. Queueing for marking was the main cause of under-employment when it occurred at all. The pupils were fairly industrious, and in some classes industrious to the point of enthusiasm.

In general, it can be said that the teachers in cluster O were efficient at performing a very limited task. Their weakness lay not so much in what they did but in what, for whatever reason, they did not even attempt to do. Where they differed considerably amongst themselves was in respect of the amount of contact they had with pupils and of the amount of feedback provided. Teacher 31 stood out in respect of the high quality of her questioning, her very good provision of feedback, her sensitivity, and her presenting work as a matter of intrinsic interest. However, she was the one, along with teacher 33, who had, through queueing, the greatest time wastage.

Cluster P

This cluster and the only other cluster remaining to be

110

discussed—cluster Q—share one characteristic, their remoteness from all other clusters, and indeed from each other. Cluster P's least distant neighbour is in fact cluster M. Despite the fact that the mean distance of its members from those in other clusters is exaggerated by the inclusion in it of teacher 127, whose characteristics were so extreme as to place him at a substantial distance from all the other teachers observed,[15] this cluster must be regarded as an extreme one. As Table 6 shows, its teachers combined high levels of coercion and poor relationships with pupils with a total lack of any attempt to develop pupil responsibility, with low levels of motivation, with poor feedback, and with 'teaching skills' that are classified as 'weak'. It is important, however, to realise that the weaknesses in 'teaching skill' were not uniform. Teacher 101, for instance, might perhaps a century ago have been seen as an excellent teacher. (His pupils certainly did learn thoroughly lists of names of rivers and answered with some keenness questions on what they had memorised; pages from the geography textbook were read aloud numerous times by various pupils, and every arithmetic example a pupil attempted was marked before he was allowed to do any more. Moreover the teacher treated his task with the utmost seriousness, and his pupils, clearly accepting the need to 'get things right', accepted also what the present writer noted at the time as his 'unbridled criticism of errors'. Teacher 127, on the other hand, simply answered his own extremely low level questions or, having told his pupils what to do, a little later told them what the answers should be.

All the teachers in this cluster took teacher-centredness to an extreme degree: everything had to be done by every pupil at the same time and in the same way. Amounts of work covered were very small and amounts of time wasted very great. All clearly wished to dominate their classes, but their success in doing so varied widely. Teachers 9 and 101, for instance, maintained a control that was absolute, whereas teacher 127 spent a high proportion of his time in endeavouring to maintain what he manifestly saw as a constantly threatened authority. (There can be little doubt that extreme insecurity led him to do everything himself, not trusting a pupil so much as to hand out books.) Even those with secure authority, however, minimised pupil freedom of movement and access to resources.

For all their dominance, real or attempted, these teachers—with

[15] His least distant neighbours were teachers 101 and 124—both in the same cluster—and teacher 77 in cluster Q.

the exception of teacher 101—secured from their pupils little application to work, and deliberate avoidance of work on the part of pupils was far from uncommon. This was often the consequence of boredom, as in the case of teacher 9, who, for all her superficial air of competence, conducted work so slowly and at, for most of the class, so unchallenging a level, that her pupils had nothing to maintain their interest.

Pupil motivation was probably further undermined, the observers believed, by the sheer unpleasantness of the way in which several of these teachers — notably 9, 124, and 127 — addressed their classes. How far this unpleasantness was damaging to pupils' self confidence is hard to say. The pupils of teacher 127 seemed well accustomed to his hectoring speech and they appeared to regard him with a mixture of indifference and contempt. Nevertheless, he did from time to time provoke hostility, and respond to hostility with hostility — as did teacher 9 and, to a lesser extent, teacher 124. Even teacher 75, who was less extreme in respect of some of the characteristics she shared with other members of this cluster and who, in particular, did provide her pupils with work differentiated to some degree according to ability,[16] appeared quite unable to display any liking for her class.

That any pupils should have to make do with teaching such as found in this cluster is indeed disturbing.

Cluster Q

As has been previously noted, this is a remote cluster, its nearest neighbours, clusters K and L, lying at a very substantial distance (Table 5). As Table 6 shows, teachers in this cluster were characterised by being the poorest of all in respect of management and disciplinary control. In other areas, they were similar to cluster P. The fact that they are shown as having been less coercive than cluster P and as having had somewhat better relationship with pupils results largely from variance within the cluster: whereas the observers perceived two of the teachers (59 and 77) to be cold, insensitive, and unpleasant to at least some of their pupils, the remainder were, in general, reasonably pleasant — most notably teacher 42, who showed sensitivity to pupils' feelings. All seemed to be in large measure ineffectual.

In the area of 'teaching skills', teacher 97 stood out as the best, though, since her levels in respect of the relevant variables were

[16] Although teacher 75 did have pupils seated in groups, the class was generally taught as a whole and worked at not more than two difficulty levels.

themselves low, this serves only to underline how extremely poor the remainder in fact were. Their exposition was poor even though they aspired to nothing more than a wholly mechanical approach to learning; low level questioning went hand in hand with a total lack of inventiveness and clarity. Their own grasp of their subject-matter was often questionable. Several of them were heavily dependent on their text-books. Generally the classes were taught as a whole or in two large groups, though teachers 59 and 97 taught medium sized groups. However, in view of the low level of teaching instruction and indifferent feedback, it is hard to see how group size could have significantly affected the situation for better or worse. All the classes lacked motivation and indeed any significant participative role, and, at best, only some of the pupils applied themselves more than intermittently. (In teacher 42's class, work avoidance by pupils was commonplace and his inefficiency stood out even in so inefficient a group.) That three of the teachers (44, 59, and 77) appeared themselves to lack interest in what they were doing was no doubt a factor contributory to this situation, though it may in part have been the result of it also.

That these teachers showed low awareness of what individual pupils were doing in part reflected the difficulty of monitoring so chaotic a situation. Poor class control made the situation more difficult for several of them: the time and effort spent by teacher 97 and, even more notably, by teacher 59, in attempting to maintain control seriously impeded their getting on with their teaching. The use of time-consuming administrative procedures—almost certainly as a control mechanism—by teachers 77 and 97 similarly interfered with the progress of work and in turn acted as demotivating forces.

Even when one's role is the relatively detached one of observer and analyser of data, it is difficult not to feel strongly about the situation of pupils who suffer all at once restrictive control, boredom, and unskilled and ill-organised instruction, as did those taught by the teachers in this fortunately not large cluster.

CHAPTER 9

OUTCOMES: 1

There is an obvious need to draw together the many points of general importance that have surfaced in the course of the cluster descriptions in the preceding chapter, for the clusters, and indeed the individual teachers making them up, are of significance only in so far as they serve to illuminate for us the nature of the teacher's craft. This is, nonetheless, postponed until Chapter 11 in order that account may be taken of the researchers' attempts to measure a few of the outcomes of different teaching styles or strategies. *Those readers whose interest lies solely in the conclusions drawn from this research may, however, feel it preferable to proceed at this point straight to Chapter 11.*

At the same time as the first version of the SCOTS schedule was being revised after its first use in 1974/75, the research team turned its attention to measuring some of the changes in pupils' performance and outlook that would occur during the year in which the final observations would take place (1977/78). Their hope was, of course, that particular types of change might be found to occur in association with certain types of teaching but with no others. Such an association if established would, of course, have been no proof of causation, but it might have lent some support to judgements the researchers would make on the basis of their observations.

Decisions about what should be measured were not easy to make, and it was clear that even the most strenuous efforts would permit the measurement of but little of what it would have been interesting to measure. No doubt the most obvious candidates for measurement were attainment, particularly in subject areas common to all classes. However, it was recognised that 'before and after' scores in any subject area would be much affected not only by curricular differences—which might not be very great—but by the time at which particular curricular elements were introduced: pupils were likely to show increments in learning whenever new work was introduced and these increments were likely to outweigh, or at least obscure, any increments arising from the ways in which pupils were taught. To have assessed separately pupils from P5, P6, and P7 would not have overcome this problem.

It was in the light of these considerations that it was decided to attempt to assess

114

a) the attitudes of pupils to school and learning.

b) application to work.

c) the relationship between the development of computational skill in arithmetic and the acquisition of the concepts involved.

Initially an endeavour was made to find existing tests suitable for making the desired measurements. Failure to find ones meeting the researcher's exact requirements led to the undertaking of a considerable programme of test development. This may, in retrospect, be seen as having been over-ambitious, for although much success was achieved in a period of less than two years and contemporaneously with the tasks already referred to, the time for employing the tests in the research programme arrived before the test instruments could be claimed to be themselves fully tested. They had, in the event, to be used as they were.

Since, moreover, the ultimate objective of linking changes (as measured by the tests) with cluster membership was, in large measure, unsuccessful, the tests themselves and the ways in which they were employed will be described fairly briefly, and comment restricted to what may be learned from the experience. It seems clear, however, that failure to find links with cluster membership was not entirely, or even mainly, attributable to shortcomings in the tests. Much of the difficulty almost certainly arose from a failure to foresee how complex would be the teacher differences between, and even within, clusters. There was, of course, some evidence of this complexity in the 1974/75 SCOTS data, but it was not discovered. It might indeed have been, had the 1974/75 SCOTS data been analysed to the extent that the 1977/78 data were in due course, but there was neither adequate time to do this nor recognition that it was necessary.[1] A cluster analysis of the 1974/75 data was in fact carried out, but not the time-consuming work subsequently undertaken in respect of the 1977/78 data.

What measurements were undertaken will now be described, not least because they are of interest in their own right. They will, however, receive far less attention than at one time was intended, for what can be learned from them proved to be not only different from what was aimed at, but of a different nature.

---

[1] The SCOTS schedule was the means of discovering this complexity—not its cause. The schedule was designed to measure a wide range of variables, whose inter-relationships could only be guessed at. The complexity was there to be discovered whenever means of recording it were created.

ATTITUDES AND APPLICATION TO WORK

The great advantage of attitudes and of application to work as areas for investigation is that the effects of curricular differences—so troublesome in measuring changes in attainment—do not arise. On the other hand, it is obvious that the extraneous influences that affect them are numerous: parents, peers, and the school as a whole are obvious ones. However, since parental influence on attitude may reasonably be different for each pupil, it seems reasonable to suppose that, *in terms of effect on the class as a whole*, parental influence—and particularly *changes* in it—will be self-cancelling. Such, at least, were our assumptions and the tests were framed on the basis of them. For the same reason, subsequent analyses of data were based on the performance of each class—or, where necessary, a section of it—and not on that of individuals.

ATTITUDES

Another supposition, one underlying the decision to attempt to measure pupil attitudes before and after their exposure to the teaching they experienced in the first two terms of the session 1977/78, was that improvements in attitude to school would be conducive to improvements in learning (and perhaps a reflection of them too) and that measuring change in attitude would therefore serve as an indirect assessment of change in attainment both at the time and in at least the immediate future. In retrospect, this supposition seems naïve in its simplicity.

However, once it had been decided to measure attitudes to school, an effort was made to find an existing test that would serve the purpose. To this end, a substantial number of measures were examined, among them one by Joan Barker Lunn[2], which made use of the actual words spoken by pupils when describing their attitudes. Although this measure was eventually discarded because it was thought not to cover all the attitudes most relevant to the interests of the research, it was found a useful guide and checklist.

The eventual outcome was a decision to produce an attitude scale tailored to what was conceived to be necessary and, at the same time, to be usable by the youngest of the children whose attitudes were to be recorded, namely pupils who, at the time of the pre-testing, would be just completing P4 (and thus 8-9 years old). In short, the scale had, so far as possible, to be suitable for the group-

[2] See Barker-Lunn (1970), especially pp 307-9.

116

testing even of children whose reading skills were very limited. The scale produced is reprinted in Appendix F (where pre-test and post-test distributions, expressed as percentages, are also given.) Perusal of the scale shows that its 16 items each has four options in multiple-choice form. In order to minimise the problems arising from the inadequate reading skill of some of the pupils, the test was administered (always by the same researcher) by reading each of the 16 sets of options aloud twice, the pupils being asked not to record their choice before the reading aloud of the options for the second time had been completed. The pupils, who had in front of them the full text as shown in Appendix F, had, therefore, need only to be able to follow the text as it was read, and weak readers were thus protected from the task of independent reading.

The reading aloud had another important advantage, for it was possible

a) to eliminate, or at least reduce, differences of interpretation of the words by reading the options in a way that pointed the interpretation intended, and

b) to use the tone of the voice to underline the feelings expressed by the words—eg, feelings of pleasure or revulsion—and thus to control the affective as well as the cognitive aspects of the options.

It was, of course, because of the importance of reading the options in an unvarying way that it was important to have the same researcher administer the test on every occasion it was used.

A critical feature of the construction of the test was, of course, not only the selection of attitudes to be measured but the choice of the wordings of the item options. Trials were carried out with non-sample classes and with individual pupils. Administration of the draft instrument to individual pupils gave opportunity for the pupils concerned to explain their choices either in retrospect or as they were making them—and thus it was possible to detect, and subsequently amend, flaws in the wording of options, and, in general, endeavour to ensure that the choices made did reflect the attitudes the children believed they held. Time did not, however, permit the undertaking of measures to establish validity in other ways.

It is, of course, common in multiple-choice instruments to repeat some items at intervals as a check on the consistency and thus, indirectly, the accuracy of the responses. To do so was found to be impractible in the case of this scale, since repetitions exact enough to be useful would have been obvious to the pupils. It was possible, however, to detect when responses to certain items were wholly incompatible with those to certain others, and use was made of this by subjecting each pupil's responses to a test—carried out by computer—of mutual compatibility. If more than a certain degree of virtual self-contradiction was detected, a pupil's record was eliminated.

Although all pupils in relevant classes were tested at both pre-test and post-test stages, scripts were eliminated for any one of the following three reasons:

1. inconsistency of responses (see above)
2. word knowledge inadequate (as indicated by failure to achieve a minimum score on a simple multiple-choice vocabulary test).
3. absence for any testing session.

From the 128 post-test classes, 2544 sets of usable scores were obtained. It is interesting to note that no pupil whose responses were deemed mutually consistent at pre-test was found to fail the consistency criteria at post-test. (There was, of course, no means of detecting any pupil who had on either or both occasions given responses that were untruthful but mutually consistent.)

This is not to say, however, that all problems associated with assessing attitudes had been overcome even in the case of pupils who endeavoured to respond truthfully, for what they thought of as being their attitudes may not have corresponded fully to the 'real' attitudes that in practice influenced their conduct. They may, for instance, have been inclined to present as their own attitudes ones that they saw as being approved of by authority figures such as parents and teachers. In addition to this, there were no data on the stability over time of these children's attitudes, either 'real' or expressed. There was always a possibility, for instance, of a recent incident in their classroom having coloured their attitudes, albeit temporarily.

It is clearly necessary to gain some familiarity with the attitude scale itself, and to do this we must look briefly at the 16 items of which it is comprised (Appendix F). Each item is clearly distinct from all others, but some items are clearly mutually related more closely than others. The degree of relationship *where this is linear* can be assessed by their inter-correlations, and hence such inter-correlations were calculated in respect of a) the pre-test data

(May/June 1977), b) the post-test data (May/June 1978), and c) the change scores (ie, the differences between 'a' and 'b'). The inter-item correlations varied greatly—from approximately 0 to .75—though on which of the three sets of data they were based (a, b, or c) made little difference. Correlations between items 3, 9, 14 and 15 on the one hand, and all other items on the other were, as would be expected, typically negative since, in respect of favourability/unfavourability, the options ran in the opposite direction. For the purpose of analysis, certain items were grouped as follows:

1. Items relating to *application to work*—1, 8, 11
2. Items relating to *liking for teacher or school*—3, 5, 9, 16
3. Items relating to *academic confidence*—4, 10, 13
4. Items relating to *value of school/interest in learning*—2, 7, 14

(That there is a good basis for grouping these items in this way is shown by the fact that the within-group inter-correlations range from .4 to .7, save in the case of groups three and four, in each of which a correlation of as low as .3 is encountered.[3] It will be noted that items 6, 12 and 15 fall into none of these groups.)

The following descriptions of these groups of items should be read in conjunction with Appendix F.

1) *Items relating to application to work (items 1, 8, and 11).*

Item 8 amounts to self-report on how conscientiously (or keenly) the pupil works; item 11 is very similar but brings in an additional element: care concerning the quality of work done. Item 1 looks at much the same situation but focusses on the opposite aspect: the pleasure—or displeasure—of wasting time and engaging in non-work pursuits. In short, it lays greater emphasis on affective aspects of working or not working.

2) *Items relating to liking for teacher or school (items 3, 5, 9, and 16)*

Items 3 and 9 are, of all the items, the ones that came nearest to being parallel to one another. However, there are differences: if 3 is the science, 9 is the applied science. The relationship between items 5 and 16 is one of a similar nature, but the differences are almost certainly greater. (Both items relate to attitude to teachers in general. The wish of the researchers had in fact been to record the attitude of the pupils to their own teacher, but since the test instrument was seen by many of the teachers involved, it was feared that

[3] ie, the correlations between items 10 and 13 and between items 2 and 14.

119

doing so would offend some. It was hoped, however, that attitude to teachers in general would in fact be influenced considerably by attitude to the class teacher.) It should, incidentally, be noted that whereas item 5 relates to attitudes to teachers as individual people, item 16 relates to attitude to authority and hence to teachers as authority figures.

3) *Items relating to academic confidence (items 4, 10, and 13)*

In this group, items 4 and 10 are obviously the most similar, but there are differences: item 4 gives a general picture of the degree of success in school *as perceived by the pupil*, while item 10 concentrates on the situation when difficulty or error is encountered. Responses to both items may of course in part reflect pupils' ability—a highly intelligent pupil is probably more likely than others to choose response 'd'—but it appears possible for levels of self-confidence higher or lower than would otherwise be the case to be engendered in the same pupils by, for example, factors relating to the teacher's skill in teaching or his relationship with pupils.

It seems probable that responses to item 13 may be a reflection of personality characteristics, but, at the same time, there seems to be a possibility of these characteristics being reinforced or diminished in their effects by experience, including that in the classroom.

4) *Items relating to value of school and interest in learning (items 2, 7, 14)*

The importance of interest in motivating learning is something few would dispute. Many of the social class differences often found associated with success in school may well reflect the degree to which pupils of different backgrounds have developed interests in the sort of thing the school seeks to provide. Nonetheless, it is a role of the teacher to enhance existing interests and promote new ones. Item 2 seeks to measure the current general level of interest as perceived by the pupils. Interest may, however, itself be influenced to some degree by pupils' perception of the instrumental value of learning in general or of learning particular things. Item 14 seeks to measure pupils' general view of the instrumental value of the learning the school provides or makes possible, and item 7, what might be seen as recording an outcome: pupils' perception of the importance of doing work well.

5) *Ungrouped Items (6, 12, 15)*

Item 6 is concerned with enjoyment of, or distaste for, facing up to difficulty. It does not appear to fit into any of the four groups of items, though it does appear to have limited links with individual variables within them, namely items 3, 5, 8, 9 and 14.

It has an obvious relationship to what we attempted to measure with our second main test instrument, the one used to record actual application to work in an experimental situation (see page 132).

Item 15, which deals with liking for prominence in class—and thus indirectly with social confidence—deals with matters closely related to the personalities of individual pupils and therefore one would expect there to be considerable within-class variation in respect of this item. On the other hand, it seems entirely plausible that teachers can either contribute to or diminish pupils' social confidence by the way they act. Ridicule, sarcasm etc. may well, for example, diminish social confidence. However, it is important to bear in mind that the psychological characteristics involved are complex ones: thus, for example, showing-off in class—being a 'lime-light' case—may point to feelings of insecurity rather than self-confidence. Moreover a socially confident pupil may feel no need to seek approbation and therefore be happy to hide his light under a bushel.

Item 12 is concerned with pupil anxiety (or lack of anxiety) over work. Although teacher relations with pupils may well have a bearing on the level of pupil anxiety, the data are difficult to interpret if only because of an inherent uncertainty about the significance of selecting option 'd': a low level of anxiety may result from indifference to outcomes or from confidence in getting work right. When changes in attitude were examined in respect of individual classes, it became apparent that any general trend there might be in respect of other items was reflected in item 12.

The Test Data

The distribution of the responses for each item in the scale is given in Table 7. Perusal of this table reveals not only that the the distributions were fairly similar on the two occasions of testing but that in both cases the responses for each item tended to be concentrated in only two categories, the two which both pupils and others were likely to see as representing the most favourable attitudes (categories 'a' and 'b' for items 3, 9, 14 and 15, and 'c' and 'd' for all other items). It is perhaps notable that the only item where the distribution is more even across all categories—item 15—is one where favourability/unfavourability is a more debatable issue. It should be noted, however, that item 12 has the same general bias of distribution despite the fact that its categories have no obvious link with favourability/unfavourability and may perhaps therefore be taken readily at their face value. It is also extremely important to note that in at least some cases—for example, items 15 and 16—a coding of 'c' might well be judged to be more favourable than one of 'd'.

Whether the other responses should be taken at their face value is, it would seem, a more difficult issue, for one wonders how far in expressing attitudes conventionally judged to be good the pupils were expressing their real attitudes or whether they were, in many cases, biasing their responses in the direction of what they saw as being approved of by parents and teachers. The minority who recorded responses conventionally seen as unfavourable could, of course, have been deliberately rejecting conventional values and consequently as biasing their responses in the opposite direction—though the very fact of wishing to reject the conventional response might in any case indicate an unfavourable attitude to all matters related to school.

The *validity* of the scale obviously hangs on whether the pupils' responses were, to any significant extent, in fact biased in the direction of attitudes they saw as conventionally judged to be good, when their actual attitudes were different. Unfortunately it was impractible (in terms of workload) for the researchers to collect any independent data bearing on this question other than what was yielded by observing the classes being taught. It certainly appeared to the present writer that most classes were extremely tolerant of whatever teaching they received—good or bad, interesting or tedious—and that the views they expressed in their responses to the attitude scale may well have reflected a tendency to accept conventional values and, within limits, act in accordance with them. If this is so, their responses may have been quite accurate but their expressed attitudes may also have been relatively unresponsive to differences in the ways they were taught.

A very limited attempt—all that time permitted—was made when the attitude scale was being piloted in schools not involved in the main study to assess the *reliability* of the scale by re-testing two classes after two weeks—ie, after time had been allowed for forgetting the earlier responses but before genuine and lasting changes in attitude were likely to have taken place. *Re-testing with the same instrument after so short interval* was probably, however, a demotivating experience and it seems very likely that, on the

TABLE 7

ATTITUDE SCALE: PERCENTAGE DISTRIBUTION OF RESPONSES
(N = 2544)

	PRE-TEST (May/June 1977)				POST-TEST (May/June 1978)			
Item	(a)	(b)	(c)	(d)	(a)	(b)	(c)	(d)
1	3	6	55	36	2	6	68	24
2	5	20	43	32	4	22	51	23
3	15	58	12	15	8	66	16	9
4	2	12	53	34	1	9	59	30
5	6	22	26	46	5	25	31	38
6	6	20	34	40	4	16	45	35
7	3	10	43	43	3	9	47	41
8	4	20	52	23	4	22	57	18
9	21	37	20	23	13	46	24	17
10	6	20	43	31	4	19	54	23
11	2	4	40	53	2	2	50	46
12	13	21	43	24	10	20	53	17
13	4	14	59	24	2	11	68	19
14	63	28	4	5	59	33	5	4
15	21	28	29	22	13	28	39	20
16	8	18	25	49	6	24	34	36

(The Scale is given in Appendix F).

second occasion, at least, many of the pupils involved—all drawn, it so happened, from a school in a socially disadvantaged area—did not treat the test with the seriousness that the researchers had hoped for. Certainly some gross inconsistencies between the two occasions occurred in the case of some of the pupils and it was difficult to know whether to reject the scale as unreliable or regard the test of reliability as itself invalid.

123

Re-testing after an interval of a year, as was the case with the pupils involved in the main study, was probably less demotivating and the fact that *all* pupils whose scores showed internal consistency in the pre-test showed the same consistency in the post-test tends to confirm this. On the other hand, the reliability of the instrument was not formally established and there would clearly be formidable difficulties in doing so, since a) there is no parallel form of the test, b) it is hard to concieve of how a valid parallel form could be produced that would appear to the pupils to be significantly different from the first, and c) comparisons with data derived from wholly independent attitude scales would be difficult to interpret. Since formal data of instrument reliability are lacking, the data themselves must clearly be viewed with caution.

What is beyond dispute is that the concentration of responses in only two categories was a major cause of difficulty in finding any association between the type of teaching the pupils experienced and the attitudes they expressed. (Had all the responses in the minority category been concentrated in classes falling into just a few clusters, conclusions might, of course, have been easy to draw, but, as we shall see, this was not the case.)

Before we look at the relationships between class attitudes and cluster membership, it is worthwhile to pause for a moment to look further at Table 7 to see what changes in distribution of responses for all classes taken together occurred between pre-test and post-test—during which time all the pupils involved aged by one year. This perusal of the table reveals a slight but consistent trend across all items to make less use of the highest and the lowest categories. On the other hand, save in the case of item 15 (which we have already noted to have been generally anomalous) the percentages in the outer pairs (ie, a + b and c + d) remained remarkably constant in aggregate.

The Relationship of Attitudes to the Teaching Received

It must be emphasised that the research was *not* designed to study the attitude changes of individual pupils. Not only was it thought that the scale was likely to have insufficient reliability, when administered as a group-test, to permit conclusions to be drawn about individuals, but it was recognised that the individual attitudes might be strongly affected by factors wholly external to the school. The aim was to look at general changes of attitude in a class—ie, something arising from a common influence, the teacher.

It was recognised from the outset that for this purpose mere comparison of post-test attitude scores would be of little value. The reasons for this were:

1. The absolute level of class attitudes would be likely to be affected by factors arising from the social background or backgrounds of the pupils, and, insofar as this was so, would obscure any effect teachers had on attitudes.
2. Likewise, the personalities of the pupils might well have affected what was attainable in any particular class.
3. The teacher in the preceding year might well have developed a set of unusually favourable attitudes—or unusually unfavourable ones—and consequently might have given the current teacher a good or a bad start.

Since it seemed likely that the same teachers teaching two different classes in two different schools, or even in the same school, would produce two different sets of attitudinal outcomes, it was seen as essential to take the starting-point into account—hence the need for the pre-test data, data that would show what the class was like before it came under the influence of the teacher in whose effects we were interested and that would, presumably, be the product of environmental factors, the personalities of the pupils in the class, and the type of teaching previously received. The interest therefore had to be on the change produced, or, if the starting point was particularly favourable or unfavourable, whether any change had occurred during the year.

To this end, the data for each class were displayed as exemplified in Figure 3. To enable this to be done, it was necessary to transform the data in certain ways. In the first place, numerical values on a 1-4 scale replaced the alphabetic characters defining the item categories and this was done such that, in all cases, 1 represented the 'least favourable' category and 4 the 'most favourable'. (For most items this meant that $a = 1$, $b = 2$, $c = 3$, and $d = 4$, but for items 3, 9, 14 and 15 it was the reverse: $a = 4$, $b = 3$, $c = 2$, and $d = 1$.)[4] Once these numerical values were attached, it was possible to calculate mean pre-test and post-test scores for each class or section of a class. (Some classes were made up of pupils drawn from different classes in the previous year and it appeared better to treat these sub-groups separately.) These mean (or average) scores were then converted into deviations from the pre-test means for all

---

[4] The application of this practice to items 12 and 15 is of course questionable for reasons previously given.

FIGURE 3

*SAMPLE OF GRAPHICAL REPRESENTATION OF ATTITUDE DATA FOR
A SINGLE CLASS*

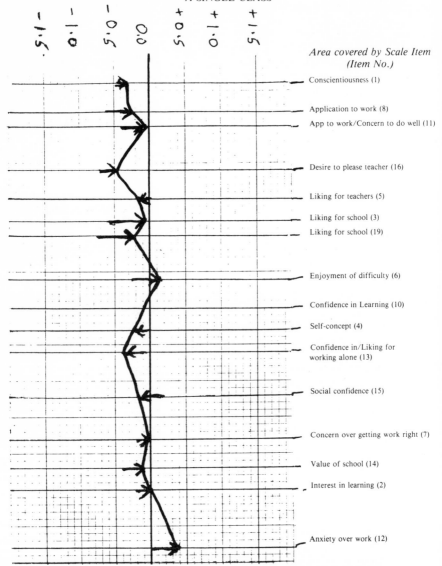

*Area covered by Scale Item
(Item No.)*

Conscientiousness (1)

Application to work (8)
App to work/Concern to do well (11)

Desire to please teacher (16)

Liking for teachers (5)

Liking for school (3)
Liking for school (19)

Enjoyment of difficulty (6)

Confidence in Learning (10)

Self-concept (4)

Confidence in/Liking for
working alone (13)

Social confidence (15)

Concern over getting work right (7)

Value of school (14)

Interest in learning (2)

Anxiety over work (12)

NOTE: Scores are represented as deviations from mean for all classes on the pre-
test. The graph shows *post-test* deviation scores.* The arrows indicate the
extent of change from pre-test. Those pointing to the right indicate
'improvement' in attitude; those to the left, 'deterioration', except *for items
12* and, perhaps, 15 (see p 122).

* The sign of the deviation was reversed for items 3, 9, 14, and 15.

classes taken together[5], this having the advantage of relating all item data to a common mean of zero. Pre-test and post-test scores were than plotted on graph paper, the post-test ones being linked by a line to show a profile. The extent of change was shown by drawing arrows from the pre-test points to the post-test ones—ie, in the direction of the profile line. Arrows pointing from left to right thus indicated improvements in attitude.

One useful way of assessing whether the data were reliable and whether they did in fact represent the influence of the teacher plus that of all other factors was, it was thought, to look at the data relating to those classes or sections of classes that had in fact been taught by the same teacher during the preceding year, for in these cases it seemed reasonable to hypothesise that a) no attitude change would occur (ie, that external factors such as parental ones would, *on average*, probably not differ from year to year and b) the teaching style was likely to be much the same). In all, there were 23 classes that had had the same teacher in the preceding year and seven more had a sub-group (of at least four pupils) that had been taught by the same teacher. Of the 23 complete classes, 10 showed virtually no change in respect of any item (ie, the arrows showing change were very short or were non-existent) and a further seven only quite small ones. The remaining six classes showed quite substantial changes—indeed in one case quite large ones. In the seven cases where just a section of class had been taught by the same teacher in the preceding year these sections all showed some change, though in three cases this appeared to represent their adoption of the attitudes of the other section(s) of the class.

These facts had, of course, to be evaluated relative to the data relating to those classes where the teacher taking the class in the year preceding the observations was *not* the same. There can be no question that, whereas some of these other classes did themselves display little or no change of attitude, this was the case much less frequently than in the classes retaining the same teacher. The evidence, which was far from conclusive, did therefore lend some support to the hypothesis that the teacher as well as other factors influenced attitudes. The seven instances where the whole class had the same teacher the previous year but nonetheless changed their attitudes remain unexplained. Relationships between teacher and class can, of course, evolve over time and teaching styles may

[5] ie, the mean score for all classes together for an item was deducted from the individual class mean score on that item. Above average class scores were therefore positive and below average ones negative. Positive scores thus represented more 'favourable' attitudes.

change, but in these instances no more than speculation was possible.

On the basis of the limited evidence on reliability (and validity) described in the preceding paragraph, it was possible to consider the question which was central to the interests of the researchers: did teachers sharing a teaching style or strategy—ie, those found in the same cluster—have any common effect on attitudes?

In pursuing this issue the researchers did, of course, have to make one major assumption, namely that the style of teaching observed and recorded (necessarily in a period of approximately one week, sometime between October and April) was indeed representative of that occurring throughout the year. *If it was and if the measurements were soundly based, the conclusion seemed to be a clear one: there was NOT any systematic relationship between the factors recorded using the SCOTS schedule and the pupils' expressed attitudes as recorded using the attitude scale.*

This conclusion was reached in a number of ways. In the first place, the attitude data plotted as in Figure 3 was examined in respect of all the teachers, taken cluster by cluster, but no consistent pattern could be detected in any cluster; rather the contrary. Of course, the concentration of so many cases in only two categories (see Table 7) made it difficult to find change, but the very fact that classes remained within these two categories suggests that they were not particularly prone to change. It was, therefore, of some importance to look at some individual cases.

When one looked at the recorded attitudes of the classes of those teachers who were not only extremely skilled and able (as judged by the criteria used throughout Chapter 8) and whose classes had been observed to respond to them with a keenness and enthusiasm that could only be described as impressive, notably favourable attitudes were typically *not* found; in some instances indeed even the contrary was found. Teacher 117 (cluster B), for instance, whose class had the previous year had attitudes that had been close to average, had deteriorated slightly in attitude by the time she had taught them for a year, yet she had been described by the researcher who observed her as 'positive' and 'enthusiastic', as motivating her pupils to a high degree, and as suggesting 'imaginative use of resources, so making all work interesting'. Had she perhaps taught her class to be critical and independent in judgement and hence to avoid claiming to have attitudes that were merely pious ideals? It was possible only to speculate.

The post-test attitudes of the class of teacher 21 (cluster A), though little changed, were nonetheless below average despite an unusually privileged social background and a teacher who was both highly skilled and willing to give her pupils considerable freedom. (It is, of course, important to realise that even somewhat below average attitudes were, in absolute terms, still quite favourable because of the high level of the average.) Teacher 106 (also cluster A), whose class enjoyed none of the privileged social background of teacher 21's, had, on the other hand, attitudes about average in their favourability. There were indeed notable differences in the teaching styles of the two teachers—see Chapter 8, pp 77-78—but did these explain the differences? Or were the less socially privileged children more anxious to appear to be virtuous in their attitudes? Again these were speculations. Teacher 122 (cluster C), whose class was noted by the observer and by the present writer as appearing to be very highly motivated and whose teaching was perhaps the most impressive—especially in respect of interest and questioning skill—of the teachers giving instruction either to the complete class or two large groups, apparently induced somewhat different attitudes in the two sections of her P6/7 class, the P6 section dropping slightly to around average for all attitude items but the (smaller) P7 section rising sharply to very well above average in respect of liking for teachers and desire to please them, and also in respect of interest in learning. Did her approach suit the older section of her class better? Whatever may have been the case, there could be little doubt that this teacher's pupils were well able to understand the choices they were making when they indicated their attitudes.

A survey of clusters P and Q showed clearly that even some of the weakest teachers had not induced responses that were particularly unfavourable attitudes of the class taught by teacher 9 (cluster P) class whose attitudes improved substantially to a level well above average. Moreover, although the class taught by teacher 77 (cluster Q) had expressed unfavourable attitudes, these may well have been due not to her low level of competence but to what was judged to be her total insensitivity to the feelings of her pupils, and similarly the unfavourable attitudes of the class taught by teacher 9 (cluster P) might have been due less to her weak organisation than to what the observers felt to be her overbearingness.

Whatever the true explanations may be, being kind, pleasant, and dedicated to pupils' welfare does not necessarily, it would seem, bring forth expression of favourable attitudes—teacher 65 has already been instanced and teacher 37 could be too. Nor, it would seem, does a teacher's being critical prevent a favourable attitude to teachers, for teachers 3 and 101 are instances of the contrary. Teacher 3's emphasis on what she expected of her class may well have induced the very attitude she was seeking; teacher 101 by his old-fashioned approach — and his conscientiousness and high expectations — may have had a very similar effect. Yet again, teacher 80 seems to have been able to make his pupils think well of teachers, like school, and enjoy difficulty. Was it the result of his criticism and his demand for standards? Or may it have been his teasing manner and his fondness for challenging individuals?

Speculations such as these most certainly do not provide secure answers, but they do point to the mass of ways in which teachers may influence pupils' attitudes.

Discrepencies between pupils' expressed attitudes and their 'real' ones, a faulty schedule, and many other matters could be adduced as the reason for the failure to find any systematic and uniform link between teaching style (ie, cluster membership) and class attitudes, but it seems to the present writer more plausible that neither teaching style nor teaching efficiency are major determinants of pupil attitudes. This is not to claim that teachers do not influence the attitudes of their pupils but that the means by which they do so are extremely variable and not necessarily uniform with respect to all pupils in a class. Factors of personality may, for instance, be of key importance. On the other hand, factors of convention may make impervious to influence many of the attitudes of children— and particularily the ones they express.

Failure to find clear links between teaching styles and pupil attitudes could of course be attributed to inept clustering. However, the extensive correlational studies that were undertaken seeking to elicit any relationships there might be between the attitudes the pupils expressed and the ratings of their teachers on both single and grouped items of the SCOTS schedule served only to underline the conclusion already reached: that teaching characteristics as measured by the SCOTS schedule, whatever their effect on particular pupils and in particular circumstances, do *not* appear to have been a major factor in determining the attitudes to school of complete classes.

APPLICATION TO WORK

As in the case of the attitude scale, the researchers' objective in measuring application to work was to record changes in the pupils' outlook relative to school work and to learning in general, rather than to record how well they applied themselves to work in the classroom while under the direct supervision of their teacher.

It was recognised from the outset that adults tend to apply their efforts selectively, giving the greatest application to activities that interest them or that are important to them in some way, and pupils were expected to be no different. How interesting pupils found the work they did in school would, we were confident, have bearing on the degree to which they applied themselves to school work. How important they saw school work as being to themselves seemed likely also to have such a bearing. But of course the school situation is substantially different from that in which adults—and children out of school—generally operate. In particular, the importance of what is undertaken in school is something pupils are in a very poor position to assess, for the importance often has to be judged in terms of utility later in life. (In advanced societies, preparation for life and the life that is prepared for typically stand far apart.) Pupils' judgements of the importance of what they do in school are, therefore, likely to be heavily dependent on the views of others—parents, teachers, peers etc.—though pupils can, and almost certainly do, assess in the light of their own limited experience the arguments put forward by others. There are, then, on the face of it, grounds for supposing that teachers may, intentionally or unintentionally, alter pupils application to school-type work both by influencing their level of motivation and by influencing their assessment of the importance of such work. The interests of the research team lay in finding evidence of whether this was in fact so *in any systematic way.*

It was also recognised from the outset that willingness to apply one's efforts to one sort of task does not necessarily imply willingness in respect of another sort. Accordingly interest was focussed on two contrasting sorts of task, one involving repetitious work and one involving struggling to understand what one has failed to grasp at the first attempt, and work on producing suitable tests was undertaken. The test developed for the first of these two purposes was eventually abandoned as a failure, but the other one was utilised in the subsequent research programme.

The test that was abandoned will be described briefly since the reasons for its failure are of some interest. It consisted of a series of multiplication sums, and was thus highly repetitious. The measurement was concerned not with the rightness of the answers but with maintained work-rate, which was perceived as a measure of application. Since work-rate was the key factor, it was important that variation in difficulty should not cause variation in work-rate. Accordingly the multiplication sums, all involving multiplication by a single digit and all utilising four of the five digits 3,4,5,6 and 7, were devised such that the operations involved —eg, multiplying 6 by 7—were constantly and regularly repeated, as can be seen in the following examples, which constituted the first seven items of the test:

1) 675×4; 2) 576×3; 3) 347×6; 4) 473×5;
5) 653×4; 6) 563×4; 7) 475×3.

The test was applied as follows:

1. The pupils worked at the test for 5 minutes.
2. At the end of this time, they were stopped and asked to mark how far they had reached.
3. They were then restarted, and, after 5 minutes, again stopped and asked to record how far they had reached.
4. Step 3 was then repeated.

The rationale of the test was that step 1 would provide a base rate and that subsequently work-rate would fall off differentially and thus provide a measure of application to this repetitious task. In the event, the rationale proved unsound. Once pupils realised the amount of work they had completed within a time-span was being recorded, they were motivated to race with one another and were observed to compare amount done. Far from the work-rate declining, it rose dramatically! The pupils created the competition themselves and clearly enjoyed it!

Testing application to overcome difficulties of understanding posed novel problems for the researchers. The first difficulty related to the fact that a task that might tax one pupil would pose no problem for another. If pupils were to be faced with the situation with which the test was concerned, all pupils had to be confronted with problems matched to their own abilities—matched in being just difficult enough to require them to struggle but not so difficult as to be beyond their capacity. To meet this problem a number of steps were taken:

1. Twelve 'puzzles' in the form of programmed texts were devised. (Examples of these are given in Appendix G.) Each puzzle had a number of sections. In the first, the pupil was able to attempt the puzzle unaided. When he had recorded an answer, he had then to remove an adhesive label that covered

the correct answer in order to see if he was correct. If he was not, he had to go on to the next section, where some explanation was given before he was asked another question designed to test his understanding. His answer was then checked, again by removing an adhesive label. If he did not have the correct answer this time, there was a third section following the same pattern as the second but giving even more help.

2. These puzzles, which had been designed to vary in difficulty, were then piloted in order to ascertain empirically their relative difficulties so that they could be ranked in order of difficulty.

3. A system was then devised whereby pupils undergoing the test would work through the puzzles, starting with the easiest, until they came to one they did not get correct at the first attempt (ie, on page 1 of the puzzle). To speed this progress, those getting a puzzle right at this first stage—ie, without help from the text—skipped the immediately following puzzles, and those requiring only the help provided by the second section skipped a smaller number. Only those requiring to cover all three sections skipped none.

4. Finally a system was devised for observing and recording how the pupils applied themselves.

The behaviours on which attentions was focussed related to a) cheating—ie, seeking the right answer without first seeking to understand how it was reached; b) application/non-application to task; c) working independently or seeking help from other pupils and/or the test administrator. (The specific behaviours are shown in Figure 4.) Recording such behaviours required close observation, and it was found practicable for an observer to record the behaviour of no more than 8 pupils. These 8 pupils' activity was recorded sequentially throughout the time of testing. Thus, as soon as an observer had recorded the current behaviour of one pupil, he turned his attention to the second, and so on until all 8 had been recorded. He then returned to the first. (At each recording, the puzzle on which the pupil was working and the exact point in it then reached were noted.)

Since it was possible to provide no more than two trained observers to work with a temporary member of the research time— an experienced teacher—who instructed the pupils how to proceed and answered pupils' questions, it was not possible to test more

FIGURE 4

*APPLICATION TO WORK TEST—EXAMPLE OF COMPLETED OBSERVATION SCHEDULE**

OBSERVER'S CODING	1	4	3	3	4	5	6	4
PUPIL NUMBER	1	2	3	4 (11.58)	5 (11.56)	6 (11.58)	7 (11.55)	8
A. Peels answer before answering.								
B. Peels answer then changes answer.		Doubtful case	(6/1? [illegible])	[illegible]		11/1	4/1, 9/1, 12/5,	[illegible]
C. Looks through label then writes answer.		6/1, 9/1,			9/1?, 10/1, 11/2			6/1, 10/1?, 11/1, 12/1,
D. Looks ahead for answer then writes it in.								
E. Copies from neighbour.		-	(10/1?)	(4/1?), 6/1,		9/1?,	4/1, 10/2, 10/3? 11/1	
F. Tries to look through label.							10/3, 12/3	9/1, 11/1
G. Looks ahead for clue.								
H. Looks around for help/inspiration.							4/1	
I. Answers quickly (doubtful case).		6/1? (changed ans)		4/3, [illegible]	12/1	6/1, 9/1,		[illegible]
J. Insists on co-operating with another.				4/2				
K. Insists on disturbing another child.								
L. Seeks help from teacher.				4/1, 6/1, 11/4, 11/4				
M. Daydreams./Plays.								
N. Peels answer after answering.	[illegible], 5/1, 6/1, 7/1, 9/1, 9/1,	[illegible], 4/1, 5/1, 10/1	[illegible], 4/1, 12/1,	[illegible], 4/1, 6/1, 9/1?, 11/1, 12/1	4/1, 4/1, 7/1, 8/1, 9/1,	[illegible], 4/1, 5/1, 10/1, [illegible]	10/1, 11/1	[illegible], 3/1?, 5/1, 9/1,
O. Writes in answer with working.					[illegible]	4/1, 5/1,		5/1, 5/3, 9/1,
P. Goes back and revises.								
Q. Works methodically.	4/2, 4/3, 4/2, 4/3, 7/2, 7/3, 7/4, 9/2, 12/4	4/2, 4/3, 5/1, 5/4, 6/1, 9/1, 10/2, 10/3, [illegible]	4/2, 6/1?, 9/1, 10/2, 4/3, 10/4	4/3?, 5/2, 9/2?, 9/3?, 11/2, 11/4, 11/4, 12/2	4/1, 4/2, 4/3, 7/2, 7/3, 7/4	4/2, 4/2, 10/1, 10/2, 12/3, 12/5		4/2, 4/2, 4/4, 5/2, 9/4, 10/1?,
R. Stuck and (perseveres)	[illegible] 9/1, 9/2, 9/3, 9/4	(12/3), 7/4	(10/3)	(11/4)			(10/1)	(9/1)
S. Reads Puzzle.								
T. Seeks help from another child.								

NOTE: Save for those in the top row, the hand-written figures—eg, 4/3—indicate which puzzle, and which page of that puzzle, the pupil was working on at the time when the particular activity category was recorded.

* The devising of this schedule was the work of Finlay Coupar and Graham McAvoy.

than 16 pupils in a class. In order that these 16 might be representative of the range of ability/attainment in each class, they were selected using the Word Knowledge scores. Thus pupils were ranked according to Word Knowledge score and then, if, for example, the class numbered 24, every third pupil was dropped and the remainder tested at the pre-test stage. Absence of pupils or the effects of reconstruction of classes tended to reduce the number tested to below 16 at post-test stage. Those tested at both stages numbered 1776. They were drawn from 125 of the 128 classes.

For the post-test stage, a parallel form of the test instrument was used. (The "puzzles" for the two versions of the test were exactly parallel in that exactly the same lines of reasoning had to be followed—only the examples, the superficial characteristics, varied.) This was done in order to avoid the risk of any answer being remembered and to minimimse demotivation resulting from the repetition. The puzzles involving numeric/alphabetic series were identical in both forms of the test, since recalling any specific series after a year was clearly impossible.

The coding form used (Figure 4) yielded, of course, only frequency counts of the various behaviours specified. These frequencies were the basis of the observers' subsequently placing the pupils on a 6-point scale, on which '1' represented the highest level of application and '6' the lowest. (In some instances where observers had noted uncertainty about exactly what a pupil was doing at a particular instant, clarification was possible by making subsequent reference to the appropriate point in the pupil's puzzle script.)

Reliability

The most obvious questions that arise when one considers a test such as this relate to observer reliability and to the relationships between the behaviour observed under test conditions and that occurring at other times.

In order to assess observer reliability, a total of 58 pupils from 13 classes were observed by both observers. In some cases this involved having two test sessions instead of one, with approximately 12 pupils tested on each occasion. (With a group of 12 pupils it was possible for 4 pupils to be covered by both observers.) In other instances, where the total number of pupils available to be tested fell well below 16, it was possible to have some double observations during a single testing session. A very high level of agreement was achieved between the observers, their means for a group of children from a class being virtually identical. For 44 of the 58 pupils, codings by the two observers were in fact identical. In 13 other cases, there was a discrepancy of one scale point, and in one case of two scale points. Comparisons of the raw recordings on which these codings were based also showed a close correspondence despite the fact that the specific times when the two observers recorded the behaviour of an individual pupil would not, in general, have been identical. There was some evidence, however, that what one observer recorded as 'looks around for help/inspiration' was recorded by another as 'daydreams/plays'. Less prominent or less frequent behaviours were sometimes recorded by one observer and not by the other.

Validity

The behaviours observed and recorded pose relatively few problems of interpretation and a close agreement between the observers tends to confirm this. Any question about the validity of the test lies not so much in the validity of what was recorded as in the representativeness of the *behaviour evoked by the test situation*. The level of interest of the test items may have been quite different from that of learning tasks either in the classroom or in life at large, and pupils may have seen the puzzles as either less or more important than routine school work. Yet again, working under the direction of a stranger may have affected their behaviour. There is no clear-cut answer to such questions.

The Pupils' Application in the Test Situation

It will be recalled that the prime objective of the test was not to record whether the pupils worked or not but whether they persisted at seeking to understand whatever caused them some difficulty. Although a small proportion of the pupils made little effort, the vast majority appeared keen to get the right answer. However, although in the case of about 60% of the pupils this keenness involved a high degree of effort to understand, and in some instances extreme determination, the remaining 40% (those coded 3-6) appeared concerned mainly to get the right answer irrespective of whether understanding was achieved. Thus they cheated when they got into difficulty—some more often or more readily than others. They did so by removing the labels covering the answer before attempting to answer themselves, or by holding the sheet up to the light to read the answer through the covering label, or simply by copying from neighbours. By so doing, they seemed to indicate either that they saw understanding the problem as unimportant or that they despaired of getting the right answer no matter how hard they might try.

Stability of Pupils' Application in the Test Situation

Table 8 shows the relationship between pre-test and post-test codings for all the pupils observed. 641 (36%) of the 1776 pupils observed were coded identically on both occasions, no less than

TABLE 8

APPLICATION TEST: PRE-TEST CODINGS BY POST-TEST CODINGS (PERCENT)

	CODING	1	2	3	4	5	6	TOTAL
				PRE-TEST				
P O S T	1	25.8	10.0	3.9	3.2	2.4	1.2	46.5
	2	6.3	3.5	2.3	0.8	0.8	0.5	14.2
	3	5.9	2.9	2.7	1.2	1.0	1.6	15.3
T E S T	4	2.7	1.8	2.4	0.9	1.0	1.0	9.7
	5	1.5	1.0	0.7	1.1	0.5	0.9	5.6
	6	0.9	1.4	1.5	1.2	0.9	2.7	8.6
	TOTAL	43.0	20.6	13.5	8.4	6.6	7.8	100.0

(N = 1776)

NOTE: The codings run from 1 (high application) to 6 (low application).

458 of these being coded '1' on both occasions. A further 513 (29%) were coded differently by only one point. On the other hand 139 (8%) moved up or down by as much as 4 or 5 points. The question arises of whether those who changed did so in response to the type of teaching they had received.

Relationship to Teaching Received

What was seen as a crucial test of whether the changes between pre-test and post-test were associated systematically with the type of teaching received was whether the changes in the classes that had the same teacher as in the preceding year were less than in other classes, since if the degree of change was virtually the same, it was entirely credible that whatever accounted for the change in the former classes accounted for it also in the latter. When the mean change for each class was calculated, it was found that *if the direction of change was ignored* the mean change for all class with the same teacher was .55 and that for all others .60. This was clearly too small a difference to be of any practical significance. When the mean change-scores, together with the post-test mean scores, were tabulated for each cluster, it was obvious that the variance within clusters was freqeuntly large or very large. Mean post-test scores ranged from 1.0 (the minimum possible since it represented everyone of the 13 pupils tested as coded as 1) to 4.44, and the highest mean change score was -2.17. Those cases with extreme scores were individually examined, but although in some instances it was possible to hazard an explanation, it was quite impossible to apply the same explanation to other cases with the same score characteristic. The only conclusion that it seemed reasonable to draw from the evidence was, therefore, that no systematic linkage had been found between teaching received and application to work as measured by this test. This conclusion, it must be stressed, does not, however, preclude the possibility of individual teachers having, in a highly individual way, an impact on the ways in which their pupils apply themselves to work.

The Relationship between Application and Attitudes

In view of the fact that, as we have already seen, those who were coded less favourably for application were not, in general, idle, but concerned to get the right answer *by any means*, it is not surprising that no association could be found between application scores and those items of the attitude scale that related to application to work (1, 6, 7, 8 and 11). A very high proportion of those coded as '1' for application did indeed describe themselves on the attitude scale as being conscientious over work, but an equally high proportion of those coded 2, 3, 4, 5, or 6 did so too. Those who on the attitude scale had claimed to apply themselves to work but who were coded as 4, 5 or 6 on the application scale were not necessarily dishonest or mistaken in their responses on the attitude scale, for getting the right answer would have been seen by them as tantamount to application.

Conclusion

The supposition that led the researchers to measure attitudes and application to work, namely that attitudes and application are important mediating variables between teaching and pupil performance, receives no support from the evidence accumulated in this research. If teaching styles have *systematic* effects on attitudes and on application to seeking to understand, this research failed to elicit them.

CHAPTER 10

OUTCOMES: 2

In this chapter, we shall be concerned with the two remaining tests that were designed to record change in pupil performance during the year in which the teachers were observed (1977/78), namely the two arithmetic tests, one concerned with computational arithmetic and the other with knowledge/understanding of related arithmetic concepts.

It has already been explained (see page 114) that performance on these tests—and particularly the former of them—would, at any moment in time, be much influenced by *opportunity to learn* (ie, by whether a particular topic, such as multiplication of decimals, had been taught) and that it was thought probable that this effect would outweigh differences in performance that were the outcome of differences in the teaching style experienced. It was, moreover, known to the researchers that there were considerable differences amongst teachers as to when they introduced particular topics for the first time, and that hence any comparison of class performance that assumed that by the end of a school year all P6 pupils, for example, would have completed the same range of topics would be unsoundly based. It was judged essential, therefore, that both tests should cover all likely curricular elements, but that the performance of the classes should be assessed only relative to those test items that related to work that they had been taught. Furthermore, by comparing the performance of pupils in respect of the same curricular items in the computational test and in the tests of concepts, it was hoped to ascertain whether the employment of particular teaching styles might be conducive to pupils' acquiring greater understanding of the arithmetic processes that they were taught to use.

It was, of course, well known to the researchers that some teachers laid far more explicit emphasis on the acquisition of arithmetic concepts than did others and that, although many used, perhaps involuntarily, a text-book that emphasised the acquisition of concepts, it was the case, as had been noted during the 1974/75 observations, that it was used with widely different degrees of commitment and skill. Teaching style was unlikely to be the only factor.

In order that the proposed testing could be carried out, two tests were produced. The test of concepts confined itself to addition, subtraction, multiplication, division, and place value (all in respect of both integers and of decimal numbers), to fractions, and to the relationship between decimals and fractions. Its approach was thus essentially numeric and reflected the type of teaching of arithmetic concepts that had been observed to occur. The test of arithmetic computation closely matched the concept test in terms of the arithmetic processes covered.

THE TEST OF ARITHMETIC CONCEPTS

The concept ('Look and Tell') test (Appendix H) was a multiple choice one, with four options for each of its 58 items. For each item a number or an arithmetic expression appeared in column A and another in Column B and the pupil was required to indicate by a tick whether A was larger than B, B larger than A, or both equal. The fourth option was 'Don't know'. Pupils were not allowed to do any calculation on the test sheet, and great emphasis was placed by the test administrator (an experienced teacher who temporarily joined the research team during both the pre-test and the post-test periods in 1977/78) on the need for them to judge what the answers should be without working out the arithmetic expressions.

A multiple choice test of this sort is, of course, open to guessing and copying by neighbours. The latter was, so far as possible, prevented by the test administrator, and specific steps were taken to control the effects of the former. Thus all items in the test were paired (as shown in Table 9) and a correct response was recorded only when *both* these items were answered correctly. (The paired items were always well separated from each other. In one instance, four—instead of two—items had to be answered correctly.) These measures to reduce the effects of guessing must, incidentally, have reduced the effects of all but sustained copying.

A 'Don't know' response is, of course, one that may be either over- or under-used. The instructions given to the pupils were to the effect that this response should be used only when they had no idea what the correct answer was. If they thought they had an answer that might be right, they were asked to record it.

Both this and the computational test were administered without formal limit of time, since it was desired that pupils should answer as many items as they could, though practical considerations made it necessary from time to time to end the testing session when one or more pupils who had made abnormally slow progress were still unfinished. So far as the concept test was concerned, this lack of

TABLE 9

ARITHMETIC TESTS: TOPIC AREAS AND RELATED ITEM NUMBERS

TOPIC AREAS	CONCEPT ITEM NUMBERS (The item numbers are those adopted when test items were paired.* The numbers in brackets are those of the test items combined and thus correspond to the items in Appendix H)	COMPUTATION ITEM NUMBERS
Integers		
Addition	8(4 + 10), 9(16 + 24) 26(15 + 23)	1, 2, 3, 4, 5, 6
Subtraction	6(3 + 9), 7(20 + 28)	12, 13, 16, 17
Multiplication	10(15 + 11 + 19 + 27), 11(17 + 25), 12(37 + 46)	14, 15, 18
Division	13(6 + 12), 14(32 + 41), 3(18 + 16), 28(52 + 58)	3, 5, 7, 8, 9
Place Value	1(1 + 7), 2(13 + 21)	
Fractions		
Equivalence	17(36 + 45), 27(48 + 54)	19, 20
Addition	—	21
Subtraction	—	22
Multiplication	15(29 + 38), 16(33 + 42)	23, 24
Division	18(47 + 53)	25, 26
Decimals		
Money	4(2 + 8), 5(14 + 22)	10, 11
Place Value	19(31 + 40), 20(34 + 43)	27, 32, 34
Addition and Subtraction	—	32, 33, 34
Multiplication	22(51 + 57)	35, 43, 44
Division	—	36, 37
Decimal/Fractions		
Equivalence/conversion	21(35 + 44), 23(30 + 39), 24(49 + 55), 25(50 + 56)	28, 29, 30, 31, 37, 38
Brackets	12(37 + 46), 28(52 + 58)	39, 40, 41, 42

* In the case of item 10, four parallel test items were linked.

142

time limitation did have one major disadvantage, that of allowing time for undertaking illicit computation.

THE TEST OF COMPUTATION

The computation test (Appendix J) requires few comments, on account of its familiar nature. The areas to which its items refer are set out in Table 9. Scoring it was, however, a complex and time-consuming operation, a matter to which we shall return later in this chapter. In order that the type of scoring envisaged could be undertaken, the pupils were required to show all working on the test sheets.

Both the concept and the computation tests covered a larger syllabus than the younger classes were likely to have covered. They did, however, give pupils an opportunity to demonstrate what they could do.

PERFORMANCE ON THE CONCEPT TEST

Table 10 shows the mean scores for all the 2650 pupils present for the concept and computation tests at both pre-testing and post-testing and in a class having pupils belonging to a single year group.[1]

It can readily be seen from this table that there are very few differences between successive year groups at the same stage. Thus P6 pre-test scores and P5 post-test scores—both of which were the results of tests administered at the same stage (the end of the P5 year) in two successive years—are almost identical, as are P7 pre-test scores and P6 post-test scores. Over the year 1977/78, however, there is a clear pattern of growth of mean score for each year group—ie, between their pre-test and their post-test scores.

It is worth noting that, where more than one item is a measure of a single area (eg, the multiplication of fractions), the mean scores sometimes differed substantially. Since this must represent a difference in item difficulty, the items must either relate to somewhat different concepts *or*, if they relate to the same concept, must do so in a context that requires a grasp of the concept to different degrees.

For each year group, these means provided a basis for assessing

[1] 374 pupils who satisfied the first of these criteria but not the second were excluded to facilitate the computation of these means. For a variety of reasons, three of the classes that had been observed were not tested at the post-test stage.

TABLE 10

ARITHMETIC CONCEPTS TEST: MEAN SCORES BY YEAR GROUP

(I) OPERATIONS WITH INTEGERS

Item Nos.†	Addition 8 9	Subtraction 6 7	Addition and Subtraction 26	Multiplication 10 11 12	Division 13 14 3 28	Place Value 1 2
Year Group						
P5 (Pre-test*	42 34	47 27	17	12 5 6	40 15 15 9	75 61
(Post-test	58 46	70 48	26	26 18 15	55 32 32 17	88 81
P6 (Pre-test*	60 51	66 47	27	27 17 14	52 37 37 7	87 78
(Post-test	70 58	80 63	33	39 31 26	62 52 53 11	93 90
P7 (Pre-test*	68 59	77 60	34	35 26 21	59 46 47 7	92 85
(Post-test	75 64	87 72	44	45 41 32	69 63 64 13	95 92

* Pre-test at end of preceding school year
† These item numbers relate to paired items. For the test items constituting these pairs, see Table 9.

TABLE 10 (contd.)

(ii) OPERATIONS WITH FRACTIONS, DECIMALS AND BRACKETS

	Fractions			Conversion (Fract./Dec.)	Money	Decimals		Brackets: Use of
	Equivalence	*Multiplication*	*Division*			*Multiplication*	*Place Value*	
Item Nos.	17 27	15 16	18	21 23 25 24	4 5	22	19 20	12 28
Year Group								
P5 (Pre-test*	35 2	64 9	12	6 3 17 2	46 34	8	5 8	6 9
(Post-test	37 6	72 19	21	12 11 21 2	17	15 26	15 17	
P6 (Pre-test*	33 6	70 26	22	10 8 21 3	59 36	16	13 25	14 7
(Post-test	34 12	73 38	33	26 22 31 9	72 38	37	36 48	26 11
P7 (Pre-test*	31 12	73 33	25	28 23 32 10	69 38	35	33 45	21 7
(Post-test	45 18	74 46	37	40 37 45 20	78 47	54	49 61	32 13

(P5: N = 781; P6: N = 873; P7: N = 996)

* Pre-test at end of preceding school year

145

whether the classes in a particular cluster were above or below average at pre-test and at post-test.

Where a class was made up of sub-groups each of which had been taught by different teachers in the preceding (ie, pre-test) year, the sub-groups had to be compared separately. Since, moreover, it was desired to compare all these statistics with corresponding ones from the computation test, it was necessary to exclude all pupils who had not taken any of the four tests (ie, concept pre-test and post-test, and computation pre-test and post-test). Where the resulting sub-groups had less than four pupils, they were disregarded, and others with small numbers had to be treated with considerable caution.

We shall return to the consideration of the comparisons after performance on the test of computation has been described.

PERFORMANCE ON THE COMPUTATION TEST

Whereas the responses for the concept test were multiple choice categories, and therefore susceptible to scoring by computer once they had been recorded on punched cards, the first stage of the scoring of the computation test had to be undertaken manually. The reasons for this will quickly become apparent.

Had interest been confined to whether the correct answer had been obtained for each test item, scoring would have been easy. However, there appeared to be a strong case for ascertaining where the process employed by the pupil was correct even if a 'slip' had led to an incorrect answer. Accordingly, where an answer could not be coded as correct, the pupil's working was examined. In some instances it was possible to determine beyond doubt whether the process was right or wrong, but in some others there was insufficient evidence to be sure. Where doubt existed, account was therefore taken of whether the process in question had been used correctly in other items. To this end, the scorer coded each item as a) wholly correct, or b) as wrong in answer but correct in process, or c) as wrong in answer and possibly correct in process, or d) as wrong in answer and certainly incorrect in process. These codings were then revised by computer such that a coding of 'c' was changed into one of 'b' if the same process had been used correctly in at least two other items (ie, if two other items involving the same process had been coded 'a' or 'b'). Thus—at the cost of arduous coding—doubtful cases were, so far as possible, resolved. Once the performance of the pupil on each item of the test had been finally coded, it was possible to compute, for each class, mean scores for each topic area—both in respect of fully correct responses and of ones where only process was correct. The maximum score for each topic area equalled the number of items relating to that topic area. Equivalent scores were computed for each year group (eg, P5) and these are shown in Table 11.

Perusal of this table shows the same stability of performance from one year to another for pupils at the same stage (eg, P6 post-test and P7 pre-test) as was found (in Table 10) for the concept test, and a similar growth over the year for each year-group of pupils.

THE RELATIONSHIP OF CONCEPT AND COMPUTATION SCORES TO CLUSTER MEMBERSHIP

It will readily be appreciated that the comparisons to be made between clusters in respect of change in performance over the year were of considerable complexity, especially as account had to be taken of difference in starting point (ie, pre-test score) and difference in opportunity to learn (ie, difference in time of introducing specific elements in the curriculum).

Since it was indeed judged to be impracticable to use statistical techniques to provide a few indices that would in themselves summarise what it was desired to know, it was found necessary to write a computer programme that would serve to set out the relevant data for each class in such a way that they could be readily inspected on a class by class (or sub-group by sub-group) basis. Figure 5 demonstrates this layout for a single class.

It will be noted from Figure 5 that it is possible readily to compare scores for concepts and for computation within each subject area—eg, in respect of the multiplication of integers. In each case, scores on pre-test or post-test that were above or below the pre-test year means by more than three arbitrarily determined margins were distinctly marked by hand in two colours, one colour for those above the mean and the second for those below it. Similarly two sorts of arrows, each in two colours, were used to mark changes up or down in excess of each of two arbitrary amounts.

In this way, it was made easy to see at a glance where moderate or large rises (or falls) in mean class score had arisen and where pre-test and post-test mean class scores were, to varying degrees, above or below the mean year scores shown in Table 10 (Concept) and Table 11 (Computation).

147

TABLE 11

ARITHMETIC COMPUTATION TEST: MEAN SCORES BY YEAR GROUP

(I) OPERATIONS WITH INTEGERS

	Addition 4	Subtraction 2	Multipln 1* 2	Multipln 2† 2	Division 1* 2	Division 2† 1	Place Value 5
Possible Score							
Mean Scores							
P5 (Pre-test**	2.6	1.0	1.1	0.3	0.9	0.0	2.8
(Post-test	3.4	1.5	1.6	1.0	1.4	0.2	3.9
P6 (Pre-test**	3.5	1.5	1.5	1.1	1.4	0.3	4.0
(Post-test	3.6	1.7	1.7	1.4	1.7	0.5	4.3
P7 (Pre-test**	3.6	1.6	1.7	1.4	1.6	0.5	4.3
(Post-test	3.7	1.8	1.8	1.6	1.8	0.7	4.5

* By single figure number
† By two figure number
** Pre-test at end of preceding school year

148

TABLE 11 (contd.)

II) OPERATIONS WITH FRACTIONS, DECIMALS, AND BRACKETS

Possible Score	Fractions Equivalence	Addn/ Subtn	Multipn	Divn	Conversion (Fract/ Dec)	Money	Decimals Addn/ Subtn	Multipn	Divn	Brackets Place Value	
	2	2	2	2	6	2	3	3	2	3	4
Mean Scores											
P5 (Pre-test	0.4	0.0	0.1	0.0	0.7	0.4	0.7	0.0	0.0	0.6	0.4
(Post-test	1.1	0.5	0.2	0.0	1.4	0.8	1.3	0.1	0.0	1.2	1.2
P6 (Pre-test	1.1	0.5	0.2	0.0	1.6	0.8	1.5	0.2	0.0	1.3	1.4
(Post-test	1.6	1.0	0.5	0.3	2.8	1.0	2.1	0.6	0.2	2.1	2.2
P7 (Pre-test	1.5	1.0	0.6	0.3	2.7	0.9	2.1	0.8	0.2	2.1	2.2
(Post-test	1.7	1.4	1.0	0.6	3.7	1.1	2.5	1.4	0.5	2.5	2.9

NOTES: 1) Test items contributing to each subscore can be identified by making reference to Table 9.
2) Scores relate to items with fully correct answers. Some scores would be augmented by 0.1 to 0.4 if credit were given for process only correct.

149

FIGURE 5

SAMPLES OF COMPUTATION AND ARITHMETIC CONCEPT DATA FOR A SINGLE (P7) CLASS SET OUT FOR EXAMINATION OF TRENDS AND RELATIONSHIPS

	ADD ✓	SUB ✓	A/S(ADV) ✓	MULT1 ✓	MULT2 ✓N	DIV1 ✓	DIV2 ✓	FR(EQUIV) ✓	FR(AD/SB) ✓	FR(MULT) ✓N	FR(DIV)
CMP(POS)	4	2	2	2	2	2	1	2	2	2	2
CMP(PRE)	3.1(0.2)	1.2(0.2)		1.4(0.1)	0.6(0.0)(0.3)	1.4(0.0)	0.4(0.0)	1.2	0.3(0.0)	0.1(0.0)	0.0(0.0)(0.0)
CMP(POST)	3.6(0.2)	1.6(0.1)		1.7(0.2)	1.5(0.3)	1.5(0.0)	0.7(0.0)	1.5	1.0(0.3)	0.6(0.0)	0.0(0.0)(0.0)
	%	%	%	%	%	%	%	%	%	%	%
CON(PRE)	60 / 43	30	34	47 / 12	21 / 4	47 / 69	12 / 4	26 / 12	8	87 / 69	12 / 34
CON(POST)	60 / √65	√52	26	39 / √34	34 / √26	√69 / √34	√34	17	12	16 / 15	18
CON(ITEM)	8 / 9	7	6	10	11 / 12	3 / 13 / 14	28	17	27	16 / 15	18

	DEC(MNY)	CNVT(DC/FR) ✓	DEC(A/S) ✓	DEC(MULT) ✓N	DEC(DIV) ✓N	DEC(PV) ✓	PL VAL	BRKTS ✓
CMP(POS)	2	6	3	3	2	3	5(1)	4
CMP(PRE)	0.3(0.5)(0.3)	0.8(0.0)	1.3(0.2)	0.1(0.1)	0.0(0.0)	3.4(0.0)	1.0	1.4
CMP(POST)	0.8(0.4)(0.3)	3.1(0.0)	2.2(0.2)	1.1(0.5)	0.5(0.0)	4.0(0.0)	2.0	2.6
	%	%	%	%	%	%	%	%
CON(PRE)	60 / 34	8 / 4 / 17	17	12		17 / 21	78 / 73	4 / 4
CON(POST)	69 / 47	21 / √26 / 8	21 / √26 / 8	√43		30 / √52	82 / 91	√26 / 4
CON(ITEM)	5 / 4	21 23 25 24	24	22		19 / 20	1 / 2	12 / 28

NOTES ON SYMBOLS: a *tick* above a topic area indicates that there is evidence from computation scores of the topic's having been taught. When it is accompanied by an 'N', it indicates that this teaching apparently occurred *after* the pre-test and is therefore 'new'. Underlinings (—, —— and ===) indicate that the score is *below* the year's mean by various margins. (In some other classes, as appropriate, similar underlinings—distinguished by colour, indicate scores *above* the year mean.) The downward pointing arrows indicate improvements. (Upward pointing ones would indicate deterioration.) The juxtaposition of computation and concept scores relating to the same topic area facilitates comparison. The relationship between the concept item numbers and concept best items is shown in Table 9 (p 160). *MULT 1* indicates multiplication by a single digit number; *MULT 2*, by a two-digit number. CNVT = Convert; BRKTS—Brackets; A/S(Adv) = 'Advanced' adding and subtracting. PL VAL and PV = Place Value.

Since the sets of records for each class (or, where necessary, each sub-group of a class containing at least four pupils) were grouped together according to the cluster membership, it was possible to note any signs of trends common to individual clusters.

Thereafter, the first step taken was to construct Table 12. This was done on a judgemental basis because of the large number of factors to be taken into account. Most importantly, the assessments were arrived at relative only to those topic areas that had been taught. (Whether they had been taught had been marked manually on the computer print-out as exemplified in Figure 5 on the basis of the score for computation: if there was a computation score significantly[2] greater than zero, either at pre-test or post-test, it was assumed that the topic had been taught, though if only the post-test score was significantly greater than zero, the item was further marked as relating to a topic first taught in the session 1977/78.) It is important to emphasise that the 'improvements' in score recorded in Table 12 were judged on a relative basis: in particular, only those items on which improvement was possible were taken into consideration. (Thus, for example, a P5 class was judged in respect of only those items/topic areas that had been marked as having been studied and a P7 class only in respect of those items/topic areas for which improvement was possible, for if, for instance, 90% of a class had been correct at pre-test for a particular concept item, no more than a very small improvement was possible.)

It will be seen from Table 12 that the classes in each cluster were classified (separately for concept and for computation) on a five-

---

[2] In this context, this term does NOT imply statistical significance.

point scale ranging from 'none' to 'substantial'. It has, of course, to be admitted that a degree of error of judgement is virtually certain where such relative judgements are being made, and not least so when allowance is being made for so many factors. On the other hand, it can be argued that

a) occasional errors of up to one category would not greatly distort the general picture obtained

b) the task was greatly facilitated by the manual markings—in distinct colours—that have been described above, which served to direct the eye to all relevant factors

c) it would be wholly impracticable to make allowance for so many relevant factors if more objective means were employed. (The heart quakes at the thought of attempting to devise an algorithm that would permit a computer to undertake the task with complete consistency!)

Perusal of Table 12 at once reveals that there is little correspondence between cluster membership and the level of 'improvement' recorded. Those classes showing the greatest improvements in performance in respect of either concept or computation are distributed over many clusters, some of them extremely diverse in nature, and the variation among classes within each is typically large. It is further to be noted that larger improvements are considerably more numerous in respect of computation than of concept. This suggests that relatively few teachers achieved—or perhaps even aimed at—greater understanding of concepts in a range of topic areas.

Further perusal of Table 12 itself shows that the most uniform clusters were O and C. Most noticeably, both had achieved high computational performance, though clearly by very different means, for whereas the cluster C teachers required pupils to think for themselves, cluster O teachers, in laying emphasis on performance of the class *as a whole*, sought to achieve a high level of computational performance, even in the less able, by laying stress on the mechanical means of securing correct answers.[3] To these differences in means employed might have readily been ascribed the generally lower scores of cluster O in respect of concepts, but the ascription would have been more soundly based had it been possible to demonstrate comparable relationships in other clusters. However, the within-cluster variance that was found

[3] It will be recalled that a number of the teachers in this cluster taught in schools where it was policy to hold weekly arithmetic tests.

TABLE 12

IMPROVEMENT IN ARITHMETIC PERFORMANCE BETWEEN PRE-TEST AND POST-TEST, BY CLUSTER

	Concept					Computation				
	None	V.Little	Little	Some	Substantial	None	V.Little	Little	Some	Substantial
Cluster A	0	0	1	0	1	0	0	0	1	1
Cluster B	1	1	2	2	0	0	0	0	1	5
Cluster C	0	0	1	1	2	0	0	0	0	4
Cluster D	0	1	0	1	0	0	0	2	0	0
Cluster E	1	0	7	0	1	0	2	0	2	5
Cluster F	0	2	0	7	1	0	1	2	5	2
Cluster G	1	1	1	2	1	0	2	1	1	2
Cluster H	0	0	4	3	4	0	1	1	3	6
Cluster I	0	1	3	2	1	0	0	3	2	2
Cluster J	0	1	0	1	3	0	0	0	1	4
Cluster K	1	0	4	1	0	0	2	2	2	2
Cluster L	1	0	10	4	1	1	3	1	4	6
Cluster M	0	3	3	2	2	0	0	3	4	5
Cluster N	0	3	2	3	1	1	0	1	3	2
Cluster O	0	0	6	3	1	0	0	0	0	9
Cluster P	2	1	1	2	1	1	0	2	1	3
Cluster Q	1	1	1	2	0	1	0	2	1	1
Total	8	15	46	36	20	4	11	20	31	59

in most clusters and the disparities between the clusters that might have been expected to be most similar to one another, all pointed to there being little, if any, *systematic* relationship between cluster membership and improvement of performance in the two arithmetic tests.

Subsequent to the preparation of Table 12 further information was assembled in an attempt to see what links there might be between teaching input and improvement achieved. One might, for instance, have expected to find some relationship between improvement in concept performance and improvement in computational performance, at least in those cases where the former was achieved. In fact, however, it was found that, save in a few cases, improvements in concept scores frequently fell in topic areas where there were no improvements in computational scores to indicate the likelihood of there having been teaching of those topics. This fact seems to be sufficient cause for questioning whether some of the improvements in concept score did in fact have their origin in the class teacher.

None of the data available could offer an answer to that question, but some of the thirteen classes that were identified as ones where there was considerable correspondence between improvements in the one and in the other did yield a few diverse pointers. First of all, three of these teachers belonged to cluster C, a four-teacher cluster characterised above all by the fact that the teachers in it required their pupils to think for themselves, were very skilled in questioning, and were highly stimulating. Indeed at least a few others of the 13 had been noted by the observers as requiring their pupils to think for themselves. On the other hand, many of the rest of the thirteen teachers—teachers 77 and 101 in particular—in no way resembled the teachers in cluster C in teaching style. Teacher 101 is the one who was described in Chapter 8 as being one who, by the standards of former years, might have been judged a very good teacher. It would seem from this evidence that, though the education received by his class was extremely narrow in scope, through his rigorous questioning and through his painstaking explanations of computational procedures he must have in some way prepared his pupils to manage successfully many of the concept questions.

Perhaps it is significant that a further three of the thirteen teachers, though belonging to different clusters, all taught in the same school—one which made general use of the concept-oriented text-book previously alluded to. One of these three teachers was specifically noted by an observer to have set all work from this text-book and as having habitually referred any pupil experiencing difficulty back to the explanations given in this book. How much, one may wonder, of the attainment in respect of understanding of concepts was derived directly from this text-book rather than from the teacher?[4] How many parents, perhaps aided by this text-book, had been the source of the understanding their children had acquired? Whatever the answers to these questions may be, it would be unwise to assume that pupils learn from their teachers only.

How teacher 77 (cluster Q) came to be one of the thirteen teachers beggars explanation, unless it be that either the class received some teaching from another teacher or that teacher 77's own teaching was very different at other times from what it was when it was observed.

GENERAL CONCLUSIONS

The data derived from these two tests, being such as it is, certainly allows no sweeping inferences to be drawn, and certainly gives no support to any hypothesis that teaching style has in itself any major role in accounting for pupil acquisition of concepts.

In retrospect, it is clear that it was over-ambitious to attempt to explore the teaching of arithmetic in the course of a study of teaching in general. It is abundantly evident that the measures of input left unrecorded many relevant factors. In particular, how the teaching of arithmetic was undertaken required more detailed recording over a far longer period than was done, or than it was possible to undertake. Unfortunately, this shortcoming was compounded by a failure to realise soon enough that many teachers stressed concepts in some subject areas—eg, English—but not in others. The observers noted this fact in many cases and indeed found it a source of difficulty in coding item 11 of the SCOTS schedule for teachers who differed from subject to subject in this respect.

Nonetheless, certain conclusions may be tentatively drawn from the work undertaken.

1) There was a strong emphasis placed by most teachers on computation, though they differed in respect of the extent to

---

[4] Unfortunately, which of the teachers in this study used this text-book was not systematically recorded.

which they were prepared to seek mechanical proficiency at the expense of comprehension.

2) The widespread mismatch between topic areas in which particular classes made gains in score in computation and those in which they made gains in concept scores suggests either that the teaching of concepts was undertaken separately from the teaching of computation or that the pupils improved their grasp of concepts by other means.

3) There was some limited evidence that these other means might be the study of a text-book oriented to concepts and the undertaking of exercises from that text-book, with or without appreciable aid from the teacher.

4) The fact that classes receiving what was almost certainly inadequate teaching[5] did in *some* cases (see Table 12) achieve as much as classes taught by apparently far better teachers may be explicable in terms of a carry-over effect from better teaching in the preceding year and/or in terms of there being many sources of learning available to pupils other than the teaching provided by the class teacher. It is worth noting that many teachers were observed to evoke enthusiasm in their pupils, even when their own skills in exposition and explanation appeared very limited. Such enthusiasm may well result in pupils seeking aid in other quarters.

[5] These include most, if not all, those in clusters P and Q.

CHAPTER 11

CONCLUSIONS

In this chapter, the author seeks to reflect on what he has learned by being involved in the research reported in this book. In doing so, he makes judgements and draws conclusions that have not, in any formal sense, been established by the research. He does so in the belief that the person who is in the best position to learn from a piece of research is the one who performs it and that it is his duty, so far as he is able, to pass on what he believes he has learned—even at the risk of some degree of error. The function of research is not to provide certain answers, for that can seldom be done save in respect of trivial matters, but to diminish error and to provide new understanding. The researcher does, of course, have to question his own judgements and test them as rigorously as he is able against the evidence he has gathered—not least by seeking for any contra-indications in his data. This the present writer has endeavoured to do.

*　*　*　*

The SCOTS schedule, by virtue of the large number of aspects of teaching performance that it makes possible to record, has in the research reported in this book revealed something of the immense complexity of the variation in the ways teachers teach. To reveal such complexity is important, but, at the same time, it is important not to allow it to obscure practical issues with which every teacher has to come to terms. The product of this research is not a series of prescriptions but a basis for thinking afresh about many of the practices commonly adopted by teachers. *It thus provides a basis for teachers to look again at their objectives and the ways by which they seek to achieve them.*

A broad issue that underlies many narrower ones is the relationship of teaching to learning. Two opposite dangers exist. On the one hand is the danger of the teacher's being so preoccupied with his own activity, teaching, as to give pupils little opportunity to learn: being taught does not necessarily mean that one learns. On the other hand is the danger of assuming, because children need to learn, that they are best left to get on on their own, a view that ignores both the need to maintain motivation and to transmit at least some knowledge and concepts. (Children do not have time to rediscover the wheel; nor can the transmittible experience

157

mankind be acquired by a child entirely through his own experience.) This is not to say, however, that the knowledge and concepts can be acquired without some direct personal experience to make them meaningful; nor is it to say that knowledge and understanding are acquired in any real sense unless one has made them 'one's own' by fitting them into, or reconciling them with, the conceptual structures one has already adopted in order to make sense of sensory experience and verbal communication. The process of education is one of continual extension and adaptation of the beliefs and concepts that make up one's view of the world and one's own relationship to it. Although children as well as adults have to make these extensions and adaptations for themselves, they can be helped to do it. It is therefore necessary for every teacher to find ways in which each child can learn in a *variety* of ways. Teaching is, or should be, helping others to learn and to understand.

General principles such as those set out in the immediately preceding paragraphs are of fundamental importance in informing action, but they do not in themselves show what that action should be. The classroom teacher has a practical task involving solving many problems and reconciling a variety of objectives that may seem less than fully compatible with one another.

There is much evidence that different individuals have different learning styles, or at least different preferred ways of learning[1]. Nevertheless it is probable that almost everyone learns principally in four distinct sets of circumstances and benefits from each in different ways:

1) by receiving information and explanations from others seeking to transmit information and/or concepts

2) by interacting with others, arguing out some issue

3) by thinking a problem out for oneself or by seeking to apprehend some concept

4) through having direct experience, thus ensuring that knowledge and concepts acquired are related to both one's sensory experience and to the way one operates in the world.

It is clear from Chapter 8 that teachers differ considerably in the importance they attach to these four modes of learning and in the opportunities they give for them to occur. Moreover, these opportunities differ not only quantitatively but qualitatively.

It will be recalled, for instance, that the teachers in cluster I

[1] See, for instance, Entwistle (1981) and Spencer E (1983)

laid particular stress on the first two of these modes. They did so, it may be inferred, because they saw their task as being to pass on ideas and concepts and because they wished their pupils to understand and not merely memorise. Their strength lay in clear, well-reasoned exposition and in questioning that required their pupils to think. They appeared to be generally successful in securing the acquisition of the sets of facts and concepts that they believed it necessary for their pupils to have. They typically employed whole-class instruction because, it may be supposed, they did not see any need for differentiation amongst pupils save in respect of varying the difficulty level in the 'practice' undertaken by their pupils. They were challenging and treated all they taught as important and as interesting in its own right, and, probably as a result, the pupils appeared to accept their values and to be well motivated. Nor did their pupils typically lack training in respect of 'study-skills': study of texts and the use of books of reference readily fitted into the pattern of teaching to which they were exposed. They may even have had also a limited exposure to the third mode of learning in that they may have found it necessary to think out for themselves any point that they had not fully grasped at the time of its exposition. What they certainly did tend to lack was experience of following an argument wherever it might lead: their learning was essentially convergent. In this their position stood in contrast to that of the pupils taught by the teachers in cluster C, for these teachers were prepared to exploit any opportunity that arose and to encourage pupils to reach their own conclusions. Teacher 122 was most notable in this, and not least because of the way she encouraged pupils to revise their opinions by leading them to think again about the soundness of an initial conclusion. For children in her class, knowledge and ideas were open-ended, originality was something to be valued, and their own views and interests counted. We thus see in these two instances that what was provided for pupils by two groups of teachers—both of which were clearly above average in ability and knowledge— yielded a substantially different learning experience and that the difference had its origin in two different views of the type of learning that should take place.

Indeed it was the type of open-ended, questing learning experience that the cluster C teachers gave their pupils — together with their special type of teacher-centredness that allowed pupils still to exercise initiative and influence the course of events — that both gave their cluster its homogeneity and so strongly distinguished it from cluster I. It must, in particular, be remembered that this homogeneity transcended the fact that, while three of the four cluster C teachers used group methods, the fourth used predominantly whole-class teaching. Despite this apparently great difference, all the cluster C teachers interacted strongly with each individual pupil in their classes, adapted their approach to individuals in the light of their knowledge of them, secured a high level of pupil involvement, and encouraged open-ended thinking. Even when teacher 122 was engaged in whole-class teaching, she maintained a clear differentiation amongst her pupils as individuals. Her class and the classes of the other three teachers were at once both teacher-centred and pupil-centred.

It is instructive to consider also what the difference would have been if, for instance, teacher 122 (cluster C) had adopted group methods. What would have been the gains and what the losses? A possible loss would have been of the sustained high level of stimulation that she maintained. Had she worked with groups as did the other members of her cluster, she was unlikely to have been any less stimulating to whichever group she worked with, but she would on average have stimulated any one group for a much shorter time. On the other hand, it would have been easier for her to ensure that *every* pupil was engaged interactively for at least part of the time, and more pupils would have had the opportunity to acquire understanding through personal struggle. All approaches to teaching have to sacrifice some ends in the interest of securing others. Priorities have to be established relative to the children taught—and weaknesses in each approach compensated for as far as possible.

It is unfortunately the case, however, that the adoption of whole-class (or large-group) teaching does not guarantee stimulation and that small group methods do not guarantee either differentiation of work to meet individual needs or the opportunity for pupils to be actively involved in making ideas and facts 'their own'. The potential benefits of either approach are achieved by the skills brought to bear by teachers—but unfortunately not by all teachers.

Where failure to achieve the characteristic virtues of group teaching—notably differentiation of activity to match individual needs and the opportunity for *all* pupils to learn actively and co-operatively—occurs, it is, the experience of the research suggests, largely due to one or both of two factors:

i) that the teachers employ group methods because it is the conventional wisdom that they should be used and not because of being committed to, or even understanding, their purposes, and

ii) that they lack the necessary organisational skill, and perhaps also prepare inadequately.

It was clear from the research that the number of teachers was small who used group methods in ways that secured from those methods advantages that it is difficult or impossible to obtain otherwise. Teacher 106 (cluster A) is, perhaps, the best example that can be cited from this research of a teacher who had not only found a solution to the central problem of how to distribute his own time when having a class working in groups but had established groups that worked as co-operative units: he worked with individual groups in a stimulating way, he ensured that all groups could organise activities for themselves and be self-supporting, he ensured that they had interesting tasks to undertake, and he did not require them to work alone for periods longer than they could sustain. (He in fact had some activities conducted on a whole-class basis and thus eased his task of maintaining interest and motivation.)

In contrast, classes in which group methods were employed unprofitably were characterised by

a) over-involvement of the teacher in a limited range of tasks, such as correction, and/or

b) pupils' being left for long periods either doing repetitive work, or 'stuck' with a problem, or simply unmotivated, and/or

c) failure to provide a range of interesting tasks and/or material to carry them out, and/or

d) lack of training of pupils in organising their own time and in undertaking for themselves responsibilities that otherwise fall on an over-burdened teacher.

It is not being argued here that the solution adopted by teacher 106 is the only one available; nor is it necessarily an ideal. Many other practices may contribute to solving the organisational problems of group teaching. Thus, for example, a teacher may 'stagger' new work, so that only one or two groups are at any one time at a stage where the personal involvement of the teacher may be required for substantial periods; activities for different groups can be scheduled such that ones requiring much teacher involvement and ones requiring virtually none coincide; combining self-correcting facilities with good record keeping can both reduce the

161

time the teacher has to devote to teaching and, at the same time, permit monitoring of individual progress; and a breakdown service can be organised to provide aid to pupils who have failed to overcome their own problems.

It will not have escaped the notice of those who have read Chapter 8 with care how few of the teachers observed who were employing group methods were, even if their organisation of their own time was satisfactory, doing so in ways that afforded advantages unobtainable through whole-class (or large-group) instruction, nor that the more skilled of the teachers employing whole-class (or large-group) instruction secured *by different means* at least some of the advantages—eg, in respect of individualisation —normally associated with group methods. Indeed, it might be argued that those who failed to overcome the problems specific to small-group methods would have lost little, if anything, had they abandoned them in favour of a less demanding approach.

Unfortunately, the evidence presented in this book also shows quite clearly that the successes of the most able 'whole-class' teachers were not shared by all those who instructed their classes on a whole-class basis. Weakness in 'teaching skills' (as defined in Chapter 8), poor feedback, dullness, excessive allocation of time to work so repetitive as to serve little function other than that of keeping pupils occupied, and failure to identify and respond to individual differences were found both where group methods were employed and where they were not. Queues of pupils waiting for correction of their work, time-wasting transitions from one task to another, and lack of pupil-training to permit them to operate efficiently without constant direction are, alas, found in both situations.

Simon and Galton[2] have argued on the basis of the ORACLE study—which involved studies of teaching employing observations instruments that differed from SCOTS in concentrating attention on narrower aspects of the teaching process—that there is a need to maximise inter-action between teachers and pupils, that this can best be done by employing whole-class teaching, and that group methods can profitably be used in conjunction with such whole-class teaching. (Wholly individualised instruction they rejected on the grounds that, unless classes are extremely small, adequate teacher-pupil interaction can in no way be achieved.) The findings of the research described in this book lend general support to this view, but it is important to remember that many of the problems

[2] Simon and Galton (1980)

162

that teachers have to solve exist wholly independently of whether whole-class, group, or individualised approaches are employed. It is, therefore, to issues that inform and underlie these problems that we must now devote attention.

OPERATION OF SYSTEMS

No teacher can operate a class as an efficient organisation without the active and informed participation of the pupils in operating whatever system the teacher decides to adopt. It was manifest to the observers that in well-run classes the pupils knew what was expected of them, knew how to proceed in various circumstances, could operate effectively for periods of time even in the absence of the teacher, and, because they did not have to make many enquiries of the teacher about how to proceed or about how to overcome routine problems, left the teacher free to teach or interact with individuals or groups as proved necessary. This knowledge of procedures did not come by chance: the classes concerned had been informed of these procedures and trained in operating them at the very beginning of their time with their current teacher. It is of fundamental importance therefore that teachers should have well thought-out operational procedures and that they should ensure early in the school year that pupils are familiar with them and know how to operate them. Only in this way can a teacher optimise the use of his own time and avoid constant involvement in trivia.

DIRECT AND INDIRECT CONTROL

It is a fallacy to suppose that teachers have an option of renouncing control in order to allow pupils to follow their own bent. For a teacher to abrogate control is to renounce all responsibility for the education of the pupils entrusted to him. The real options lie in how control is exercised and particularly in whether it is effected directly or indirectly. In the short term at least, direct control is the easier to implement, for there is an exact and obvious relationship between the instruction given and the desired effects. On the other hand, direct instruction has some inherent disadvantages:

a) it involves action by the teacher at every step or transition;

b) both ends and means are *overtly* dictated to pupils

c) pupils are, therefore, the less likely to adopt the teacher's ends as their own.

It would be unwise to over-stress the last of these points since this research affords numerous instances – e.g. the teachers of cluster I or even the far more extreme case of teacher 101 (cluster P)—of classes apparently accepting wholly imposed means and ends. On the other hand, there were many instances of pupils working without enthusiasm, and a few of classes where a substantial proportion of the pupils were either apathetic or even hostile to the teacher's objectives. It is clearly essential that, by one means or another, every class broadly share the teacher's objectives.

Some would argue that this can best be achieved by giving pupils real choice in what they do. However, there are obvious dangers that pupils' choices will be based on criteria that ignore their long-term interests, if only because they lack any basis for knowing what their long-term interests are, and teachers are, in any case, rarely willing to forego control. What is commonly forgotten, however, is that the giving of pupil choice does not necessarily imply the renouncement of teacher control. For this there are two principal reasons. The first is that by skilfully structuring the context in which pupil choice is exercised, teachers can influence very heavily indeed the choices made. The second is that the options offered to pupils can all be compatible with the fulfilment of the teacher's objectives. In short, pupils may choose freely, or at least have the impression of choosing freely, while remaining effectively under teacher control. For them to have that impression may be important, for a sense of involvement in where they are going may very well be a major factor in avoiding the development of pupil disaffection, especially in the longer term. However, it has to be noted that there were many instances of pupils displaying obvious involvement despite the lack of exercise of choice

It is particularly important to realise that pupil choice does not need to be individual: a discussion leading to consensus concerning, say, a topic for discussion can give the pupils a feeling that what they are doing is what they have jointly chosen to do. On the other hand, it is equally important to realise that nominal choices where all the options pre-determined by the teacher seem equally un-attractive (as can, for example, be the case where a choice of essentially similar work-cards is offered) do not confer the advantages usually associated with the exercise of choice.

A specific instance of a practice where many of these issues arise is that of the so-called 'integrated day/week', where work to be undertaken by pupils during a pre-determined period—eg, a day or week—is set down (usually on a blackboard). A common supposition is that this not only permits pupils to work at their own pace and motivates them to work hard so that they may move on to optional activities of their own choice, but allows them to exercise effective choice. While this supposition is well-founded in certain instances, it is frequently not so, for often the teacher requires the work to be undertaken in a pre-determined order and the only variation amongst pupils is in pace of working. Often it is manifest that the integrated day/week is used simply as a means of exerting pressure on pupils to complete a set amount of work in a given time, the penalty for non-completion being deprivation from participation in some generally preferred activities and/or a requirement to do unfinished work at home. Thus here too appearances may be deceptive.

(There is, of course, inherent in the use of the integrated day/week the risk of leaving pupils relatively unstimulated for substantial periods of time—and this may be so even when correction/feedback/aid is available concurrently.)

MOTIVATION

Choice, even if apparent rather than real, and indeed anything that leads to a sharing of objectives by teacher and class, are clearly important means of securing pupils motivation. However, the SCOTS schedule and the observation based upon it draw attention to other means by which motivation can be established and maintained.

One such way is, as we have seen in Chapter 8, to exploit opportunities—eg, a chance event or some matter happening to arise in the course of class work—by abandoning planned work for the meantime and pursuing the matter of interest while interest is still aroused. Such exploitation of opportunities, however, pre-supposes an appropriate attitude of mind in the class teacher and the possession of a wide range of knowledge that can be called on on the spur of the moment. Thus, for instance, in contrast to the cluster C teachers who readily seized such opportunities, the teachers of cluster H displayed rigidity of purpose and an un-willingness to deviate at all from their pre-determined programme. It is not difficult to see that the cluster C teachers provided a far more stimulating learning situation than did the cluster H teachers, and, in addition, were the more able to draw on special knowledge possessed by individual pupils. The shared enthusiasms that were generated helped to produce in the cluster C classes what appeared to be a sense of one-ness that encompassed the teacher as well as the pupils.

Another important means of maintaining motivation is reinforcement of desired conduct by ensuring that it is regularly praised. However, the observations made it clear that while the opposite—habitual criticism—was in some cases either a demotivating or alienating factor, even sharp criticism of pupil work did not necessarily demotivate. Much seemed to depend on the basic relationship between teacher and class: a teacher who was liked by the class or perceived of as generally well-disposed to the class could criticise bluntly either work or conduct without causing offence and consequent demotivation. Indeed, self-confident and able pupils were noted to be stirred to fresh effort by sharp criticism. It appeared to be in recognition of this fact that some teachers—such as teacher 90 (cluster I)—differentiated their comments such that the able incurred criticism and the less able, encouragement.

RELATIONSHIPS BETWEEN TEACHER AND PUPILS

It has already been demonstrated in the preceding paragraph that teacher-pupil relationships have a bearing on how pupils react in various circumstances. There appear, however, to be two partially related aspects of such relationships. The first aspect relates to the formality/informality of the relationships and the second to the similarity/disparity of social background, interests, etc.

Extreme informality, where pupils treated the teacher as a social equal, was confined to a very small number of teachers. This informality did not appear to result in the teacher's enjoying notable popularity, though it has to be said that this may have been due less to the informality itself than to other characteristics such as irritability when over-extended—e.g., teacher 5 (cluster N)—or an unwillingness to be bothered with the less able—e.g., teacher 26 (cluster K). It has also to be noted that many teachers who were obviously very well-liked by their pupils did maintain a well-defined social difference between themselves and their pupils. There is, however, a clear distinction to be drawn between the degree of social distance that may command respect and that which implies indifference or even hostility. The latter typically caused pupils to keep their distance or, in some cases, themselves to display hostility.

Disparity of social background between teacher and class can, of course, make it more difficult for the two to share interests, and, moreover, may possibly make it more difficult for the pupils to see the teacher as having characteristics that it would be good to emulate. Disparity of social background is obviously likely to be most acute in schools where the pupils are drawn from severely under-privileged social backgrounds. The case of teacher 39 (cluster B) has been cited in Chapter 8 as an example of one who not only lived in the same underprivileged area as his pupils but spoke with the same accent, used similar speech patterns, and shared with them some non-standard usages (such as 'he done it'.) This teacher certainly had a good relationship with his class, but whether the fact that his style of speech—and, by inference, his social background—was not notably different from theirs did in any significant way contribute to their good relationship or indeed to their willingness to learn, it was not possible to glean.

DEVELOPING PUPIL RESPONSIBILITY

Almost all the teachers seemed concerned that their pupils should display a responsible attitude to their school work. Rather fewer appeared to be equally concerned about helping them to become adults with a sense of responsibility.

Some of those who did little to develop pupil responsibility clearly viewed their pupils as being in any case irresponsible and untrustworthy and as unlikely to develop responsibility. That their own manifest distrust might in fact induce irresponsible behaviour in their pupils was something of which they showed no awareness.

Where distrust was perceived to be at its greatest, as in the case of teacher 127 (cluster P), fear of disorder appeared to be the major reason for giving pupils virtually no duties to perform. Others gave pupils tasks to perform, but supervised so closely as to deny any genuine responsibility to the pupils executing them.

Those who did give pupils responsibilities fell into three broad categories. The first encompasses those who trusted pupils to behave responsibly and saw the giving of responsibility as a means of promoting it. (The trust of such teachers did not appear to be abused even by pupils who were known to have been a source of trouble to a teacher in a preceding year—though this finding could be explained in terms of those whose trust had been abused having ceased to trust.) The second category includes those teachers who gave responsibilities out—usually on a rota basis—but placed clear limits on the extent of their trust. Those in the third category gave responsibilities only to those seen as both competent and keen: in short they appeared to be interested in exploiting the assistance of those who could be depended upon to act responsibly rather than in developing responsibility in the remainder.

There seemed to be some evidence that teacher training had done more to communicate the techniques by which responsibilities could be widely distributed—eg, duty rosters—than to impart understanding of how responsibility might be developed.

TEACHER KNOWLEDGE AND SKILLS

a) Knowledge

The background of knowledge that the teachers brought to their tasks varied very greatly. The most knowledgeable were clearly persons of high ability and wide interest and were able to provide informed comment on virtually any topic that arose. At the other extreme were those who were clearly ill-informed and who communicated to their pupils inaccurate information. Some of them were, unfortunately, also inclined to be dogmatic—and to be unwilling to look up what they were unsure about.

It was possible to ascertain that amongst teachers who were themselves most knowledgeable in many spheres were some who showed weaknesses in respect of numeracy. These teachers were typically well aware of their weaknesses, but their reaction was frequently to minimise the time they spent on arithmetic in order to be able to spend more time on activities where they felt more secure.

While it would be foolish to argue that extent of knowledge is the major factor in teacher quality, inadequacy of knowledge is something for which other skills and qualities cannot wholly compensate. It is important that weakness in important areas such as numeracy should be detected and rectified during pre-service training.

b) Teaching Skill

Since almost universally the first step when a teacher seeks to introduce new work to a class or group is some form of presentation of facts and ideas, skill in exposition is clearly of fundamental importance. (Even when 'discovery methods' are employed, there is, in the presentation of the material and in the way the teacher responds to pupils' attempts, some sort of implied exposition.) Exposition does not, of course, necessarily imply the teacher's making statements: the teacher may, for instance, pose questions and the pupils attempt to provide the statements. But, whatever the precise process adopted, unless the teacher is providing some structuring of the knowledge, he is contributing little to the pupils' learning. Obviously, however, if a teacher does not have sufficient understanding of what he is seeking to teach to be able to provide a useful structure, he inevitably fails in this vital step. This then is a point at which the teacher's knowledge and depth of understanding of subject matter is almost certain to be of crucial importance.

However, even a well-structured piece of teaching is unlikely to achieve immediate and sustained learning by every pupil. In any case, new learning has to be related to old, and the old is unlikely to be the same for all pupils either in respect of knowledge or of structuring. The teacher may therefore need to explore the interface between what he is seeking to teach and what the individual pupil already knows. Much may depend on his ability to see the current situation through each pupil's eyes, so that old and new knowledge and structures may interlock. Doing so may require finding an alternative structuring of what has been already taught. It is at this second stage that teachers appear most often to fail: many seem to be able to find one structure— not necessarily an optimal one—but not two. There thus seems to be a strong case for providing teachers with specific training designed to enhance their skills in the structuring and restructuring of ideas and associated information.

It must be stressed that ability to structure is unlikely to be independent of knowledge and understanding of what has to be structured, but flexibility of approach is something that it may be possible to foster.

The same flexibility is likely to be helpful to teachers in enabling them to recognise different learning styles in pupils and either to adapt presentations to those learning styles or to seek to modify the learning styles themselves.

In this connection, it is important to realise that the correction of pupil work should wherever possible be treated as a diagnostic task, such that feedback may not only be provided but adapted to individual needs.

INTEGRATION OF KNOWLEDGE

It might seem that, in the primary school where the teaching of virtually all subjects is usually undertaken by the same teacher, it would be easy to link together teaching in different subject areas. Yet in the observations it was a rare experience to record a serious effort to integrate what is taught in one area with that taught in another, even by the very simple means of recalling, while teaching in one area, what was taught in another.

'Project-work' was widely undertaken and it provided an opportunity for the integration of knowledge and skills. The integration that was found, however, was commonly superficial— and often little more than an easy way of finding something for pupils to draw.

COOPERATIVE LEARNING

Projects also give an opportunity for cooperative work, and indeed this was quite óften found. Unfortunately the cooperation most often involved sharing out different parts of a task rather than cooperative learning. Thus although some social training may have been provided, the interplay of minds was frequently not facilitated.

Much of the difficulty seems to lie in a deeply entrenched view that, if pupils are set to work together, one or two will do all the work and thinking, and that the others will merely copy. However, although it is clearly desirable to avoid virtual inactivity on the part of some pupils, it is unwise to ignore the opportunties there are for pupils to learn from one another—though of course some monitoring of what is being learned is clearly essential if the transmission of error is to be avoided. The other factor that seems to inhibit teachers from encouraging or even permitting co-operative learning is the fear of losing disciplinary control. Such fear, however, smacks of defeatism. It is true that pupils may not spontaneously learn co-operatively but they can be trained to do so. It is merely one element in the process of learning to learn. Similarly skills in working alone and using reference tools have to be taught and learned.

The mention of co-operative learning brings us back to the topic of learning in groups. Perhaps one of the prime teaching skills is to know how best to divide time between whole-class and group learning in such a way that

a) the teacher does not waste time repeatedly communicating the same thing to different individuals and groups

b) the pupil has the maximum individual stimulation and the maximum opportunity to inter-act with both teacher and other pupils

c) the pupil has adequate time to reflect on and consolidate what he has learned and to discover where he has difficulties with which he needs help.

Fulfilling such a variety of objectives calls for balance and compromise; it calls also for *awareness, sensitivity,* and *flexibility.* It is more important that the teacher should succeed in these three respects than that any particular teaching style or practices be adopted. The writer is convinced on the basis of his observations that there are many different ways of excelling in teaching.

Perhaps it is because the skills of a teacher need to be so various and so adaptable that it seems necessary to describe teaching as an art rather than a science. There is, however, a danger as well as an advantage in that term, for the art involves the employment of many specific skills—such as questioning—that can be studied and taught. There is a clear distinction to be drawn between the acquisition of specific skills and the optimal application of them in the complex classroom stituation where conflicting demands exist and where conflicting objectives have to be reconciled week by week, day by day, and hour by hour.

* * * *

It was said in the opening chapter that the research described in this book was a journey of discovery, a journey adventurous enough to make some failures well-nigh certain. And failures there have been: the traveller returns certainly sadder and, it is to be hoped, wiser. In particular, though the complexity of the teaching situation was appreciated early and the SCOTS schedule created in an attempt to reflect it, the attempt to relate outcomes to particular teaching styles proved simplistic. That teaching styles can be related to pupil progress had been previously asserted in the research literature, in Britain most notably by Bennett.[3] The present writer, in company with many others, questioned the soundness of Bennett's specific findings soon after they were published[4], but the

[3] Bennett (1976)
[4] Powell (1976). Similar criticisms of the revised findings of Bennett's study arising from a new statistical analysis of his data—Aitken, Bennett, and Hesketh (1981) —have been made by Gray and Satterly (1981).

idea of associating teaching style and outcomes seemed a reasonable one, even in the light of the warnings by writers such as Rosenshine[5] of the difficulties and limitations of process-product studies. It is now clear, however, that the failure in this research to find associations between, on the one hand, the styles of teaching observed and described and, on the other, attitudes, application to work, and relative progress in acquiring concepts and computational skills in arithmetic is primarily attributable to two factors in addition to the technical ones that have been referred to in Chapter 9:

    a) the complexity of variation in how teachers teach gave rise to considerable within-group variance even when as many as 17 clusters were used to classify 128 teachers

    b) the large number of factors other than those encompassed in teaching style that contribute to the performance of classes.

The question does, therefore, have to be faced of whether the whole approach adopted in the research—notably the attempt to look at and record, by employing the SCOTS schedule, a wide range of data concerning the multifarious aspects of classroom activity rather than concentrating, as so many others have done, on single aspects—is a useful one. Reflecting on the research described in this book leads the author to conclude that the two approaches are complementary. Many of the generalisations made in this chapter required to be tested and, where necessary, modified by further detailed studies; equally such detailed studies have to be seen as limited by the very fact of their having to ignore and leave uncontrolled the many interacting factors that make any classroom what it is. To relate and reconcile findings from approaches so different, it is necessary for each to be qualified by the other—something that requires the exercise of informed judgement. Skilfully done, this may enhance our understanding of complex matters.

*   *   *   *

As was emphasised at the beginning of this chapter, the conclusions that have been drawn and presented—largely in Chapter 8 and in this final chapter—constitute insights that lack the backing of any form of proof. They are, however, based on disciplined observation and on the interpretation of observations

[5] Rosenshine (1971)

172

by a team of researchers who were themselves teachers.[6] Whether their interpretations and the wider ones the writer has based on them in this book have been distorting or illuminating, whether prejudice has misled and values biased, it is for the reader to decide.

[6] It was pointed out in Chapter 3 that even the statistics derived with a minimum of inference in the course of interaction studies are themselves the subject of interpretation in ways that are themselves subjective. See pp 17-18.

REFERENCES

AITKEN Murray, BENNETT S Neville, and HESKETH Jane (1981). "Teaching Styles and Pupil Progress: a Re-analysis", in *Brit. J. of Educ. Psych.*, 51, pp 170-186.

BENNETT S Neville (1976). *Teaching Style and Pupil Progress*, Open Books, London.

BARKER-LUNN Joan C (1970). *Streaming in the Primary School*, NFER, Slough.

DUNKIN Michael J and BIDDLE Bruce (1974). *The Study of Teaching*, Holt, Rinehart and Winston, Inc., New York.

ENTWISTLE Noel (1981). *Styles of Learning and Teaching*, John Wiley & Sons, London.

FLANDERS Ned A (1970). *Analyzing Teaching Behaviour*, Addison-Wesley Publishing Co., Reading, Massachussetts.

GALTON Maurice and SIMON Brian (eds) (1980). *Progress and Performance in the Primary Classroom*, Routledge and Kegan Paul, London.

GRAY J and SATTERLY D (1981). "Formal or Informal? A Review of British Evidence", in *Brit. J. of Educ. Psych.*, 51, pp 187-196.

MORRISON Arnold and McINTYRE Donald (1969). *Teachers and Teaching*, Penguin Books Ltd., Harmondsworth, Middlesex.

POWELL John L (1976). "After Lancaster: some reflections on the progressive-traditional controversy", in *Research in Education*, 16, SCRE, Edinburgh.

POWELL John L (1984). *Objectivity, Subjectivity and Value Judgements in the Context of the Classroom Observation of Teaching Styles*, a paper delivered at the Annual Meeting of the American Educational Research Association, New Orleans, April 1984.

ROSENSHINE Barak (1971). *Teaching Behaviours and Student Achievement*, NFER, London.

SPENCER Ernest (1983). *Writing Matters across the Curriculum*, SCRE, Edinburgh.

TRAVERS R M W (ed) (1973). *Second Handbook on Research on Teaching*, Rand McNally, Chicago.

WISHART David (1978). *Clustan User Manual* (Third Edition), Inter-University Research Council Series, Report 47.

SYSTEM FOR CLASSROOM OBSERVATION OF TEACHING STRATEGIES
(SCOTS)
(1977 Revision)

JOHN L POWELL and MABEL N G SCRIMGEOUR

NOTES

1) The items of this schedule are discussed in detail in Chapter 3.

2) Where item options were combined after the use of the schedule in 1977/78, this is shown, together with all necessary item re-numberings.

3) The data arising from the 1977/78 observations (Appendix D) refers to item-options as *re-numbered*.

4) The five columns to the right of all items are for recording the observer's codings in each of five observations extending for approximately one quarter of a school day. Where the letter T appears at the head of one of these columns, it indicates that information concerning the item is to be sought from the teacher at the end of that observation.

5) Where the symbol S appears above an item, it indicates that there is a distinct form of the item for summarising the codings from the five observations. (These summative forms are given in Appendix B.)

6) The figures in the left-hand margin are the frequencies for each option in 1977/78 when 128 teachers were observed. It must be stressed that these figures relate to final summative codings, *not* to provisional recordings during a single observation. (It is for this reason that the frequencies for items marked S are given in Appendix B.)

I ITEMS REQUIRING INFORMATION FROM BOTH TEACHER AND OBSERVATION**

1) VISIBLE DIFFERENTIATION BY ABILITY/ACHIEVEMENT

	T				

1) Pupils seated in rank order in accordance with test results or teacher's current assessment of each pupil's relative merit OR as '2', but that the status of the individual strongly underlined by the teacher either by prominent promotions/demotions or by regular pejoritive references to particular groups.

2) Pupils seated for most of the time in ability groups whose composition does not change from subject to subject. (Transfer from group to group may occur from time to time in view of teacher's assessment of performance.)

3) Pupils seated in ability groups for at least a significant part of the time but with membership of groups varied according to subject OR as '4', but with the relative status of the groups regularly and strongly underlined by the teacher.

4) Work undertaken in ability groups for at least some subjects, but these groups have no intentional correspondence with seating groups.

5) No intentional correspondence between seating position and ability/achievement AND no regular work undertaken in groups of identifiable ability level.

Observer's Notes:

Observation 1)

....

Observation 2)

....

Observation 3)

....

Observation 4)

....

Observation 5)

....

** Columns marked 'T' indicate the observation at the end of which enquiries should be addressed to the teacher. Wherever possible the observer should clarify/confirm the teacher's statements by recalling for discussion relevant instances that have been observed.

176

2) USUAL NUMBER OF WORK DIFFICULTY LEVELS FOR ARITHMETIC/MATHS

			T	
27 1) One work level for class.				
40 2) Two work levels for class.				
47 3) Three or four work levels for class.				
3 4) Five or more work levels for class (excluding situation described in '5').				
11 5) Multiplicity of work levels, such that work is allocated mainly on an individual basis.				

3) USUAL NUMBER OF WORK DIFFICULTY LEVELS FOR ENGLISH (EXCLUDING READING PRACTICE)

			T	
42 1) One work level for class.				
48 2) Two work levels for class.				
36 3) Three or four work levels for class.				
1 4) Five or more work levels for class (excluding situation described in '5').				
1 5) Multiplicity of work levels, such that work is allocated mainly on an individual basis.				

4) VARIATION OF TREATMENT ACCORDING TO PUPIL NEEDS

33

			T	
1) No variety of treatment amongst pupils (level of work may vary but approach is identical for all pupils.)

64

2) Some variety of treatment, but for low OR high ability pupils only.

22

3) Treatment varies for the extremes of low AND high ability pupils from that used for class in general.

4

4) Treatment varies with instructional groups.

5

5) Treatment varies with individual pupil need.

Observer's Notes:

Observation 1)

....

Observation 2)

....

Observation 3)

....

Observation 4)

....

Observation 5)

....

5) <u>TEACHER OBJECTIVES (RELATING TO COGNITIVE OUTCOMES)</u>

47

1) Teacher aims to have all pupils, including the
   most able, reach the highest level of which
   they are capable.   Work is differentiated
   accordingly in both level and breadth.

75

2) Teacher aims to have all pupils (save the very
   weakest) attain a common basic standard.   Pace
   of basic work is therefore that of the middle
   group.   Those who can proceed faster are <u>not</u>
   permitted to undertake work at a higher level,
   though they may be permitted to broaden their
   work (at the same level) or undertake additional
   peripheral work.

6

3) Work is geared to a low level so that most of
   the weaker pupils can cope with the work.
   Additional work may be given to some more able
   pupils.

<u>NOTE</u>:

If the teacher's response cannot be accurately represented by one of
the above three categories, a brief explanatory note should be
appended below.   Any relevant information derived from observation
should also be recorded.

II DIRECTION/CONTROL OF WORK

6) DIRECTNESS OF TEACHER CONTROL OF PUPILS' LEARNING ACTIVITIES

1) Control of pupils by teacher is entirely direct; pupils show no sign of training in managing work activities.

2) As '1' save that in some limited contexts a significant proportion of the class operate in ways showing a lesser dependence upon the teacher. (Note: merely repeating an operation a number of times without further instructions should not be taken as evidence of lesser dependence.)

3) Although the teacher intervenes substantially to maintain the operation of the working system, pupils also show a substantial competence in work management.   Most pupils show themselves able and willing to sustain even non-routine work for at least a short while in the absence of the teacher or in the absence of teacher support.

4) As '5', save that the role of the teacher in keeping the wheels turning is rather more apparent. In particular the teacher apparently finds it necessary to intervene from time to time - eg, because pupil work operations are seen as faltering. (Note: class lessons and class discussions should not be regarded as teacher-intervention.)

5) There are very few signs of direct teacher-control of pupils' work activities (other than basic instructions infrequently given, concerning work to be undertaken) and yet nearly all pupils work purposefully, clearly knowing how to operate the system in use.   (Work is typically unaffected by the absence of the teacher.   The teacher is usually consulted only when significant problems of comprehension arise.   Such consultations normally involve pupils taking an active role.)

7) PUPIL RESPONSIBILITY FOR MANAGING OWN WORK

49

    1) Pupil has no control of own work. Tasks are almost always instructed by the teacher singly. The time spent is controlled entirely by the teacher, as is the way in which the work is undertaken.

58

    2) As '1', save that, at least sometimes, more than one task is instructed by the teacher at a time. When more than one task is instructed, the pupils have to do them in a given sequence and the teacher often intervenes to ensure that time spent on each task is that intended. (Control may not be exercised by the teacher in a minority of subject areas that the teacher considers peripheral.* 'Filler' tasks may also be uncontrolled.)

11

    3) Most work is instructed by the teacher as in '1' or '2'. Pupils are however sometimes given responsibility either over a short period (up to approximately one quarter of a school day) for allocating time to each of a small number of tasks and for determining their sequence or for a longer period (up to a whole day) for allocating time to tasks but not controlling their sequence.

9

    4) Pupils are given a programme of work to be covered over a period of time (usually ½ day or 1 day.) The distribution of time is left to the pupils save that the teacher may intervene whenever a pupil is thought to be devoting too much time to any one activity with the result that the amount - and quality - of work in other areas is suffering. The intervention normally takes the form of direct instructions as to what the pupil is to do.

1

    5) As '4', save that teacher intervention is infrequent and different in type. Thus the teacher does not intervene until there is evidence available (eg, from a pupil's own work record) that a pupil's work is suffering through failure to allocate time satisfactorily. Typically, however, the intervention will take the form of indicating to a pupil the nature of the failure and of a request to ensure that it does not recur. (More direct and more frequent intervention as described in '4' may, however, be applied to a small minority of pupils who have proved unable to respond to the normal type of intervention.) Despite the low level of intervention, the teacher is likely to devote time to advising pupils, before they start working, of the standards to be met.

* Usually art and projects, but this may when necessary be checked by asking the teacher obliquely.

8) AUTHORITARIAN/DEMOCRATIC PRACTICES

42

1) Teacher totally authoritarian: the work to be
undertaken is determined by the teacher without even
a semblance of consulting pupil wishes or allowing
pupil choice (save in 'fill-in' activities.)

65

2) As '1', save that limited degree of pupil choice may
be permitted in very limited contexts (eg, projects,
art, selecting work-card from a prescribed set.)

11

3) Practice varies: whereas some children are treated
as in '4' (or even '5'), approximately as many are
treated as in '2' (or even '1').

10

4) Children are encouraged to express preference for
work topic and/or work mode (even though choice may
be from a restricted range of options and may be very
limited in material effect.)

0

5) As '4', save that children often make suggestions
that are taken up by teacher and that have an effect
on the work of the class that is more than nominal.

9) TEACHER PRESSURE ON PUPILS TO SECURE WORK

3

1) Teacher constantly drives pupils, seeking to secure
effort and/or high work standards.

18

2) Teacher presses pupils to secure effort and/or high
work standards, but not constantly. Pressure
tends to be applied selectively. However, lapses
in pupil effort are seldom allowed.

33

3) Teacher presses pupils from time to time to secure
effort and/or high work standards. However, lapses
in pupil effort do occur and go unchallenged. Demand
for high work standards is less strong than in '1'
and '2' (but slipshod work is not tolerated.)

49

4) Most pupils are not pressed to secure effort and
work standards, but such pressure as there is is
likely to be directed at those whose activity is
falling off OR at a minority who, experience has
apparently shown, do not work satisfactorily unless
regularly reminded.

25

5) There is little sign of pressure on any pupil though
activity may be encouraged in the inactive. The
teacher is, however, likely to be available to
respond to children's needs.

8.

10) INTEGRATION OF KNOWLEDGE

Note all signs of integration of work across subject barriers, carefully distinguishing between the superficial and the profound.   In each case the subjects and/or work activities should be noted.

Observation 1

Observation 2

Observation 3

Observation 4

Observation 5

11) TEACHING FOR MEMORISATION/UNDERSTANDING

1) The emphasis is almost entirely on rote-learning (eg, of tables, spelling, etc) and on the acquisition by pupils of mechanical competence. The focus is on obtaining the correct answer, and there is little sign of any attempt to discover whether any understanding of the underlying principles and concepts is being acquired.

2) As '1', save that sporadic attempts are made to ascertain whether understanding of underlying principles and concepts is being acquired.

3) Some emphasis is laid on pupils' acquiring an understanding of the principles and concepts relating to the areas of competence with which their learning is concerned. Nevertheless rote-learning (eg, of tables, spelling, etc) and the acquisition of mechanical competence is also prominent.

4) The emphasis is predominantly on the acquisition of understanding of principles and concepts. Nevertheless, rote-learning (eg, of tables, spelling, etc) does occur to some extent, and 'rule of thumb' procedures, designed to avoid accidental mechanical errors in the application of understood principles, may be found.

5) The main emphasis is on the acquisition of understanding of principles and concepts. There is no rote-learning since the pupils are expected to look up required necessary facts and to memorise these simply through familiarity in usage. Failure to establish the correct answer is treated as less important than demonstration of understanding of how to obtain it. 'Rule of thumb' procedures are accepted only when the pupil can demonstrate understanding of the principal underlying the rule or when the alternative would be total failure (ie, neither mechanical performance nor understanding of principle.)

184

12) ENCOURAGEMENT/PREVENTION OF DIFFERENCE

16

1) The work of the class is characterised by conformity to the teacher's dictates. In consequence, inventiveness, discovery, and doing things differently are prevented or strongly discouraged. Suggestions from pupils not welcomed and not used.

90 3

2) Suggestions from children are listened to and kindly dealt with but rarely, if ever, used. Teacher seems to be paying 'lip service' to idea of participation but in fact shows why his ideas are better without permitting children to find this out for themselves. Thus, in practice, the pupils have to follow the teacher's dictates.

3) The work of the class is characterised by a fair degree of conformity in that the teacher, while not preventing, rarely encourages inventiveness, discovery, or doing things differently. Difference is therefore able to occur but is unlikely to manifest itself often or in many pupils but may possibly give substantial encouragement within one or two subject areas, probably ones thought peripheral.

21

4) Teacher encourages children to suggest ideas for work and ways of carrying out work. Inventive individuals are encouraged to try out their ideas and consider the appropriacy of them. Teacher does not always insist on conformity of work and work method - however teacher normally suggests basic approach to work so that those devoid of ideas may participate. Likely to be marked by teacher showing pleasure at good ideas.

1

5) The work of the class is characterised by very little conformity and the teacher strongly encourages curiosity, discovery, and inventiveness, and differences in learning mode are commended if at all sensible.

NOTE: By discovery is meant finding things out for oneself.

By differences in learning mode is meant difference in approach to work, in arriving at answers, etc.

13) TEACHER'S MODE OF COGNITIVE QUESTIONING

1

1) Unless a correct answer is obtained instantly, the teacher either abandons the question he has posed or personally provides the answer. Alternatively the first partially correct answer is accepted. (The questions thus functionally constitute shallowly disguised teacher-statements.)

32

2) Teacher is concerned to get the correct answer as quickly as possible from any pupil. (No individual pupil is pressed for an answer.) If no correct answer is obtained, the first partially correct answer is accepted - though a better answer may then be offered by the teacher.

40

3) The teacher is concerned to get an answer from the pupil to whom any question has been addressed (ie, the questions are intended to find out what the pupils know/think/can deduce), but if the pupil fails to respond the teacher soon gives up and either directs the question to another pupil or provides his own answer.

36

4) Teacher is concerned to get correct answer and/or to get the child (or possibly children) questioned to make an effort, to think about what the answer should be. To this end he repeats the question, though without significant variation, until the required answer is obtained or until he eventually finds it necessary to provide the answer himself or direct the pupil(s) to a source from which an answer can be obtained.

19

5) As '4', but when the question is pursued it is re-presented in many different ways in order to lead pupils to reason out a correct answer. In the last resort an answer is provided by the teacher or by consultation of a written source.

14) <u>CLARITY OF EXPOSITION OF BASIC PRINCIPLES</u>

10

1) When explaining any point*, the teacher presents facts in such a way that the underlying principles will not be apparent to anyone not conversant with them already. Irrelevant facts may be brought in and essential ones omitted.

47

2) When explaining any point*, the teacher relates facts presented to underlying principles to some degree, but the stress is on either the practical/mechanical or the superficial rather than the basic principles. Examples of other applications of the principles are wholly lacking and consequently the opportunities for the pupils to generalise or to transfer the 'training' to other areas are minimal.

38

3) When explaining any point*, the teacher presents the facts in a clear logical order so that the underlying principles are made readily apparent or alternatively presents principles and applies them to cases so that the nature of the principles is made apparent. However, the teacher shows signs of underestimating the difficulties many of the pupils have in grasping key intermediate steps.

33

4) As '3', save that the teacher is sensitive to the types of difficulties experienced by many pupils and appears to be able to pin-point most of the areas of difficulty experienced by <u>individual pupils</u> and to deal with these simply, clearly, and appropriately.

0

0) Insufficient exposition to permit coding.

*

This variable covers any explanations, whether in initial teaching, in revision, or in dealing with any misunderstanding or failure to understand. These explanations may be directed to individuals, to groups of pupils, or to a complete class. Even when a group or class is being instructed, there may be a 'target population' within the class/group to which the teacher is primarily directing his effort at that time. The clarity of his exposition must, therefore, be judged in terms of each 'target population' observed.

15) TEACHER VARIETY AND INVENTIVENESS IN EXPLANATION

14

2 1) If initial explanation is unsuccessful the teacher
         repeats the original explanation; no sign of
         trying a different approach.

95 3 { 2) Most points are explained in only one way, but
              there are occasional cases of an alternative
              explanation or mode of exposition.

         3) Teacher explains most points in more than one way
              to aid pupil comprehension, but no great inventive-
              ness displayed, the types of explanation are
              fairly stereotyped.

14   4) Teacher uses a variety of ways of explaining most
              points, endeavouring to overcome most of the
              failure of comprehension; these ways are
              characterised by considerable inventiveness.

5   5) Teacher uses a great variety of ways of explaining,
              endeavouring to find some way of overcoming every
              difficulty experienced by pupils; these ways are
              characterised by great inventiveness.

         0) No instances of teacher explaining anything.

NOTE: This variable applies equally to teaching of class, group, or
       individual. It relates exclusively to cognitive activities.

16) NATURE AND FREQUENCY OF TEACHER CONTACTS WITH INDIVIDUAL
     PUPILS   (S)

     1) Individual or quasi-individual instruction given
         but in no great depth: simply the making of a
         few simple points (or even one simple point.)

     2) Substantial individual or quasi-individual
         instruction going beyond making a few simple
         points and almost certainly extending over a
         period of time.

NOTE: The observer should endeavour to note the extent of the
       occurrence of '1' and/or '2', but should supplement this in
       the notes he takes.

14.

17) <u>FEEDBACK TO PUPILS</u> (S)

   a) <u>Concurrent</u>

   1) There is virtually no significant concurrent
      feedback to pupils. There are no self-
      correcting facilities and teacher's responses
      to pupils' questions about the work they are
      currently doing are minimal.

   2) Limited feedback is provided by teacher and/or
      through self-correction facilities. Thus
      pupils can find out, perhaps after some delay,
      whether their work is right. However, guidance
      to those in difficulty is brief and at a
      superficial level <u>or</u> restricted to very few
      pupils. If lessons on faults observed by the
      teacher are given to the class (or groups), these
      occur only after the faults have been occurring
      for some time.

   3) Every effort appears to be made to give individuals
      on-going guidance and comment. However,
      organisation is not equal to the demands of the
      pupils. The result is delay, with some pupils
      getting more help than others. Lessons to class/
      groups on frequently observed faults are given
      more promptly than in '2'.

   4) Through selective and economical use of his own
      time, and through such measures as the careful
      scheduling of class-work to spread the load on
      himself, the teacher provides an optimised system
      of concurrent feedback unimpaired by personal
      over-involvement. Help for pupils who cannot
      provide it for themselves is thus provided with
      minimal delay.

<u>Observer's Notes</u>:

Observation 1)

      ....

Observation 2)

      ....

Observation 3)

      ....

Observation 4)

      ....

Observation 5)

      ....

17) FEEDBACK TO PUPILS ⓢ

b) Retrospective

1) Written work that has not been already adequately marked concurrently is frequently left unmarked. When marking is undertaken, it resembles that described in '2'.

2) Although written work that has not been already adequately corrected concurrently is normally marked, it is examined and assessed so cursorily that pupils lack specific guidance. Typically ticks and/or marks and/or very general comments (such as 'poor' or 'good') are the only writing by the teacher on pupil's work. Oral follow-up with individuals is not found. Class and/or group instruction may, however, be given on errors etc found to be prevalent in pupils' work.

3) Written work that has not been already adequately marked concurrently is subsequently marked with care. Explanations of errors (if any) are terse and pupils have to make of them what they can. Oral follow-up with individuals and/or the requesting of pupils to do further work to demonstrate their understanding of errors marked are observed rarely, if at all. Class and/or group instruction, may, however, be given on errors etc found to be prevalent in pupils' work.

4) As '5' save that the explanation of errors (whether written or oral) are much less full.

5) Written work that has not been already adequately marked is subsequently marked with care. Explanations of pupils' errors, corrections etc are either given fully and clearly in writing, or pupils subsequently are given substantial help in overcoming their difficulties through individual, group, or class instruction. The teacher thus does not confine his attention to commonly experienced errors/difficulties.

Observer's Notes:

Observation 1)
....

Observation 2)
....

Observation 3)
....

Observation 4)
....

Observation 5)
....

IV. MOTIVATION, CONTROL, AND DISCIPLINE

18) TEACHING (OR TEACHING SITUATION) STIMULATIVE/DULL

2

1) Teaching/teaching situation dull and unstimulating: teacher apparently bored, weary, or uninterested in task or class.

20

2) Teaching/teaching situation evokes only occasional interest in pupils; pupils unlikely to sustain concentration and effort.

60

3) Teaching/teaching situation evokes fairly consistent interest in most pupils for much of the time but the pupils' enthusiasm is not aroused.

41

4) Teaching/teaching situation is bright and interesting; teacher's interest and enthusiasm is communicated to the class.

5

5) Teaching/teaching situation is outstandingly bright, interesting, and challenging; a high level of enthusiasm is communicated to the class, most of whom become deeply involved in the work.

NOTE: The alternative, teaching/teaching situation, is used so as to cover both teacher-centred and non-teacher-centred situations.

19) TEACHER SENSITIVITY TO PUPIL SELF-CONFIDENCE AND/OR SELF-ESTEEM

1

1) Teacher shows gross insensitivity to the feelings of at least some pupils such that there are clear signs of pupils' self-confidence and/or self-esteem being undermined.

13

2) Teacher lacks any significant sign of sensitivity, but there is much less sign than in '1' of pupil self-confidence and/or self-esteem being undermined. Nevertheless, effects on pupils are more than slight and almost certainly more than temporary.

51

3) Teacher shows no marked signs of sensitivity or lack of it; his/her effect on the self-confidence and/or self-esteem of pupils is slight OR, if more than slight, of short duration.

49

4) The teacher shows clear signs of sensitivity and there is no indication of any undermining of pupils' self-confidence or self-esteem; any forthrightness etc on the teacher's part is off-set by a generally high level of rapport with pupils.

14

5) Teacher shows great sensitivity in all contact with pupils; any work or action that might genuinely threaten a pupil's self-confidence and/or self-esteem does not occur.

20) <u>FOSTERING A SENSE OF RESPONSIBILITY</u>

1) Pupils have no responsibility for their actions
(eg, teacher himself may even count pencils,
rulers, etc, daily.)   Teacher also supervises
all aspects of school life.   If pupils are
given any duties to perform (eg, giving out
jotters), these are given as chores rather
than responsibilities and the teacher closely
supervises their execution.

3

2) As '1', except that a selected minority of pupils
is trusted to perform chores without direct
supervision.   Even these pupils, however, are
subject to the teacher's checking (usually by
asking) that assigned duties have in fact been
carried out.

8

3) Pupils given duties to perform are not <u>closely</u>
supervised but are expected to perform them well
and responsibly.   On the other hand, teacher
makes no attempt to foster responsibility,
duties being allocated only to those showing
signs of wanting them or thought likely to
perform them well.   Any pupil found not to
have acted responsibly is, however, 'written-off'
for at least a considerable time.

39

4) Teacher makes an effort to make pupils responsible
individuals.   For this reason duties and
responsibilities are widely spread throughout the
class.   (A rota is likely for all <u>main</u> duties.)
Jobs are not, however, deliberately matched to
pupils' interests and abilities, the teacher
being less sensitive to such matters than in '5'.
Consequently some pupils are likely to find
themselves with responsibilities they do not wish
to have.

57

5) The teacher, apparently effortlessly, allocates
to virtually all pupils duties well-matched to
their interests and capabilities and guides them
unostentatiously.   Even the most unpromising
pupils get something appropriate to do.   All
appear to be trusted.

21

192

21) EXTRINSIC/INTRINSIC MOTIVATION

5

1) The incentives to work provided by the teacher
    are all extrinsic - marks, points, rewards, etc.
    The teacher fails to indicate that work may be
    satisfying in itself.   Work is, either
    explicitly or implicitly, presented to pupils
    as a pain rather than a pleasure.

24

2) Extrinsic incentives are used no less extensively
    than in '1', and indeed receive considerable
    emphasis, but the teacher reveals that some of
    the work may be interesting.   He may, for
    example, indicate that some of the pupils will
    want to do a particular piece of work because
    it is especially interesting.   In contrast much
    of the work is presented as a chore that it is
    necessary to stick at.

65

3) Extrinsic incentives are used and, although they
    play a much less prominent part in the life of
    the class than they do in '2', they are given
    sufficient emphasis to show that they are part
    of the teacher's individualised system.   There
    is a tacit assumption that the work will be
    generally interesting to pupils but indications
    that pupils don't like particular tasks are
    accepted as natural.

27

4) Extrinsic incentives (if any) are no more than a
    formality.   Little time is devoted to them, and
    the pupils show little interest in them.   On the
    other hand, pupils are, at least, very willing
    to undertake work.   Their motivation is therefore
    presumably intrinsic.

7

0) No extrinsic incentives employed and, since signs
    of any motivation in the pupils is notably lacking,
    it would be unwise to assume that there is any
    intrinsic motivation either.

193

22) COMPETITION

1

1) Competition amongst children is intense and of a
'cut-throat' nature. It pervades almost all the work
of the class, and, except for pupils who 'opt out',
the struggle is constant. At least some of the
children may, nonetheless, appear to enjoy the
competition.

3

2) Competition amongst children is a prominent feature
of the class, but it is less 'cut-throat' than in '1'.
Children may spontaneously indulge in 'races' with
others in the class (if only with immediate neighbour(s).
Though there is so much effort to be 'better' than
others (in work, speed, or behaviour), it is friendly
and enjoyed by most children.

12

3) Competition is marked but 'criterion-referenced' -
not 'cut-throat'. The emphasis is on all attaining a
'good' standard (relative to ability): the teacher is
anxious to see as many as possible do well rather than
to see some reach a higher standard than others.

35

4) Competition such as that described in '3' is a feature
of only a few activities OR, from time to time, of
most activities.

77

5) No sign of any competition (other than in games.)

23) TEACHER USE OF RATIONAL ARGUMENTS TO SUPPORT COMMANDS/REQUESTS

2

1) Teacher never supports commands or requests with any
form of explanation or argument.

OR

10

Teacher supports commands or requests only by claiming
them to be of long-term advantage to the pupils (eg,
'You'll need to be able to do this when you're grown up');
otherwise no support given.

113 *3*

2) Teacher only very occasionally supports commands or
requests with reasoned argument relating to the present
or immediate future; otherwise teacher either gives no
explanation or makes dubious claims of the long-term
advantage of compliance.

3) Teacher quite often supports commands with carefully and
validly reasoned arguments relating to the present and
immediately future situation. (More dubious claims of
the long-term advantages of compliance may also be used.)

5

4) Teacher habitually supports commands or requests with
carefully and validly reasoned arguments relating to
present and immediately future situations. (Dubious
claims of long-term advantages of compliance are NOT used.)

NOTE: This variable covers exhortations relating to work etc as well as to
discipline.

194

24) TEACHER'S MODE OF EXERCISING CONTROL

6

1) Teacher coerces pupils; control is almost entirely by deterrence.

28

2) Although control is generally exercised by coercive means, some pupils (probably the better behaved of more co-operative ones) are influenced by persuasive means.

59

3) Neither coercion nor persuasion predominates. (The teacher may, however, display a wide repertoire of control techniques.) Which technique is employed on each occasion probably represents what the teacher expects or hopes to be effective. The ways of treating pupils (or groups of pupils, or the complete class), are not necessarily mutually consistent.

26

4) Although coercion is applied to a minority of pupils (or even to most pupils occasionally), persuasion and reinforcement are the dominant modes of control.

9

5) Teacher encourages self-control by pupils. When pupils have been thoughtless or their behaviour has fallen below the standards expected of them, the teacher encourages the pupils to assess the consequences of their actions; good behaviour and thoughtfulness are however reinforced by the teacher.

25) PUPIL APPLICATION TO WORK/WORK AVOIDANCE

1

1) Lack of application to work is a prominent feature of the classroom. There are some very obvious examples of pupils not attempting prescribed work.

5

2) Some evidence of intent to work but work is slow to start at outset of sessions and/or falls away rapidly as time proceeds. Most of those completing tasks seem unenthusiastic about additional work (other than fill-in activities such as drawing.)

12

3) Class fairly evenly divided between '1' and '5' situations in terms of numbers.

45

4) As '5', except that EITHER there is a distinctive minority of the class that does not conform to the pattern and tends to avoid the work prescribed OR the general level of industry, enthusiasm etc is somewhat lower.

65

5) General air of industry. Pupils tackle all available work and appear to be not only satisfied with their work but enthusiastic about commencing new tasks. (Isolated exceptions should be disregarded.)

26) PUPIL TALK

48

    1) Class works silently except for communication with
       teacher.

59

    2) Class works silently though some talking may develop
       towards the end of an assignment or a period of work

       OR

       Talking occurs though not when teacher is addressing
       class or when it is necessary for pupils to work
       alone (eg, during test).

16

    3) Talking occurs almost all the time though not
       necessarily at unrestricted volume. Occasionally,
       however, there may be complete silence for a special
       purpose.

5

    4) Talking occurs almost always although not necessarily
       at unrestricted volume.

V. ORGANISATIONAL VARIABLES

27) UNEMPLOYMENT & UNDEREMPLOYMENT OF PUPILS

1

    1) Much pupil time is wasted through systems of working
       that either leave pupils with nothing to do or
       compel them to waste time (eg, queueing for a long
       time waiting for attention). This time-wasting is a
       major feature of the life of the class.

9

    2) As '1', but less extreme in degree.

22

    3) The systems of working are such that although a total
       lack of work to do (as in '1' or '2') is not common,
       pupils tend to experience a low level of demand on
       them, and fill-in activities that serve little purpose
       other than to keep pupils occupied are a recurrent
       feature of the scene. ('Fill-ins' near the end of
       a work-period should be weighted more lightly.)

48

    4) Situation approaches that in '5', but the organisation
       of pupil work does at times leave pupils with
       insufficient work to keep them well employed.

48

    5) Organisation of pupil work, whatever its nature,
       ensures that pupils always have plenty to do. (Any
       under-employment or non-working by pupils therefore
       represents a deliberate rejection of work opportunities
       - for whatever reason.) N.B. - Relaxed effort at
       times chosen by the teacher is not inconsistent with
       '5'.)

196

28) CLASSROOM ORGANISATION - TIME-LAG BETWEEN ACTIVITIES

1) Lengthy gaps tend to occur between tasks, such* that pupils engage in self-selected activities . (These gaps may arise either from inadequate organisation or from organisation that clearly does not have continuity of work amongst its aims.)

2) Gaps between activities are shorter/less frequent than in '1' and may be totally replaced by periods of uncertainty. (This may arise from indecision on the teacher's part and/or from his permitting 'digressions', or when individual pupils or groups of pupils control the sequencing of their own work, from failure to give pupils an appropriate response to queries or adequate guidance/support in self-management.)

3) Although pupils normally know promptly what they should do next, they from time to time find themselves impeded, (eg, by the lack of availability of materials that the teacher does have or can readily obtain.)

4) Pupils are able to pass smoothly, and normally quickly, from one activity to another and materials are always to hand. There are, however, minor hold-ups such as a requirement to consult with the teacher before changing to a new activity.

5) Transitions from one activity to another, whether at class, group, or individual level occur outstandingly smoothly. (Organisation and pupil training are both likely to be major factors in producing this situation.)

0) Changes of activity occur only at natural breaks (eg, morning intervals or lunch-time.)

*   'Self-selected activities' does not relate to work specifically allocated to be undertaken by those who finish early.

29) <u>MODE OF PERFORMING ADMINISTRATIVE FUNCTIONS</u>

0

1) Administrative functions receive great emphasis, 'ritualised' procedures being used rather than purely functional ones. Time spent on them tends to be considerable.

16

2) Administrative functions are not ritualised but are conducted with such care as to be often time-consuming. Normal work is held up while they are performed.

87

3) Administrative functions hold up normal work but are completed briskly and without ceremony, thus taking up a minimum of time.

25

4) Administrative functions are performed inconspicuously, often without any interruption of normal class work. Interference with class work is therefore minimal.

30) <u>EXTENT OF TEACHER ATTENTION TO CLASS</u>

3

1) Teacher tends to be pre-occupied for substantial period with activities that divert his attention from the bulk of the class. Whenever this is so he demonstrates, at best, only occasional awareness of what is happening elsewhere in the room.

14

2) As '1', save that the pre-occupation is far more spasmodic and consequently periods of low-awareness are frequently interspersed with periods in which teacher is alert to behaviour throughout the class.

54

3) For most of the time the teacher appears to be alert to what is happening throughout the class. Nevertheless, at times he appears to fail to notice individuals behaviour to which he normally reacts.

57

4) Teacher demonstrates a high degree of alertness such that he appears to seldom "miss a thing". This alertness is maintained even when he is engaged with individuals, groups, or private work.

<u>NOTE</u>: This variable is concerned with awareness of pupils' progress with work as well as of misbehaviour.

31) **SIZE OF TEACHING GROUPS FOR ARITHMETIC**

64
 1) Class taught as a single group.*

25
 2) Class taught in two groups.*

22
 3) Class taught in at least 3 groups with an average size of 8 or more pupils.*

9
 4) Class taught in at least 3 groups with an average size of 6-7 pupils.*

8
 5) Pupils taught in groups with an average size of 5 or less or receive instruction individually only.

* In arriving at a coding discount very small groups and individuals taught separately on account of low ability, difficult behaviour, recent absence, physical handicap, etc.

NOTE: This variable is concerned with the size of group receiving instruction, not with the number of groups.

32) **SIZE OF TEACHING GROUPS FOR ENGLISH**

78
 1) Class taught as a single group.*

27
 2) Class taught in two groups.*

14
 3) Class taught in at least 3 groups with an average size of 8 or more pupils.*

7
 4) Class taught in at least 3 groups with an average size of 6-7 pupils.*

2
 5) Pupils taught in groups with an average size of 5 or less or receive instruction individually only.

* In arriving at a coding discount very small groups and individuals taught separately on account of low ability, difficult behaviour, recent absence, physical handicap, etc.

NOTE: This variable is concerned with the size of group receiving instruction, not with the number of groups.

199

33) VARIETY OF ACTIVITIES ⟨ 3 ⟩

    1)   One activity only for class.

    2)   Two activities for class.

    3)   Three or four activities for class.

    4)   Five or six activities for class.

    5)   Seven or more activities for class.

    NOTE: Activities within the same subject area but relating to different aspects of a subject should be regarded as separate activities for the purposes of this dimension, but activities differing ONLY in difficulty level should be treated as a single activity.

34) ENCOURAGEMENT / PREVENTION OF INTER-PUPIL CO-OPERATION

57

    1)   Teacher seeks to prevent co-operation amongst pupils; there is a sustained insistence on working alone (save possibly in PT, Art, some project work, and similar activities) OR pupils show no sign of attempting to co-operate.

45

    2)   As '1', save that the total ban is not sustained OR teacher tolerates pupil co-operation but prevents it if it exceeds modest limits. (In some cases the teacher may allow a small minority greater freedom and/or totally inhibit co-operation amongst members of another such minority.)

12

    3)   As '2', but from time to time co-operation is encouraged explicitly or implicitly.

14

    4)   Teacher frequently gives implicit or explicit encouragement of co-operation. Nevertheless restrictions are imposed for some activities.

0

    5)   Teacher encourages implicitly and/or explicitly pupil co-operation whenever this is possible.

    0)   Not applicable (eg, because of testing or work that would be invalidated by co-operation.)

    (N.B. '0' is not needed in summative.)

    NOTE: For the purposes of this variable, minimal co-operation such as borrowing an eraser should be disregarded.

35) CONSTRAINT ON PUPIL MOVEMENT

3

   1) Most pupils not allowed to leave seats unless instructed by teacher.

28

   2) Most pupils free to move to teacher or for assigned functions, but no other voluntary movement allowed.

79

   3) Most pupils free to collect required materials. (May include borrowing from other pupils in class.)

18

   4) Most pupils free to move to co-operate with other pupils or to work in other areas of room.

0

   5) Most pupils free to visit areas outwith the classroom for task-related purposes (eg, to measure playground, or consult books in school central library.)

36) FREEDOM OF ACCESS TO RESOURCES

8

   1) Pupils have access to no materials other than those specified (or laid out) by the teacher for the immediate task. Requests for additional materials are usually not granted.

39

   2) In addition to those materials specified (or laid out) by the teacher for the immediate tasks, pupils may, on request, be allowed additional materials if the teacher is satisfied of a genuine need for them. (There is likely to be, however, considerable stress on economy with _all_ materials.)

88 3

   3) Teacher tends to specify the basic materials required for each task but responds readily to reasonable requests for additional ones and/or permits free access at all times to a limited range of additional items. (Scarce materials are, however, carefully shared and economy is expected with most of the materials.)

   4) A wide range of materials is in regular use and is freely available to pupils. However, there are certain materials and/or storage locations that may be accessed by pupils only when specifically instructed by the teacher.

13 4 5)

   5) Pupils have free access to all communal materials, although they may be instructed as to how and when scarce materials should be used. (Specific restrictions on access and use may be imposed in respect of dangerous items that the teacher wishes to be used only under supervision.)

VI. TEACHER PERSONALITY AND RELATIONSHIPS WITH PUPILS

37) TEACHER OVERT ANXIETY/CALMNESS

1

    1) Teacher habitually shows very marked signs of anxiety or insecurity.

3

    2) Teacher usually shows some signs of anxiety or insecurity.

    3) Teacher normally at least fairly calm, but liable to show tension occasionally.

71   3

    4) Teacher normally calm and never more than momentarily ruffled by events.

53   4

    5) Teacher is habitually calm and unruffled in all situations observed.

38) NOISY/QUIET TEACHER

0

    1) Teacher's voice heard loudly in all parts of the room whenever he/she speaks, even to individuals privately.

26

    2) Teacher's voice audible in all parts of the room whenever he/she speaks, even to individuals privately.

84

    3) Teacher clearly audible to those he/she is addressing but scarcely audible to class when speaking to individual or group.

16

    4) Teacher speaks quietly but audibly when addressing class such that all individuals must attend in order to hear him/her. Speech to groups/individuals even quieter.

2

    5) All speech to class at such an extremely low level that the class must strain to hear. Exchanges with individuals and groups are whispered.

28.

39) NEGATIVE/POSITIVE APPROACH

1) Teacher emphasises error and wrongdoing.
   Praise is almost completely absent; even
   when pupils produce good work the smallest
   defect is picked on.

2) Teacher emphasises error and wrongdoing, and
   although praise is given it tends to be
   grudging, half-hearted, or casual.

3) There are no strong indications of a positive
   or a negative approach OR both are approximately equal.

4) Teacher tends to praise rather than blame.
   The general atmosphere is supportive but the
   use of praise is less systematic than in '5'.
   (Negative instructions/comments may be
   converted into positive ones, but less
   regularly than in '5'.)

5) Teacher seeks opportunities to praise good or
   improved work/conduct and emphasises what has
   been achieved.   Criticism and prohibition are
   almost completely avoided, positive comments/
   instructions being substituted.

NOTE: Praise that is indiscriminately and cursorily conferred
      (eg, without even looking at what is praised) should be
      weighted lightly.

40) TEACHER-PUPIL SOCIAL RELATIONSHIP

1) Teacher is reserved and creates distance between
   herself and the pupils such that pupils are
   dissuaded from making any avoidable approach.

2) Teacher distant but approachable within the
   constraints of teacher-imposed formal procedures.

3) Teacher approachable, being neither distant nor
   friendly.

4) Teacher approached on social as well as school
   topics; friendly but not treated as an equal.

5) Teacher very friendly with pupils - relationship
   approaching one of equality.

203

41) APPARENT TEACHER ATTITUDE TO CLASS

0

    1)   Teacher usually shows a strong dislike to class,
        being short-tempered, easily roused, and prone
        to engaging in altercations with pupils.

5

    2)   Teacher seems unable to like class, being listless,
        dejected, and unenthusiastic about the teaching
        undertaken.

57

    3)   Teacher usually shows neither particular pleasure
        nor particular displeasure in teaching class.
        The teaching may be characterised by professional
        and business-like behaviour.

58

    4)   Teacher appears to enjoy teaching class; his/her
        behaviour is likely to be characterised by
        smiling, sympathetic interest in pupils, and/or
        a restrained/controlled enthusiasm.

8

    5)   Teacher usually shows an ebullient enthusiasm for
        teaching class; his/her approach and reactions to
        class likely to be dynamic.

42) TEACHER HOSTILITY

0

    1)   Teacher seeks confrontations with pupils and
        responds to hostility with hostility.

2

    2)   Teacher does not seek confrontation with pupils
        but nevertheless is not slow to respond to at
        least some children with marked hostility.

9

    3)   Hostility exists between teacher and one or two
        children, but relationship with rest of class is
        good; save towards the minority of one or two,
        the teacher never displays animosity - though
        annoyance may sometimes be shown.

117

    4)   Teacher does not show hostility (even when
        provoked) and is skilled at disarming pupil
        hostility, if any.

NOTE: If teacher is never observed showing hostility or being subjected
         to hostility, '4' should be coded.

43) DEGREE OF TEACHER CONTROL ACHIEVED

1) Whole or substantial part of class refuses to
accept any form of teacher control; teacher,
being impotent, has given up serious attempts
to control recalcitrant pupils.

2) Whole or substantial part of class refuses to
accept any form of teacher control; teacher
in effect impotent, but still striving to
retrieve situation.

3) Teacher apparently unable to control effectively
noise-level etc, but still manages to implement
a programme of work, though perhaps a circum-
scribed one.

4) The teacher manages to maintain control of class
and implement his programme of work; nevertheless
his time and energies are taken up to such an
extent that his teaching and/or the operation of
the class's work is almost certainly to some degree
impeded.

5) Although a certain effort in maintaining control
is apparent, the implementation of the programme
of work is not hindered significantly, if at all.

6) Class is controlled easily and effectively, thus
allowing work programme to proceed with a minimum
or friction or disturbance.

SCOTS SCHEDULE
(Summative Version)

NOTE: This appendix contains only those items of the summative version that differ from those in the classroom version (Appendix A).

10) INTEGRATION OF SUBJECT-MATTER

1) There is no significant integration; nor is indication given that knowledge from one area of study/knowledge may be valuable in another; each area of learning is treated wholly separately or, if there are any links at all made between areas, they are at so superficial a level as to provide no genuine illumination of either area.

87

2) Teacher sometimes draws pupils' attention to significant links between areas of study/knowledge but fails to make these links explicit; pupils have therefore to draw inferences for themselves, if they can, and consequently there can be no assurance that many pupils (if any) will find any genuine illumination of either area.

28

3) Significant links are established <u>explicitly</u> between areas of study/knowledge, but the practice of establishing these links is less pervasive than in '4'. The level of illumination of one subject area by another is such that pupils' depth and width of understanding is likely to be enhanced.

12

4) Integration and cross-referencing of knowledge is a regular feature of classroom life. Whenever an appropriate occasion arises, significant links between areas of study/knowledge are established, usually explicitly, such that pupils are given every chance to see all knowledge as one and at times at least, the depth and width of their understanding in specific areas is likely to be enhanced. Alternatively, this degree of integration may be attained by means of a project very carefully designed to provide links in depth with a number of subject areas in the curriculum.

NOTE: Coding of Category 3:-

In the course of five observations, there are likely to be only a few instances of integration for teachers who should be coded in this category. The <u>degree</u> to which areas of work are integrated on the occasions observed is the criterion that should separate this category from '2'. Even one instance of very thorough integration may be taken as justification for coding '3'.

16) NATURE OF TEACHER CONTACTS WITH INDIVIDUAL PUPILS

1	1)	No '1s' or '2s'	
18	2)	No '2s', only a little of '1'	
31	3)	No '2s', but '1s' occur often	
57	4)	Some occurrence of '2' (almost certainly accompanied by '1s')	
21	5)	'2s' occur often (almost certainly accompanied by '1s')	

17) FEEDBACK TO PUPILS (CONCURRENT AND RETROSPECTIVE)

			(a)	(b)	
5 3	~~1)~~		'1'	'1'	
	~~2)~~		'1'	'2'/'3'	
		OR	'2'	'1'	
63 4	3)		'2'	'2'	
		OR	'3'	'1'	
	4)		'1'	'4'	
		OR	'3'	'2'/'3'	
		OR	'2'/'3'	'3'	
25	5)		'4'	'1'/'2'	
		OR	'2'/'3'	'4'	
		OR	'1'	'5'	
29	6)		'2'/'3'	'5'	
		OR	'4'	'3'/'4'	
6	7)		'4'	'5'	

NOTE: This table enabled observers to combine their separate final codings for concurrent and retrospective feedback. Its aim sought to allow a higher level on the one to compensate to some degree for a lower level on the other.

33) VARIETY OF ACTIVITIES

Interpretation of summated scores:

26

1. More than one activity observed on no occasion (five points)

60

2. Almost certainly a maximum of three to four activities and generally two or less (six to nine points)

39

3. Minimum of three activities; at least once OR two activities every time (ten to fourteen points)

3

4. Generally at least three activities and possibly up to six on occasions (fifteen to seventeen points OR seventeen + points with no 'five')

0

5. Generally a large number of activities, with at least seven on at least one occasion (seventeen + points, with a 'five')

NOTE: The number of simultaneous activities observed to occur often varied considerably from one observation to another. To take account of this points were alloted for each observation - a coding of category 1 scored one point, of category 2, two points etc. The text above constitutes an interpretation of these points totalled - one that takes into account the various ways in which those totals might be secured.

BIOGRAPHICAL DATA
RELATING TO TEACHERS OBSERVED
(Derived from Teacher Questionnaire)

Frequencies

Post held	Headteacher—1; Assistant headteacher—7; Assistant—120.
No of Schools in which teaching post held	(1) 47; (2) 33; (3) 15; (4) 14; (5) 9; (more than 5) 10.
Years of Teaching Experience	(0-2) 13; (3-7) 51; (8-12) 25; (13-20) 14; (over 20) 25.
Age	(Under 26) 25; (26-35) 38; (36-45) 35; (46-55) 22; (56-65) 8.
Marital Status	(Single) 45; (Married) 77; (Other) 6.
Sex	(Male) 26; (Female) 102.
Time of Training	(Immediately after school) 81; (later) 47.
Degree	(BEd) 4; (MA) 12; (BSc) 1; (other degree) 5; (None) 106.
Length of paid employment *not* in teaching	(0) 79; (Up to 1 yr) 11; (2-5 yrs) 11; (6-10 yrs) 11; (more than 10 yrs) 16.
Length of time since leaving school when neither teaching nor in other form of paid employment	(0) 79; (Up to 1 yr) 7; (2-5 yrs) 17; (6-10 yrs) 19; (more than 10 yrs) 6.
Whether living in catchment area of school	(Yes) 42; (No) 86.

College of Education attended	
Aberdeen	9
Callendar Park, Falkirk	6
Craigie, Ayr	2
Craiglockhart, Edinburgh	9
Dundee	33
Hamilton	4
Jordanhill, Glasgow	16
Moray House, Edinburgh	36
Notre Dame, Glasgow	7
College in England	6

209

APPENDIX D

THE SCOTS SCHEDULE DATA: 1977/78 OBSERVATIONS

(Grouped in accordance with the subsequent clustering)

CODINGS FOR ITEMS 1-43

CLUSTER A						
45351334	43445455	64553434	53443355	33443244	546	021
45351444	43445455	65353434	53444455	44444333	546	106

CLUSTER B						
44231422	42344434	54454535	52553341	34444344	446	017
33331534	43445435	54454534	52554344	33444344	446	039
23141524	51545445	74454545	53553231	34444344	446	063
55121543	51444435	64454535	52554151	34444444	446	066
55121413	32445334	64444545	52553351	24433444	446	067
24231544	53545445	65554534	53554341	34443354	546	117

CLUSTER C						
23242321	33435454	64433533	51554444	32224244	446	038
23331522	43434445	64443534	51554433	31334344	446	041
43351442	43455454	75544534	51543412	21334544	546	045
12242322	43435444	65453434	51452422	21224344	546	122

CLUSTER D						
52151523	51545445	64553545	52553411	12434254	546	002
52152314	54445444	64554535	52343311	13334354	546	046

CLUSTER E						
33321422	41334434	53443434	51553333	31334344	446	016
33231422	41435435	63354534	51543332	31434333	346	018
33331522	41444424	64454533	52553333	31343334	446	019
23231423	41344333	54453533	52553332	24443344	446	029
33321433	41343335	43554534	42553333	32344344	446	040
43331422	52434434	63553533	52544333	22333344	446	051
33331542	51342435	74544433	51544444	43434344	546	057
22231544	51434334	53354533	52553422	22333233	346	118
43331522	52545434	63444533	41553333	31434334	346	121

CLUSTER F						
25521422	41434334	44344433	42544332	32333433	446	006
33321422	31334334	44443433	42443311	23333344	446	010
42332421	41334334	63434535	52443313	21434434	446	025
33322431	32333334	44433533	52543411	32334344	446	061
43321322	31434434	54444534	42443443	22333334	446	099
43322322	41434435	44543434	52443411	22334343	446	109
23311542	41333334	43423434	51553411	22334433	446	112
34421422	41334234	44443433	52443334	21344434	346	119
33331322	41334434	53444533	42543322	34433344	346	123
43231422	41434334	53444533	42444321	33334334	346	128

CLUSTER G						
42222224	41332234	54443533	42543322	32233334	445	028
51131332	42333334	64454534	52543311	23333344	446	030
52212424	53342135	44553434	52333211	33334444	446	052
52323422	42344434	44553444	52553322	33333444	446	065
43322424	32343343	64443434	52444311	22334244	446	068
51122312	51232223	44542435	51344311	12324444	446	085

CLUSTER H						
42122512	51333233	43433535	52443411	12334323	446	003
22112322	31435443	63333434	41443311	11333333	346	023
21122312	52334234	53344533	51243311	21334333	346	035
22122322	21334333	54453433	51442421	11332344	446	036
31222212	41333333	53443534	41434422	22333344	446	043
21122322	51434435	44443533	43443211	22433334	446	062
23112312	42444332	54443534	42543321	22333344	446	069
22212311	41334332	43233433	41443411	21224323	336	074
22222522	31333344	43442433	51543422	31334234	346	078
21112321	41333344	43543533	51544411	21224334	445	079
21122322	41334233	63343533	54443411	22323234	446	087
33112522	41332232	43334533	52343431	32334334	346	116

```
CLUSTER I
   22122521    52435444    54333331    51553411    21124333    346        012
   35331552    41414344    74342233    51553421    31334333    346        024
   31112411    23334434    74442332    51554411    11224234    446        089
   42121513    31545434    64443433    52454421    11334334    446        090
   43311512    41434334    64433534    51553433    21224343    446        100
   43222312    52432453    65333532    51453432    11334333    446        102
   41312442    22335445    74442332    51554411    31224333    446        115

CLUSTER J
   13222211    22433435    64333533    52553421    11333243    346        048
   23321221    23433444    64342432    51553422    31324233    345        081
   22221211    21314434    64333434    51542412    21213352    346        082
   23212321    22313333    63342432    51554432    21224343    446        086
   23322432    22333234    64443533    51554431    31324343    446        111

CLUSTER K
   23222242    51232222    43543534    33333332    34343534    445        001
   22221211    51333223    44233532    42422311    23433335    446        026
   52222223    51333232    42333533    33323211    34334334    446        027
   33212312    51333232    43433533    33333312    24334434    446        056
   22212322    41312232    43242533    32343222    22343323    345        076
   43311421    51534332    33314534    43443322    24433334    445        105
   42322322    42332233    42343534    33333212    22333334    345        108

CLUSTER L
   23322323    41333334    43333533    42433212    22333333    345        007
   23222311    22333334    53443433    53433221    21333444    435        011
   22122311    41335234    42433533    42323321    22333333    345        013
   22112211    31232124    52343433    42333311    12333433    345        020
   21222222    41334234    42232532    33443411    22333333    345        034
   21113112    41332224    43332333    23323211    11333334    445        050
   42212311    31434335    53344533    42444311    22333333    345        054
   52232312    31333234    42433533    32333311    22223433    445        060
   22122322    21333334    43332433    42442421    22333333    345        064
   32222322    32333334    43434533    42433311    22223234    446        072
   21121222    22333234    44333333    52333311    22233334    445        080
   33222222    31332234    42343433    42333322    22323443    345        083
   43222232    42334334    43332533    43333321    22333343    344        084
   21112212    31332235    42334532    42333311    11323334    445        088
   32221211    51434334    43323523    43443221    22324333    346        098
   21222333    32343234    43433544    32434311    32333344    446        114

CLUSTER M
   23332312    31333333    44442233    41452411    11324232    345        008
   35121111    21332233    43343433    51433411    21213233    346        022
   31222321    32332334    53333432    52553411    11223233    346        047
   51122211    21334334    53332233    42443411    11233333    345        053
   22222411    21332232    43122122    51454412    21323322    336        070
   43122211    21333233    43232332    41443421    21223323    336        071
   42212211    31213233    43342322    51552422    31223344    436        103
   42212311    31432333    43343433    52443411    21324334    346        104
   43312322    11312233    43242333    51542411    21323243    335        107
   32222322    32333233    43332332    42533311    11323333    345        110

CLUSTER N
   23222421    21332233    43333531    52543444    32333223    346        004
   35231333    42332235    43453532    32333354    43333235    445        005
   23321311    41334233    43343533    41443332    31334333    346        014
   25131422    41334234    43343533    52443351    22333333    346        032
   23341321    41334235    43443533    42443344    32334334    346        037
   45321212    41433333    53343533    42443353    22333234    345        049
   33131322    41333333    53443423    42443341    21333234    446        096
   25211422    31332333    43443433    42533452    32334334    445        113
   33321322    43333334    53443433    42443333    33333234    346        120
```

211

CLUSTER O

51122211	31335234	63444522	51243411	11224343	346	031
51122111	32213233	63343532	51242411	21213323	346	033
52112311	31332333	53343532	42444411	11313333	446	055
42222312	31233234	42342521	41443311	22223333	346	073
51122211	31333233	53333532	51553411	11223333	446	091
52222111	31232234	42330522	41442411	21313433	345	092
51122322	31333235	53432533	42543311	31223344	445	093
52222222	41333232	42340533	41543411	21333333	345	094
52212322	41333132	43343433	51444411	11333332	346	095
51112211	22332233	43332532	41443411	11223223	346	125

CLUSTER P

11123111	22212234	32221332	41342411	21113222	325	009
23311111	51213123	42210522	41403333	31224322	246	015
22222211	31212223	43322432	42433311	11224233	346	075
51112111	11213223	43221331	51342411	12223222	346	101
33222111	31312232	42230432	31342411	21323223	335	124
11112111	31213222	42320532	41223311	11213332	345	126
51112111	11211121	31211521	21232411	11111221	224	127

CLUSTER Q

51113213	51232132	32441333	14113111	24324334	344	042
51113222	41232132	42330532	32224211	22322323	234	044
22222232	41232122	42332533	34223222	34333434	344	058
23313111	41212122	32221532	24323233	32323333	243	059
22212132	31212122	41230521	23222211	22322222	234	077
22232222	51333234	42343532	24222133	22333333	343	097

NOTE: These data relate to the SCOTS Schedule (Appendices A and B) as renumbered after the amalgamation of categories (Table 2, p 60) made in the light of observer reliability data.

APPENDIX E

CHARACTERISTICS OF TEACHER CLUSTERS IN RESPECT OF GROUPED SCOTS VARIABLES

This appendix expands the information summarised in Table 6 (pp 82-83).

How to use this appendix

This appendix deals, in turn, with the groups of variables covered column by column in Table 6. Thus, for example, column 1 of Table 6 relates to the SCOTS variables relating to 'Teaching Skill'. These 'Teaching Skill' variables are dealt with first in this appendix and in the following manner:

(1) All clusters classified in Table 6 as 'Very Strong' in respect of 'Teaching Skill'—i.e. clusters A, B, C and D—are dealt with first, frequencies being given for each category of each of the variables. Note that the 'short title of item' is an abbreviation of the item title in the SCOTS schedule and that the 'predominant level' is a 'short-hand' form of the category description for the item with the highest frequency.

(2) Thereafter all clusters classified in Table 6 as 'Quite Strong', 'Somewhat Limited', and 'Weak' are successively dealt with in a similar manner.

When all clusters have been covered in respect of 'Teaching Skills', 'Feedback and Individual Aid' variables are presented similarly, and thereafter all other groups of variables.

It should be noted that for an accurate interpretation of the information presented, it is necessary to expand all 'abbreviations' by making reference to the full text of the SCOTS schedule (Appendix A). As in Appendix D, the frequencies related to SCOTS Schedule items *after* the amalgamation of categories as shown in Table 2 (p 60).

213

TEACHING SKILLS

VERY STRONG   CLUSTERS A, B, C, D   (N= 14)

SHORT TITLE OF ITEM	PREDOMINANT LEVEL	0	1	2	3	4	5	6	7
14 EXPOSITION	CLEAR, LOGICAL, TEACHER AWARE OF PUPIL DIFFICULTIES	0	0	0	1	13	0	0	0
13 QUESTIONING	OUTSTANDING	0	0	0	0	3	11	0	0
15 TEACHER INVENTIVENESS	CONSIDERABLE	0	0	0	4	6	4	0	0
4 VARIETY OF TREATMENT	TREATMENT VARIED FOR INDIVIDUALS/INSTRUCTIONAL GROUPS	0	0	2	4	3	5	0	0
10 INTEGRATION	SIGNIFICANT AND EXPLICIT	0	3	2	8	1	0	0	0
11 CONCEPT/ROTE	CONCEPT – WITH SOME ROTE	0	0	0	1	10	3	0	0
12 PUPIL DIFFERENCE AND INVENTIVENESS	ENCOURAGED, BUT BASIC APPROACH PROVIDED	0	0	0	3	10	1	0	0

QUITE STRONG   CLUSTERS E, F, G, H, I   (N= 44)

SHORT TITLE OF ITEM	PREDOMINANT LEVEL	0	1	2	3	4	5	6	7
14 EXPOSITION	CLEAR,LOGICAL BUT < HALF T'S AWARE OF PUPIL DIFFICULTIES	0	1	7	19	17	0	0	0
13 QUESTIONING	VERY GOOD	0	0	6	9	23	6	0	0
15 TEACHER INVENTIVENESS	EXPLANATIONS ARE STEREOTYPED	0	0	2	34	7	1	0	0
4 VARIETY OF TREATMENT	TREATMENT VARIED FOR MOST OR LEAST ABLE PUPILS	0	10	22	12	0	0	0	0
10 INTEGRATION	NONE / SOME, BUT IMPLICIT	0	31	11	2	0	0	0	0
11 CONCEPT/ROTE	ROTE WITH SOME CONCEPT / CONCEPT WITH SOME ROTE	0	0	1	26	15	2	0	0
12 PUPIL DIFFERENCE AND INVENTIVENESS	TOLERATED	0	1	0	33	10	0	0	0

*For most items, categories 0, 6 and 7 do not exist.

HIGH LEVEL   CLUSTERS C, E, I, J   (N= 25)

SHORT TITLE OF ITEM	PREDOMINANT LEVEL	0	1	2	3	4	5	6	7
16 CONTACT WITH PUPILS	SOME SUSTAINED	0	0	0	3	16	6	0	0
17 FEEDBACK	VERY GOOD	0	0	0	0	1	4	15	5

MODERATE LEVEL   CLUSTERS F, G, H, L, N, O   (N= 63)

SHORT TITLE OF ITEM	PREDOMINANT LEVEL	0	1	2	3	4	5	6	7
16 CONTACT WITH PUPILS	SOME SUSTAINED / FREQUENT, BUT SHORT ONLY	0	0	5	16	34	8	0	0
17 FEEDBACK	AVERAGE / GOOD	0	0	0	39	17	7	0	0

FAIRLY LOW LEVEL   CLUSTERS K, M, P, Q   (N= 30)

SHORT TITLE OF ITEM	PREDOMINANT LEVEL	0	1	2	3	4	5	6	7
16 CONTACT WITH PUPILS	OCCASIONAL, SHORT ONLY / FREQUENT, BUT SHORT ONLY	0	1	13	12	4	0	0	0
17 FEEDBACK	AVERAGE	0	0	0	5	23	2	0	0

INTEREST AND MOTIVATION

VERY HIGH LEVEL   CLUSTERS A, B, C, D, G, J   (N= 25)

SHORT TITLE OF ITEM	PREDOMINANT LEVEL	0	1	2	3	4	5	6	7
18 INTEREST AND STIMULATION	PUPILS INTERESTED AND ENTHUSIASTIC	0	0	0	1	20	4	0	0
21 INTRINSIC/EXTRINSIC MOTIVATION	WORK SEEN AS INTERESTING; MOTIV. PREDOM INTRINS / INTRINS	0	0	3	13	9	0	0	0
22 COMPETITION	NONE / MINIMAL	0	0	0	0	10	15	0	0
39 POSITIVENESS/NEGATIVENESS	T. VERY POS & REINFORCING / T. GENERALLY POS & SUPPORTIVE	0	0	0	3	18	4	0	0

SOMEWHAT LIMITED CLUSTERS J, K, L, M, O (N= 57)

PREDOMINANT LEVEL

SHORT TITLE OF ITEM		0	1	2	3	4	5	6	7
14	EXPOSITION	MECHANICAL / CLEAR,LOGICAL,BUT UNAWARE OF PUPIL DIFFICULTIES	0	2	34	18	3	0	0	0
13	QUESTIONING	GOOD / MODERATE	0	0	18	27	10	2	0	0
15	TEACHER INVENTIVENESS	STEREOTYPED	0	0	4	52	1	0	0	0
4	VARIETY OF TREATMENT	TREATMENT VARIED FOR MOST/LEAST ABLE PUPILS / NONE	0	15	36	5	1	0	0	0
10	INTEGRATION	NONE / SOME BUT IMPLICIT	0	41	14	2	0	0	0	0
11	CONCEPT/ROTE	ROTE WITH SOME CONCEPT	0	0	6	44	6	1	0	0
12	PUPIL DIFFERENCE AND INVENTIVENESS	TOLERATED	0	6	0	50	1	0	0	0

WEAK CLUSTERS P, Q (N= 13)

PREDOMINANT LEVEL

SHORT TITLE OF ITEM		0	1	2	3	4	5	6	7
14	EXPOSITION	VERY POOR / MECHANICAL	0	7	6	0	0	0	0	0
13	QUESTIONING	MODERATE / GOOD	0	1	8	4	0	0	0	0
15	TEACHER INVENTIVENESS	NONE / STEREOTYPED	0	0	8	5	0	0	0	0
4	VARIETY OF TREATMENT	NONE / TREATMENT VARIED FOR MOST/LEAST ABLE PUPILS	0	8	4	1	0	0	0	0
10	INTEGRATION	NONE	0	12	1	0	0	0	0	0
11	CONCEPT/ROTE	ROTE ONLY	0	0	11	2	0	0	0	0
12	PUPIL DIFFERENCE AND INVENTIVENESS	PREVENTED / TOLERATED	0	9	0	4	0	0	0	0

FEEDBACK AND INDIVIDUAL AID

VERY HIGH LEVEL CLUSTERS A, B, D (N= 10)

PREDOMINANT LEVEL

SHORT TITLE OF ITEM		0	1	2	3	4	5	6	7
16	CONTACT WITH PUPILS	FREQUENT AND SUSTAINED	0	0	0	0	3	7	0	0
	FEEDBACK	VERY GOOD	0	0	0	0	2	7	1

HIGH LEVEL — CLUSTERS E, F, H, I (N= 38)

PREDOMINANT LEVEL

#	SHORT TITLE OF ITEM		0	1	2	3	4	5	6	7
18	INTEREST AND STIMULATION	PUPILS INTERESTED BUT WITHOUT ENTHUSIASM / PS INT'D & ENTHUS	0	0	0	19	18	1	0	0
21	INTRINSIC/EXTRINSIC MOTIVATION	WORK SEEN AS INTERESTING;MOTIVATION PREDOM INTRINS / INTRINS	0	0	4	21	13	0	0	0
22	COMPETITION	NONE / MINIMAL	0	0	1	3	12	22	0	0
39	POSITIVENESS/NEGATIVENESS	T. NEITHER POS NOR NEG / T GENERALLY POS & SUPPORTIVE	0	0	2	24	12	0	0	0

MODERATE LEVEL — CLUSTERS K, L, M, N, O (N= 52)

PREDOMINANT LEVEL

#	SHORT TITLE OF ITEM		0	1	2	3	4	5	6	7
18	INTEREST AND STIMULATION	PS INTERESTED BUT WITHOUT ENTHUS / PS INTER'D ONLY OCCAS'LY	0	0	11	38	3	0	0	0
21	INTRINSIC/EXTRINSIC MOTIVATION	WORK INTERESTING,MOTIV PREDOM INTRINS / ONLY SOME;MTV EXTRNS	2	0	15	30	5	0	0	0
22	COMPETITION	(VERY VARIED, BUT MAJORITY. NONE/MINIMAL)	0	1	2	6	11	32	0	0
39	POSITIVENESS/NEGATIVENESS	NEITHER POSITIVE NOR NEGATIVE	0	0	6	38	8	0	0	0

LOW LEVEL — CLUSTERS P, Q (N= 13)

PREDOMINANT LEVEL

#	SHORT TITLE OF ITEM		0	1	2	3	4	5	6	7
18	INTEREST AND STIMULATION	PUPILS INTERESTED ONLY OCCASIONALLY	0	2	9	2	0	0	0	0
21	INTRINSIC/EXTRINSIC MOTIVATION	NO SIGN OF MOTIVATION / WORK TREATED AS CHORE; MOTIV EXTRINS	5	5	2	1	0	0	0	0
22	COMPETITION	(VARIED, BUT MAJORITY NONE)	0	0	0	3	2	8	0	0
39	POSITIVENESS/NEGATIVENESS	NEGATIVE / NEITHER POSITIVE NOR NEGATIVE	0	0	7	6	0	0	0	0

Q

DEVELOPMENT OF PUPIL RESPONSIBILITY

STRONG EMPHASIS · CLUSTERS A, B, D, G · (N= 16)

SHORT TITLE OF ITEM	PREDOMINANT LEVEL	0	1	2	3	4	5	6	7
6 MODE OF CONTROL OF WORK	INDIRECT, WITH INTERMITTENT DIRECT INTERVENTION	0	0	1	4	6	5	0	0
7 PUPIL RESPONSIBILITY FOR WORK	(CLASSES VARY GREATLY – AVERAGE IS MODERATE)	0	3	7	3	3	0	0	0
20 FOSTERING OF PUPIL RESPONSIBILITY	EXPERT	0	0	0	0	4	12	0	0
34 INTER-PUPIL COOPERATION	ENCOURAGED SOMETIMES	0	0	4	6	6	0	0	0
35 PUPIL FREEDOM OF MOVEMENT	ANYWHERE	0	0	1	6	9	0	0	0
36 PUPIL ACCESS TO RESOURCES	FAIRLY FREE / FREE	0	0	1	8	7	0	0	0
9 PRESSURE ON PUPILS	MINORITY ONLY / LITTLE SIGN	0	0	0	2	7	7	0	0

FAIRLY STRONG EMPHASIS · CLUSTERS E, F · (N= 19)

SHORT TITLE OF ITEM	PREDOMINANT LEVEL	0	1	2	3	4	5	6	7
6 MODE OF CONTROL OF WORK	INDIRECT, WITH INTERMITTENT DIRECT INTERVENTION	0	0	0	3	11	5	0	0
7 PUPIL RESPONSIBILITY FOR WORK	LITTLE	0	0	14	2	3	0	0	0
20 FOSTERING OF PUPIL RESPONSIBILITY	RESPONSIBILITY WIDELY SPREAD	0	0	1	2	10	6	0	0
34 INTER-PUPIL COOPERATION	(VERY VARIED – AT LEAST TOLERATED BY MOST)	0	6	8	3	2	0	0	0
35 PUPIL FREEDOM OF MOVEMENT	ONLY WITHIN DEFINED LIMITS	0	0	0	13	6	0	0	0
36 PUPIL ACCESS TO RESOURCES	FAIRLY FREE	0	0	0	15	4	0	0	0
9 PRESSURE ON PUPILS	ON MINORITY ONLY	0	0	0	3	12	4	0	0

MODERATE EMPHASIS   CLUSTERS C, H, I, K, N   (N= 39)

SHORT TITLE OF ITEM	PREDOMINANT LEVEL	0	1	2	3	4	5	6	7
6 MODE OF CONTROL OF WORK	FAIRLY DIRECT, BUT PUPILS COMPETENT IN WORK MANAGEMENT	0	0	5	19	7	8	0	0
7 PUPIL RESPONSIBILITY FOR WORK	LITTLE / NONE	0	13	21	1	3	1	0	0
20 FOSTERING OF PUPIL RESPONSIBILITY	RESPONSIBILITY WIDELY SPREAD / LIMITED TO KEEN OR EFFICIENT	0	1	0	12	23	3	0	0
34 INTER-PUPIL COOPERATION	PREVENTED / TOLERATED	0	18	14	3	4	0	0	0
35 PUPIL FREEDOM OF MOVEMENT	FREE ONLY WITHIN DEFINED LIMITS	0	1	7	28	3	0	0	0
36 PUPIL ACCESS TO RESOURCES	FAIRLY FREE	0	0	9	28	2	0	0	0
9 PRESSURE ON PUPILS	ON MINORITY ONLY / LITTLE SIGN	0	0	4	5	20	10	0	0

WEAK EMPHASIS   CLUSTERS J, L, M, O, Q   (N= 47)

SHORT TITLE OF ITEM	PREDOMINANT LEVEL	0	1	2	3	4	5	6	7
6 MODE OF CONTROL OF WORK	DIRECT / FAIRLY DIRECT, BUT PS COMPETENT IN WORK MANAGEMENT	0	6	21	18	2	0	0	0
7 PUPIL RESPONSIBILITY FOR WORK	NONE / LITTLE	0	26	16	5	0	0	0	0
20 FOSTERING OF PUPIL RESPONSIBILITY	RESPONSIBILITY LIMITED TO KEEN & EFFICIENT / RESPONSY SPREAD	0	0	3	24	20	0	0	0
34 INTER-PUPIL COOPERATION	PREVENTED / TOLERATED	0	27	18	0	2	0	0	0
35 PUPIL FREEDOM OF MOVEMENT	FREE ONLY WITHIN DEFINED LIMITS / ASSIGNED FUNCTNS & TO T.	0	0	16	31	0	0	0	0
36 PUPIL ACCESS TO RESOURCES	ONLY LIMITED / FAIRLY FREE	0	5	25	17	0	0	0	0
9 PRESSURE ON PUPILS	(VARIED, BUT MAJORITY SOME / FREQUENT)	0	1	13	20	10	3	0	0

NO EMPHASIS   CLUSTERS P   (N= 7)

SHORT TITLE OF ITEM	PREDOMINANT LEVEL	0	1	2	3	4	5	6	7
6 MODE OF CONTROL OF WORK	VERY DIRECT	0	6	1	0	0	0	0	0
7 PUPIL RESPONSIBILITY FOR WORK	NONE	0	7	0	0	0	0	0	0
20 FOSTERING OF PUPIL RESPONSIBILITY	LIMITED TO SMALL MINORITY / NONE	0	2	4	1	0	0	0	0
34 INTER-PUPIL COOPERATION	PREVENTED	0	6	1	0	0	0	0	0
35 PUPIL FREEDOM OF MOVEMENT	ASSIGNED FUNCTNS & TO T ONLY / ONLY WHEN INSTRUCTED	0	2	4	1	0	0	0	0
36 PUPIL ACCESS TO RESOURCES	ONLY LIMITED / ONLY TO THOSE SPECIFIED	0	3	4	0	0	0	0	0
9 PRESSURE ON PUPILS	(VARIED BUT THE LEAST IS SOME)	0	2	1	3	0	1	0	0

GROUP METHODS

VERY PROMINENT FEATURE   CLUSTERS A, B   (N= 8)

SHORT TITLE OF ITEM	PREDOMINANT LEVEL	0	1	2	3	4	5	6	7
31 GROUP-SIZE - ARITHMETIC	VERY SMALL / SMALL	0	0	0	1	3	4	0	0
32 GROUP-SIZE - ENGLISH	VARIED(CL13: V SMALL GRPS; CL12: ALL BUT 1, WHOLE CLASS	0	5	0	0	1	2	0	0
33 NUMBER OF SIMULTANEOUS ACTIVITIES	MEDIUM NUMBER	0	0	1	6	1	0	0	0
2 NO OF WORK-LEVELS - ARITHMETIC	MANY	0	0	0	2	2	4	0	0
3 NO OF WORK LEVELS - ENGLISH	(VARIED: CL13 = 3-4 GRPS; CL12 HAS LESS , SAVE IN ONE CLASS)	0	3	2	3	0	0	0	0

PROMINENT FEATURE   CLUSTERS C, E, N   (N= 22)

SHORT TITLE OF ITEM	PREDOMINANT LEVEL	0	1	2	3	4	5	6	7
31 GROUP-SIZE - ARITHMETIC	SMALL / MEDIUM	0	1	2	10	5	4	0	0
32 GROUP-SIZE - ENGLISH	MEDIUM / LARGE	0	2	7	8	5	0	0	0
33 NUMBER OF SIMULTANEOUS ACTIVITIES	MEDIUM NUMBER / FEW	0	0	8	12	2	0	0	0
2 NO OF WORK-LEVELS - ARITHMETIC	3-4 LEVELS	0	0	2	16	0	4	0	0
3 NO OF WORK LEVELS - ENGLIS...									

LIMITED FEATURE CLUSTERS F, G, J (N= 21)

PREDOMINANT LEVEL

SHORT TITLE OF ITEM		0	1	2	3	4	5	6	7
31 GROUP-SIZE - ARITHMETIC	WHOLE CLASS / TWO LARGE GROUPS	0	10	6	4	1	0	0	0
32 GROUP-SIZE - ENGLISH	WHOLE CLASS / TWO LARGE GROUPS	0	11	7	2	1	0	0	0
33 NUMBER OF SIMULTANEOUS ACTIVITIES	FEW / MEDIUM NUMBER	0	2	10	9	0	0	0	0
2 NO OF WORK-LEVELS - ARITHMETIC	3-4 LEVELS	0	2	5	12	1	1	0	0
3 NO OF WORK LEVELS - ENGLISH	3-4 LEVELS	0	2	6	11	1	1	0	0

VERY LIMITED FEATURE CLUSTERS H, I, K, L, M, O, Q (N= 68)

PREDOMINANT LEVEL

SHORT TITLE OF ITEM		0	1	2	3	4	5	6	7
31 GROUP-SIZE - ARITHMETIC	WHOLE CLASS / TWO LARGE GROUPS	0	45	17	6	0	0	0	0
32 GROUP-SIZE - ENGLISH	WHOLE CLASS	0	52	13	3	0	0	0	0
33 NUMBER OF SIMULTANEOUS ACTIVITIES	FEW / ONE	0	18	39	11	0	0	0	0
2 NO OF WORK-LEVELS - ARITHMETIC	TWO LEVELS / ONE LEVEL	0	21	30	15	0	2	0	0
3 NO OF WORK LEVELS - ENGLISH	TWO LEVELS / ONE LEVEL	0	29	30	9	0	0	0	0

NONE CLUSTERS D, P (N= 9)

PREDOMINANT LEVEL

SHORT TITLE OF ITEM		0	1	2	3	4	5	6	7
31 GROUP-SIZE - ARITHMETIC	WHOLE CLASS	0	8	0	1	0	0	0	0
32 GROUP-SIZE - ENGLISH	WHOLE CLASS	0	8	0	1	0	0	0	0
33 NUMBER OF SIMULTANEOUS ACTIVITIES	ONE	0	6	2	1	0	0	0	0
2 NO OF WORK-LEVELS - ARITHMETIC	ONE LEVEL / TWO LEVELS	0	4	3	2	0	0	0	0
3 NO OF WORK LEVELS - ENGLISH	ONE LEVEL	0	6	2	1	0	0	0	0

LEVEL AIMED AT

HIGH

CLUSTERS A, B, E, F, N   (N= 36)

SHORT TITLE OF ITEM   PREDOMINANT LEVEL

5 LEVEL AIMED AT   HIGH: GETTING BEST OUT OF ALL

0	1	2	3	4	5	6	7
0	32	4	0	0	0	0	0

HIGH/MIDDLE

CLUSTERS C, D, I   (N= 13)

SHORT TITLE OF ITEM   PREDOMINANT LEVEL

5 LEVEL AIMED AT   MIDDLE: WHAT MOST CAN MANAGE / HIGH: GETTING BEST OUT OF ALL

0	1	2	3	4	5	6	7
0	6	7	0	0	0	0	0

MIDDLE

CLUSTERS G, H, J, K, L, M, O, P   (N= 73)

SHORT TITLE OF ITEM   PREDOMINANT LEVEL

5 LEVEL AIMED AT   MIDDLE: WHAT MOST CAN MANAGE

0	1	2	3	4	5	6	7
0	9	61	3	0	0	0	0

MIDDLE/LOW

CLUSTERS Q   (N= 6)

SHORT TITLE OF ITEM   PREDOMINANT LEVEL

5 LEVEL AIMED AT   MIDDLE: WHAT MOST CAN MANAGE / LOW: WHAT ALL CAN MANAGE

0	1	2	3	4	5	6	7
0	0	3	3	0	0	0	0

EFFICIENCY OF MANAGEMENT

VERY HIGH — CLUSTERS B, C, D, E, I, J (N= 33)

SHORT TITLE OF ITEM	PREDOMINANT LEVEL	0	1	2	3	4	5	6	7
25 PUPIL APPLICATION	INDUSTRIOUS AND ENTHUSIASTIC	0	0	0	2	31	0	0	0
27 UNDEREMPLOYMENT	NONE	0	0	0	1	3	29	0	0
28 TRANSITIONS	VERY SMOOTH	0	0	0	0	6	27	0	0
29 MODE OF PERFORMING ADMIN FUNCTIONS	MINOR HOLD-UPS ONLY / UNOBTRUSIVE	0	0	2	19	12	0	0	0
30 ALERTNESS	HIGH / FAIRLY HIGH	0	1	1	12	19	0	0	0

HIGH — CLUSTERS A, F, G, H, M, N, O (N= 59)

SHORT TITLE OF ITEM	PREDOMINANT LEVEL	0	1	2	3	4	5	6	7
25 PUPIL APPLICATION	INDUSTRIOUS AND ENTHUSIASTIC / FAIRLY INDUSTRIOUS	0	0	1	27	31	0	0	0
27 UNDEREMPLOYMENT	SOME / NONE	0	0	3	4	33	19	0	0
28 TRANSITIONS	SMOOTH	0	0	0	6	46	7	0	0
29 MODE OF PERFORMING ADMIN FUNCTIONS	MINOR HOLD-UPS ONLY	0	0	6	43	10	0	0	0
30 ALERTNESS	HIGH / FAIRLY HIGH	0	0	2	25	32	0	0	0

MODERATE — CLUSTERS K, L, P (N= 30)

SHORT TITLE OF ITEM	PREDOMINANT LEVEL	0	1	2	3	4	5	6	7
25 PUPIL APPLICATION	FAIRLY INDUSTRIOUS / MIXED WITHIN CLASS	0	0	2	9	16	3	0	0
27 UNDEREMPLOYMENT	CONSIDERABLE / SOME	0	0	2	16	12	0	0	0
28 TRANSITIONS	SOME DELAYS / SMOOTH	1	0	5	15	9	0	0	0
29 MODE OF PERFORMING ADMIN FUNCTIONS	MINOR HOLD-UPS	0	0	6	22	2	0	0	0
30 ALERTNESS	FAIRLY HIGH	0	0	7	17	6	0	0	0

LOW   CLUSTERS Q   (N= 6)

SHORT TITLE OF ITEM	PREDOMINANT LEVEL	0	1	2	3	4	5	6	7
25 PUPIL APPLICATION	LITTLE INDUSTRY / MIXED WITHIN CLASS	0	1	3	2	0	0	0	0
27 UNDEREMPLOYMENT	MUCH	0	1	4	1	0	0	0	0
28 TRANSITIONS	SOME DELAYS	0	1	5	0	0	0	0	0
29 MODE OF PERFORMING ADMIN FUNCTIONS	MINOR HOLD-UPS / OFTEN TIME-CONSUMING	0	0	2	3	1	0	0	0
30 ALERTNESS	SOME LOW AWARENESS / MUCH LOW AWARENESS	0	2	4	0	0	0	0	0

AUTHORITARIANISM AND COERCION

VERY LOW   CLUSTERS A, B, D   (N= 10)

SHORT TITLE OF ITEM	PREDOMINANT LEVEL	0	1	2	3	4	5	6	7
8 AUTHORITARIAN/DEMOCRATIC CHOICE OF WORK	DEMOCRATIC	0	0	1	3	6	0	0	0
24 COERCION/PERSUASION	EMPHASIS ON SELF-CONTROL / PERSUASION DOMINANT	0	0	0	0	4	6	0	0

LOW   CLUSTERS C, G, K   (N= 17)

SHORT TITLE OF ITEM	PREDOMINANT LEVEL	0	1	2	3	4	5	6	7
8 AUTHORITARIAN/DEMOCRATIC CHOICE OF WORK	AUTHORITARIAN	0	3	10	1	3	0	0	0
24 COERCION/PERSUASION	PERSUASION DOMINANT	0	0	1	5	10	1	0	0

MODERATE   CLUSTERS E, F, H, L, N   (N= 56)

SHORT TITLE OF ITEM	PREDOMINANT LEVEL	0	1	2	3	4	5	6	7
8 AUTHORITARIAN/DEMOCRATIC CHOICE OF WORK	AUTHORITARIAN	0	12	38	5	1	0	0	0
24 COERCION/PERSUASION	NEITHER DOMINANT	0	1	3	40	10	2	0	0

HIGH CLUSTERS I, J, M, Q (N= 28)

SHORT TITLE OF ITEM	PREDOMINANT LEVEL	0	1	2	3	4	5	6	7
8 AUTHORITARIAN/DEMOCRATIC CHOICE OF WORK	AUTHORITARIAN / TOTALLY AUTHORITARIAN	0	14	12	2	0	0	0	0
24 COERCION/PERSUASION	COERCION DOMINANT / NEITHER DOMINANT	0	2	13	11	2	0	0	0

VERY HIGH CLUSTERS O, P (N= 17)

SHORT TITLE OF ITEM	PREDOMINANT LEVEL	0	1	2	3	4	5	6	7
8 AUTHORITARIAN/DEMOCRATIC CHOICE OF WORK	TOTALLY AUTHORITARIAN	0	13	4	0	0	0	0	0
24 COERCION/PERSUASION	COERCION DOMINANT	0	3	11	3	0	0	0	0

CLASS CONTROL

GOOD AND EASY CLUSTERS A, B, C, D, E, F, G, I, J (N= 51)

SHORT TITLE OF ITEM	PREDOMINANT LEVEL	0	1	2	3	4	5	6	7
43 CLASS CONTROL	EASY AND EFFECTIVE	0	0	0	0	0	2	49	0
42 TEACHER HOSTILITY	NONE	0	0	0	0	51	0	0	0
37 TEACHER CALMNESS/ANXIETY	VERY CALM / FAIRLY CALM	0	0	0	16	35	0	0	0

INSECURE ROR SOME CLUSTERS H, K, N, O (N= 38)

SHORT TITLE OF ITEM	PREDOMINANT LEVEL	0	1	2	3	4	5	6	7
43 CLASS CONTROL	EASY AND EFFECTIVE / SLIGHT EFFORT	0	0	0	0	0	11	27	0
42 TEACHER HOSTILITY	NONE	0	0	0	0	1	37	0	0
37 TEACHER CALMNESS/ANXIETY	FAIRLY CALM / VERY CALM	0	0	1	25	12	0	0	0

SOMEWHAT INSECURE — CLUSTERS L, M, P — (N= 33)

SHORT TITLE OF ITEM	PREDOMINANT LEVEL	0	1	2	3	4	5	6	7
43 CLASS CONTROL	SLIGHT EFFORT / EASY AND EFFECTIVE	0	0	0	0	2	19	12	0
42 TEACHER HOSTILITY	NONE / HOSTILE TO A FEW	0	0	2	6	25	0	0	0
37 TEACHER CALMNESS/ANXIETY	FAIRLY CALM / SIGNS OF ANXIETY	0	1	0	27	5	0	0	0

INSECURE — CLUSTERS Q — (N= 6)

SHORT TITLE OF ITEM	PREDOMINANT LEVEL	0	1	2	3	4	5	6	7
43 CLASS CONTROL	SLIGHT EFFORT / EFFORT REQUIRED AND WORK IMPEDED	0	0	0	2	4	0	0	0
42 TEACHER HOSTILITY	NONE / HOSTILE TO A FEW	0	0	0	2	4	0	0	0
37 TEACHER CALMNESS/ANXIETY	FAIRLY CALM	0	0	2	3	1	0	0	0

RELATIONSHIP WITH PUPILS

VERY GOOD — CLUSTERS A, B, C, D, E, F, G — (N= 39)

SHORT TITLE OF ITEM	PREDOMINANT LEVEL	0	1	2	3	4	5	6	7
19 SENSITIVITY	SENSITIVE / VERY SENSITIVE	0	0	0	4	23	12	0	0
40 APPROACHABILITY	TEACHER APPROACHED ON SOCIAL TOPICS	0	0	0	6	33	0	0	0
41 ATTITUDE TO TEACHING	ENTHUSIASTIC	0	0	0	6	25	8	0	0

GOOD

CLUSTERS H, I, K, L, N, O (N= 61)

SHORT TITLE OF ITEM	PREDOMINANT LEVEL	0	1	2	3	4	5	6	7
19 SENSITIVITY	NEITHER SENSITIVE NOR INSENSITIVE / SENSITIVE	0	0	4	32	23	2	0	0
40 APPROACHABILITY	NEITHER DISTANT NOR FRIENDLY / APPROACHED ON SOCIAL TOPICS	0	0	1	31	27	2	0	0
41 ATTITUDE TO TEACHING	BUSINESS-LIKE / ENTHUSIASTIC	0	0	0	31	30	0	0	0

FAIRLY GOOD

CLUSTERS J, M, Q (N= 21)

SHORT TITLE OF ITEM	PREDOMINANT LEVEL	0	1	2	3	4	5	6	7
19 SENSITIVITY	NEITHER SENSITIVE NOR INSENSITIVE	0	1	4	13	3	0	0	0
40 APPROACHABILITY	APPROACHABLE, BEING NEITHER DISTANT NOR FRIENDLY	0	0	4	13	4	0	0	0
41 ATTITUDE TO TEACHING	BUSINESS-LIKE	0	0	3	15	3	0	0	0

POOR

CLUSTERS P (N= 7)

SHORT TITLE OF ITEM	PREDOMINANT LEVEL	0	1	2	3	4	5	6	7
19 SENSITIVITY	FAIRLY INSENSITIVE	0	0	5	2	0	0	0	0
40 APPROACHABILITY	DISTANT	0	1	4	2	0	0	0	0
41 ATTITUDE TO TEACHING	BUSINESS-LIKE	0	0	2	5	0	0	0	0

APPENDIX F

ATTITUDE SCALE

(The parenthesised titles for each item have been added for information. They are not part of the scale)

(CONSCIENTIOUSNESS VIS-A-VIS WORK)

PRE	POST		
3	2	1) a)	I play around in class for as much of the time as I can.
6	6	b)	I work for a little while, but I soon give up, and even play around if I can.
55	68	c)	I like to get on with my work most of the time, but at times I just can't be bothered.
36	24	d)	I don't like to waste time. Almost always I'd rather get on with my work.

(INTEREST IN LEARNING)

51	4	2) a)	There are very few things that I can really be bothered to find out about.
20	22	b)	I am interested in quite a few things, but very many things bore me.
43	51	c)	I'm interested in lots of things, but after a while I do get bored.
32	23	d)	I hardly ever get bored because there are so many things that I am trying to find out about.

(LIKING FOR SCHOOL - 1)

15	8	3) a)	I like everything about school.
58	66	b)	I like most things about school, but there are a few things I don't like.
12	16	c)	There's not much I like about school.
15	9	d)	I hate everything to do with school.

(SELF-CONCEPT IN RESPECT OF SCHOOL WORK)

2	1	4) a)	I'm hopeless at school work. It's just too difficult for me.
12	9	b)	I'm not very good at school work. I can manage some of it, but some of it will always be too difficult for me.
53	59	c)	Although I am only fairly good at school work, I think I'll learn how to do most of it quite well.
34	30	d)	I do very well at school nearly all the time and I expect to be able to do most of the work I'm given.

(LIKING FOR TEACHERS)

6	5	5) a)	I don't like any teachers.
22	25	b)	One or two teachers may be all right, but I don't like most of them.
26	31	c)	I like many teachers, but there are many others who aren't very nice.
46	38	d)	I like nearly all teachers.

ⓒ SCRE 1977.

PRE	POST			
				(ENJOYMENT/DISLIKE OF DIFFICULT WORK)
6	4	6)	a)	I hate having to try difficult work and get out of it if I can.
20	16		b)	I don't really like difficult work; I prefer doing easy things.
34	45		c)	I find it interesting to do difficult work but I lose interest quite quickly if I don't get the right answer.
40	35		d)	I really enjoy trying difficult work that makes me think hard, even if I have to stick at it for a long time.
				(CONCERN OVER GETTING WORK RIGHT)
3	3	7)	a)	It never matters to me if I get my work wrong.
10	9		b)	Sometimes I try quite hard to get my work right, but often I just don't bother.
43	47		c)	I try quite hard to get my work right but a few careless mistakes don't worry me too much.
43	41		d)	I try very hard to get my work right and I get angry with myself if I spoil my work by making careless mistakes.
				(APPLICATION TO WORK)
4	4	8)	a)	A lot of the time I pretend to work, but I'm not really doing it.
20	22		b)	I work hard when I feel like it. At other times I just pretend to work.
52	57		c)	I work quite hard most of the time.
23	18		d)	I work very hard almost all the time.
				(LIKING FOR SCHOOL - 2)
21	13	9)	a)	I enjoy being at school very much.
37	46		b)	I quite like being at school, and some days I really enjoy it.
20	24		c)	I don't like school very much, but sometimes it's all right.
23	17		d)	I wish I never had to go to school at all.

229

PRE	POST		
		(CONFIDENCE IN ABILITY TO LEARN)	
6	4	10) a) When I get something wrong I can never understand why it is wrong.	
20	19	b) When I get something wrong, sometimes I find out how to put it right, but usually I can't understand why it's wrong.	
43	54	c) When I get something wrong, I'm quite likely to be able to find out how to put it right and to understand why it was wrong.	
31	23	d) When I get anything wrong, I can nearly always work out how to put it right and understand why it was wrong.	
		(APPLICATION TO WORK—2/CONCERN TO DO WELL)	
2	2	11) a) I'm careless with my work. I don't even try.	
4	2	b) I do my work, but I don't think it's important to try hard.	
40	50	c) I try to do good work, but I don't often try as hard as I could.	
53	46	d) I nearly always try to do my work as well as I possibly can.	
		(ANXIETY OVER WORK)	
13	10	12) a) Usually I feel very unhappy when work is difficult because I'm afraid I shall not manage to do it.	
21	20	b) I always feel a little anxious when work is difficult, in case I can't manage to do it.	
43	53	c) Difficult work doesn't make me anxious unless I get stuck badly.	
24	17	d) It doesn't worry me if the work is difficult and I don't really worry even if I get stuck.	
		(CONFIDENCE IN/LIKING FOR WORKING ALONE)	
4	2	13) a) I don't like working alone because I can't manage unless somebody helps me with my work.	
14	11	b) I don't like working by myself, but I can manage alone sometimes.	
59	68	c) I prefer to work on my own, but sometimes it's nice to get some help.	
24	19	d) I never like people to help me because I like to do things for myself.	

230

4.

PRE	POST		
			(BELIEF IN THE VALUE OF SCHOOL)
63	59	14) a)	I'm sure school is doing me a lot of good.
28	33	b)	I think school helps quite a lot.
4	5	c)	I don't think school is doing me much good.
5	4	d)	I don't think school is doing me any good at all.
			(LIKING FOR PROMINENCE IN CLASS)
21	13	15) a)	I really enjoy being allowed to show the rest of the class something that I can do well.
28	28	b)	I quite like being allowed to show the rest of the class something that I can do well.
29	39	c)	I'd rather not have to do anything in class when I know everyone is watching me.
22	20	d)	I hate to have to do anything in class when I know everyone is watching me.
			(DESIRE TO PLEASE TEACHERS)
8	6	16) a)	Why should teachers make you do things? I don't care what they say. I do what I want.
18	24	b)	I usually do what teachers say, but I don't see why I should have to.
25	34	c)	Usually I don't mind doing what teachers tell me because it's bad for the class if they aren't obeyed.
49	36	d)	I like to please teachers by doing what they want.

231

APPENDIX G

EXAMPLES OF THE PUZZLES USED WHEN PUPILS WERE OBSERVED FOR APPLICATION TO WORK

Puzzle 5 serves as an example of a complete puzzle, with intermediate explanations for those who need them.

Only the first pages of Puzzles 1, 2, and 12 are given.

Note that in Puzzle 5 a box around an answer indicates that it is covered with a removable adhesive label.

NOTE: *The preparation of these puzzles was, in large measure, the work of Christine Darroch.*

NAME : _____

CLASS : _____

PUZZLE 5.

L.3.

Read the puzzle carefully, then try to answer the question.

XXXXXXXXXXXXXXXXXXXXXXXXXXXXXXXXXXXXXXXXXXXXXXXXXXXXXXXXXXXXXXXXXXXXXXXXXXX

Five girls, Jane, Sara, Ann, Kate, and Betty, are each wearing a
dress of a different colour.   The colours are red, blue, yellow,
green, and purple.

> Jane is not wearing the blue or red dress.
> Ann is wearing either the yellow or blue dress.
> Kate never wears purple or yellow dresses.
> Sara is wearing the green dress.
> Jane won't wear purple dresses.

XXXXXXXXXXXXXXXXXXXXXXXXXXXXXXXXXXXXXXXXXXXXXXXXXXXXXXXXXXXXXXXXXXXXXXXXXXX

Question: *Which colour of dress is Betty wearing?*

Do any working out here:

If you know the answer, write it here.

> *Betty is wearing the* _____ *dress.*

Go to page 2 for the correct answer.

If you cannot think of any answer, go to page 2, and start reading
where you see this mark ✳ .

R   233

PUZZLE   5.

Answer: *Betty is wearing the ____purple____ dress.*

If your answer is correct, go on to Puzzle 6.

If your answer is wrong, read the rest of <u>this</u> page.

✳ Here is the puzzle again but this time you will be given some help, so that you can find out how to work out the correct answer.

%%%

%   %
%   Five girls, Jane, Sara, Ann, Kate, and Betty, are each wearing a   %
%   dress of a different colour.   The colours are red, blue, yellow,   %
%   green, and purple.   %
%   %
%   Jane is not wearing the blue or red dress.   %
%   Ann is wearing either the yellow or blue dress.   %
%   Kate never wears purple or yellow dresses.   %
%   Sara is wearing the green dress.   %
%   Jane won't wear purple dresses.   %
%   %
%%%

1) You want to find which dress Betty is wearing.

    You know that there are only five dresses for the five girls.

    So if you could find out which dress each of the other four girls is wearing, you would know which one Betty <u>must</u> be wearing.

2) You are told that Sara is wearing the green dress.

    You are told that Jane is <u>not</u> wearing the blue or the red dress, and she won't wear purple dresses.‾‾ She cannot be wearing the green dress because Sara is wearing it.

    So Jane <u>must</u> be wearing the _____ dress.

    Write your answer in the space.

    NOW LOOK AT PAGE 3.

PUZZLE 5.

Answer: *Jane must be wearing the* ___ ⌐ *yellow* ¬ ___ *dress.*

If your answer is wrong, turn to page 4.

If your answer is correct, read the rest of <u>this</u> page.

Now look again at the puzzle on page 2, and try to answer this question.

Which colour of dress is Kate wearing?

Do any working out here:

Write your answer in the space, then check it with the correct answer below.

Kate is wearing the _____ *dress.*

Answer: *Kate is wearing the* ___ ⌐ *Red* ¬ ___ *dress.*

If your answer is correct, go on to Puzzle 6.

If your answer is wrong, go to page 4.

PUZZLE 5.

Here is the puzzle again and some more help.

```
XXXXXXXXXXXXXXXXXXXXXXXXXXXXXXXXXXXXXXXXXXXXXXXXXXXXXXXXXXXXXXXXXXXXXXX
X                                                                     X
X      Five girls, Jane, Sara, Ann, Kate, and Betty, are each wearing a  X
X      dress of a different colour.    The colours are red, blue, yellow,  X
X      green, and purple.                                              X
X                                                                     X
X             Jane is not wearing the blue or red dress.              X
X             Ann is wearing either the yellow or blue dress.         X
X             Kate never wears purple or yellow dresses.              X
X             Sara is wearing the green dress.                        X
X             Jane won't wear purple dresses.                         X
X                                                                     X
XXXXXXXXXXXXXXXXXXXXXXXXXXXXXXXXXXXXXXXXXXXXXXXXXXXXXXXXXXXXXXXXXXXXXXX
```

You must find out first what colour of dress Ann is wearing.

You know Jane cannot be wearing the red, the blue or the purple dress because you have been told she is not.   She cannot be wearing the green dress because Sara is wearing it.   So Jane must be wearing the yellow dress.

You are told that Ann is wearing the yellow or the blue dress.

So Ann must be wearing the _____ *dress.*

Write your answer in the space, then check it with the correct answer below.

Answer: *Ann must be wearing the* ___ `blue` ___ *dress.*

Now we can find out what dress Kate is wearing.

We know now that other girls are wearing the yellow, green and blue dresses.

We are told that Kate does not wear the purple dress.

So she must wear the red dress.

Remember at the beginning of this puzzle you were asked which dress Betty is wearing.

You know now that Sara wears the green dress, Jane wears the yellow dress, Kate wears the red dress, and Ann the blue dress.   The only dress left is the purple one.

So Betty must be wearing the purple dress.

NOW GO ON TO PUZZLE 6.

NAME : _____

CLASS : _____

Look carefully at this list of numbers, then try to answer the question.

%%
%
%
%   2   5   8   11   ?
%
%
%%

Question: What number must you put in place of the question mark
             to complete this series of numbers?

Do any working out here:

If you know the answer write it here:

      2   5   8   11   _____

Go to page 2 for the correct answer.

If you cannot think of any answer, go to page 2 and start reading where
you see this mark ✳ .

237

(c) SCRE 1977

NAME : _____

CLASS : _____

┌─────────────────────────────┐
│   │
│   PUZZLE 2.   │
│   A.1   │
└─────────────────────────────┘

Look carefully at this list of letters, then try to answer the question.

%%
%   %
%   %
%   A   D   G   J   _?__   %
%   %
%%

Question: What letter must you put in place of the question mark to
            complete this series of letters?

Here is the alphabet - it may help you.

        A   B   C   D   E   F   G   H   I   J   K
        L   M   N   O   P   Q   R   S   T   U   V
        W   X   Y   Z

Do any working out here:

If you know the answer, write it here:

        A   D   G   J   _____

Go to page 2 for the correct answer.

If you cannot find any answer, go to page 2 and start reading where
you see this mark ✳ .

238

Name : _____

Class : _____

Look carefully at all these faces and try to decide the type of face that
should go in place of the question mark to complete the last row.   The
right answer is one of the numbered faces further down the page.

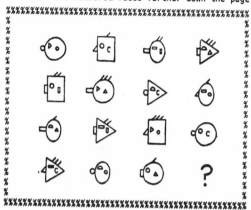

One of these faces is the correct answer. Find out which one it is.

Do any working out here:

If you know the answer, write the number of the correct picture
here: _____.

Go to page 2 for the correct answer.

If you cannot think of any answer, go to page 2 and start reading
where you see this mark ✳ .

APPENDIX H

TEST OF ARITHMETIC CONCEPTS

Name   : _____

School : _____

Class   : _____

<u>LOOK   AND   TELL</u>

We want you to tell us

If the numbers in column A are bigger than those in column B.

If the numbers in column B are bigger than those in column A.

If the numbers in columns A and B are equal.

If you don't know put a tick in the column headed Don't Know.

<u>RULES</u> :- 1. You MUST NOT try to work out the answers.

2. You CAN ANSWER by looking carefully at the numbers.

<u>EXAMPLES</u>:- Here are a few examples for you to try. The first one is done for you.

No.	A	B	A is LARGER	B is LARGER	A and B are EQUAL	Don't Know
1.	861	168	✓			
2.	945	594				
3.	2106 x 7	2106 x 5				
4.	0·14	$\frac{1}{4}$				

REMEMBER ...... Do NOT work out the answers.

No.	A	B	A is LARGER	B is LARGER	A and B are EQUAL	Don't Know
1.	4369	4871				
2.	£300	900p				
3.	789 - 535	789 - 632				
4.	300 + 70 + 5	375				
5.	63 x 5	63+63+63+63+63				
6.	362 ÷ 12	362 ÷ 13				
7.	2149	2945				
8.	600p	£200				
9.	819 - 764	819 - 467				
10.	861	600 + 80 + 1				
11.	464 x 4	464 + 464 + 464				
12.	4371 ÷ 32	4371 ÷ 23				
13.	8903	8039				
14.	£40·83	£43·08				
15.	501 - 23	391 + 23				
16.	2 + 49 + 344	2 + 11 + 444				
17.	395 x 19	395 x 18 + 395				
18.	5379 ÷ 9	5739 ÷ 9				
19.	4298 x 6	4298+6+6+6+6+6				

241

No.	A	B	A is LARGER	B is LARGER	A and B are equal	Don't know
20.	936 - 578	Take 578 from 936				
21.	6701	6017				
22.	£28·06	£26·08				
23.	761 + 59	841 - 59				
24.	9 + 19 + 245	9 + 29 + 145				
25.	861 x 16 - 861	861 x 15				
26.	4187 ÷ 7	4816 ÷ 7				
27.	3509 x 3	3+3509+3+3509+3				
28.	From 849 take 718	849 - 718				
29.	$\frac{1}{2} \times \frac{1}{2}$	$\frac{1}{4} \times \frac{1}{4}$				
30.	$\frac{1}{100}$	0·01				
31.	0·05	0·0094				
32.	3159 ÷ 19	3159 ÷ 9				
33.	$379 \times \frac{3}{4}$	$379 \times \frac{1}{4}$				
34.	0·987	1·01				
35.	six tenths	0·06				
36.	$\frac{17}{60}$	17 ÷ 60				
37.	(169 x 56) - 169	169 x 55				
38.	$\frac{1}{10} \times \frac{1}{10}$	$\frac{1}{5} \times \frac{1}{5}$				

242

No.	A	B	A is LARGER	B is LARGER	A and B are EQUAL	Don't Know
39.	$0 \cdot 100$	$\dfrac{1}{100}$				
40.	$0 \cdot 099$	$0 \cdot 8$				
41.	$4046 \div 7$	$4046 \div 15$				
42.	$583 \times \dfrac{1}{3}$	$583 \times \dfrac{2}{3}$				
43.	$2 \cdot 94$	$0 \cdot 394$				
44.	$0 \cdot 30$	three hundredths				
45.	$3 \div 8$	$\dfrac{3}{8}$				
46.	947×18	$(947 \times 19) - 18$				
47.	$763 \div 1\dfrac{1}{2}$	$763 \div \dfrac{3}{4}$				
48.	$32720 \div 8$	$(\dfrac{1}{2} \times 32720) \div 4$				
49.	$\dfrac{1}{4}$	$0 \cdot 4$				
50.	$\dfrac{1}{10}$	$0 \cdot 1 \times 10$				
51.	40×5	$40 \times 0 \cdot 5$				
52.	$(5085 \div 4)+(5085 \div 3)$	$(5085 \div 2)+(5085 \div 5)$				
53.	$583 \div \dfrac{2}{3}$	$583 \div 1\dfrac{1}{3}$				
54.	$(\dfrac{1}{4} \times 4296) \div 3$	$4296 \div 12$				
55.	$0 \cdot 25$	$\dfrac{2}{5}$				
56.	$0 \cdot 3 \times 10$	$\dfrac{3}{10}$				
57.	$80 \times 0 \cdot 125$	$80 \times 1 \cdot 25$				
58.	$(2133 \div 3)+(2133 \div 6)$	$(2133 \div 4)+(2133 \div 5)$				

243

APPENDIX J

TEST OF COMPUTATIONAL ARITHMETIC

NAME _____   DATE _____

SCHOOL _____   CLASS _____

1) 38 + 26 + 19	2) 297 + 635	3) 371 + 17 + 137
P. A.	P. A.	L. P. A.
4) 14 + 603 + 150	5) 627 - 38	6) From 538 take 469
L. P. A.	L. P. A.	L. P. A.

7) Here is a number
         6529

Which figure is the

a)   thousand .... _____

b)   unit .... _____

c)   hundred ..... ___ ___

d)   ten .... _____

P. A.

8)   Write this number in figures

One thousand three
hundred and seventy

_____

A.

9)   Here is a number
         4268

Put a ring round the figure
with the highest value

A.

10) Write in pounds

    a) 400p .... £_____

    b) 608p .... £_____

    c) 390p .... £_____

    d) 1060p .... £_____

5
A.

11) Write in pence

    a) £6 .... _____p

    b) Seven pounds forty pence

    _____p

    c) Thirty pounds and nine pence

    _____p

    d) £504 ..... _____p

4
5
A.

12) 72 x 6

P.
A.

13) 319 x 7

P.
A.

14) 715 ÷ 5

P.
A.

15) 3045 ÷ 7

P.
A.

16) 476 x 13

L.
P.
A.

17) 870 x 52

L.
P.
A.

S

18) 7105 ÷ 35

L.
P.
A.

19) $\dfrac{1}{5} = \dfrac{\boxed{}}{10}$

A.

20) $\dfrac{9}{15} = \dfrac{3}{\boxed{}}$

A.

21) $\dfrac{1}{3} + \dfrac{1}{4}$

P.
A.

22) $\dfrac{2}{3} - \dfrac{3}{8}$

P.
A.

23) $\dfrac{1}{4} \times \dfrac{1}{5}$

A.

24) $\dfrac{1}{3} \times 1935$

P.
A.

25) $9104 \div \dfrac{2}{3}$

L.
P.
A.

26) $\dfrac{2}{5} \div \dfrac{3}{4}$

L.
P.
A.

27) Here is a decimal number
 	
       0·314
 	
Which figure is
 	
a) the thousandth .... _____
 	
b) the tenth .... _____
 	
c) the hundredth ..... _____
 	
   A.
	28) Express 0·1 as a fraction
	
	   A.

	29) Express $\dfrac{3}{10}$ as a decimal A.

30) Express 0·09 as a fraction
 	
   A.
	31) Express $\dfrac{7}{100}$ as a decimal
	
	   A.

32) 4·96 + 13·08 + 0·705 L. P. A.	33) 39·84 - 17·31 P. A.
34) 107·328 - 98·472 L. P. A.	35) 35·076 x 28 L. P. A.

36) 48·298 ÷ 38 L. P. A.	37) Express $\dfrac{1}{80}$ as a decimal P. A.	38) Express 0·023 as a fraction A.
39) 4 x (384 + 31) P. A.	40) (27 + 306) x 5 P. A.	41) (783 x 3) ÷ 9 P. A.
42) 5 x (963 ÷ 9) P. A.	43) 56·23 x 1·4 L. P. A.	44) 17·52 x 0·43 L. P. A.

APPENDIX K

THE EXECUTION OF THE CLUSTER ANALYSIS

Much of the essential nature of cluster analysis was explained in Chapter 7. In that chapter also was described the nature of the inter-teacher distance measures incorporated in the distance matrix that constitutes the basis of a cluster analysis, and the choice of 'squared Euclidean distance' as the distance measure. In this appendix, the cluster analysis itself is described. First, however, it is necessary to look at one technical problem relating to the matrix of inter-teacher 'distances', that of weighting—intentional or accidental—of the variables contributing to those distances.

THE PROBLEM OF WEIGHTING

Any item can be artificially 'weighted' by being multiplied by a factor (either greater or less than one). It would be wrong, however, to assume that when no such artificial weighting has been done that all items are necessarily equally weighted. Just as when school marks are added together those subjects with marks more widely spread—those having higher standard deviations—contribute most to the rank order produced, so do items with largest standard deviations contribute most to the distance measures and thus to the clustering.

It is, of course, possible to overcome this problem by standardising all items—ie, by recalculating their value such that all have the same standard deviation—and indeed many advocate this course when a cluster analysis is to be undertaken. Unfortunately this procedure can have the effect of giving much weight to very small real differences between teachers on those items where most of the differences are small. The effect may therefore be to give considerable emphasis to differences that in educational terms are of little or no significance.

A further factor in the case of the SCOTS schedule was that, although most of the items had five-point-scales, a few had only four- or even three-point scales, and some others became so as a result of enforced category amalgamations (see page 62) and hence had smaller standard deviations than would otherwise have been the case. A case could, therefore, have been made for enlarging the standard deviations of these items (as standardisation would in fact have done in relative terms) but it is by no means certain that, in terms of educational significance, the largest possible differences on these variables were equivalent to the largest differences possible in the case of variables within a full five-point-scale. There was therefore a danger that any relative enlargement of their standard deviations would have conflicted with the intuitively based assumption on which the whole schedule is based, namely that all inter-category differences of a single unit are the same in terms of educational significance. It was accordingly decided to assume that all items with fewer categories had a smaller 'real' maximum range and therefore merited their lower weighting.

The second main factor affecting the weighting of variables is inter-correlation of items. Although in this book we have used the terms 'item' and 'variable' as almost inter-changeable, each item is in fact seeking to record a complex variable, underlying which may be many, more fundamental, but possibly unidentified, variables. In some cases these underlying variables or 'factors' are shared by more than one item in the schedule and they thus give rise to inter-correlations between the items concerned.

In so far as underlying factors are measured more than once, they are being given a degree of weighting, and, since the degree of inter-correlation was not something planned when the schedule was constructed, these weightings are to some extent random.

To overcome this problem, many advocate that before a cluster analysis is performed, the data should be 'factor analysed', and factor scores (rather than scores on items) used as the basis of distance measures. The factors produced by a factor analysis ideally represent all the basic underlying differences that, combined, produce the observed differences. Attractive as this seems, there are difficulties:

a) The factors do not identify themselves—ie, their meaning is not self-evident and can only be inferred from the size of their contribution to one or more of the original measures. The interpretation of the results of the analysis and hence indirectly of the cluster analysis is therefore made more difficult.

b) The soundness of the factor analysis depends on the soundness of the inter-correlations on which it is based. In the case of the SCOTS data, the scales on which they were based were restricted in range (the maximum being in almost all cases five used points) and often widely different in

250

distribution. If, as is likely, the inter-correlations were as a result substantially distorted, the factors produced would be inaccurate. It was accordingly decided not to use factor scores as input to the cluster analysis, but simply to survey the inter-correlation matrix for signs of any excessive over-lap between items in the schedule.

DECISIONS RELATING TO THE DROPPING OR WEIGHTING OF ITEMS

One decision was straight-forward, since it arose from a decision made long before: items 31 and 32 were each given half weight. From the outset group-size was seen as a single issue: the interest was in whether a class operated on a group basis and if so to what degree. It was recognised that there was likely to be some difference of practice (though probably mainly *in degree*) in different subject areas, and English and arithmetic were chosen because (a) they were quite likely to differ in this respect and (b) together they typically constituted a very substantial proportion of the work undertaken in most primary classes. Each half-weighted, they were together equivalent to a single group-size variable that made allowance for subject-area difference.

The same argument could have been used to justify half-weighting items 2 and 3, but action was not taken in this case. In the first place, the correlation between the two members of the pair was lower (0.48, as compared to 0.65 in the case of items 31 and 32), and, in any case, it was judged desirable to give greater weight to the matter of number of difficulty levels—something having no necessary relationship to grouping practice. Nonetheless the difference in the treatment of items 2 and 3 on the one hand, and 31 and 32 on the other does call attention to the essential arbitrariness of any such weighting of an item.

The more difficult decisions related to the possible elimination of variables from the cluster analysis basic data (ie, from the set used to calculate the distance matrix) on grounds of undue overlap.

The reasons for deciding not to solve this problem by using factors (derived from factor analysis) rather than raw ratings have been set forth earlier in this appendix. The problem however did not go away, and considerable effort was expended on various sorts of correlational analysis in an endeavour to determine whether there would be any advantage in dropping any item(s) that overlapped unduly with others.

251

In general, correlations between items were not high, the vast majority being below 0.5, and very many of these well below that figure. Indeed only six inter-correlations of 0.7 or higher were found, the highest of them being 0.79 (between items 11 and 14). However overlap was not fully measured by such correlations with other *individual* items, and accordingly the combined overlap was assessed by the calculation of multiple correlations for a few variables—11,14,19 and 25—that by virtue of having a number of moderately high correlations with other single items seemed likely to produce high multiple R's.

The multiple correlations so calculated are given in Table 13 together with a list of items contributing to each of them. (The

TABLE 13

MULTIPLE R's FOR SELECTED SCOTS VARIABLES

Item (Dependent Variable)	Multiple R	Independent Variables (in order of inclusion in regression equation)
11	.87	14, 13, 6, 21, 19
14	.86	11, 17, 18, 27, 26
19	.78	41, 39, 12, 40
25	.82	28, 43, 18, 30, 16

Note Those independent variables underlined belong to the same group of variables—see p 20—as the respective dependent variable.

items are listed in order of entry into the regression equation—ie, in their order of importance after that part of their variance that has been accounted for by their correlation with variables already in the equation has been removed or 'partialed out'.)

The ultimate decision taken was to drop item 19 only. This decision was based only to a limited extent on the multiple R's shown in Table 13, as is obvious from the fact that the three other dependent variables had higher multiple R's. The other factors taken into account were (a) how far each of the four candidates for elimination justified their retention by identifying individual teachers for whom general relationships did not hold (and justifiably so in the light of the researchers' knowledge of the individual teachers concerned) and (b) whether the variable in question belonged to a group of variables that were so numerous as to give undue emphasis to a particular aspect of a teaching style—eg, 'administrative efficiency'.

Whether the elimination of item 19 from the data used to produce the distance matrix which was itself thereafter used for the cluster analysis seems to the writer, in retrospect, very doubtful. Indeed it now seems to have been more a token gesture towards dealing with what is probably an insoluble problem, that of rationally allocating weight to particular variables in a situation where their interactions are enormously complex. [1]

WEIGHTING: GENERAL CONCLUSIONS

It seems clear that whereas the constructor of a schedule such as SCOTS can, through decisions as to what items to include in the schedule, influence in a general way the weight given to particular aspects of teachers' over-all strategy or style, any precise and rationally controlled weighting is probably too complex an operation to be undertaken, and, therefore, actual weightings must remain in part both accidental and unmeasured, and their precise effect on clusters produced, unknown.

THE ANALYSIS

Except where otherwise stated, the cluster analysis was undertaken through the use of the package of computer programs known as Clustan. [2] The reason for the decision *not* to use Clustan to produce the distance matrix but instead to read in (using a Clustan procedure) a previously computed matrix was that the former offered no satisfactory way of dealing with the small number of 'zero' codings to be found in the SCOTS data. (It will be recalled that when in the case of certain items—14, 15, 21, 28, and 34—an observer decided that he had insufficient evidence on which to make a coding, he could record a zero. [3]) Where zero codings occurred, to have taken a teacher's distance on the variable from each of the other teachers as the square of the difference between zero and each of those other teacher's coding would of course have produced nonsensical results, and even to have substituted an

---

[1] In fact a limited cluster analysis was carried out using a distance matrix where item 19 was *not* eliminated and items 31 and 32 *not* half-weighted. Comparison with an identical cluster analysis using the modified data shows that the effects of the weightings and the elimination were slight: they affected only cases where cluster membership was in any case borderline.

[2] See Wishart D, *Clustan User Manual* (Third Edition), Inter-university/Research Council Series, Report 47, 1978.

[3] In fact, zeros were recorded only for items 21 and 28—on 7 and 1 occasions respectively.

average value or a coding of 3 would have been no less arbitrary, even though the maximum error would have been smaller. The solution adopted in the program written to compute the matrix was to treat a teacher coded as zero on an item as being *in respect of that item* at a distance of zero from every other teacher no matter what coding the other teacher had. The result of this action was, of course, that any teacher coded as zero on an item had one less possible source of difference to contribute to his distances from every other teacher.

Once the distance matrix so produced had been read into Clustan, a Clustan procedure was used to carry out a 'Ward-type' cluster analysis—one which aims to produce a minimum-variance solution. This 'hierarchical' analysis takes as its starting point the situation where there are as many clusters as there are cases—in this instance, 128. Obviously with only one case per cluster there is no variance *within* any cluster: the total variance in the data is to be found in the *between cluster* variance. The first step in the Ward procedure is to reduce the number of clusters by one by combining in a single cluster whichever two cases are nearest together (or if there is more than one pair with an equal distance score at this minimum level, the first of these cases encountered by the program). Unless the distance between the two combined cases is zero, the combination produces some *within-cluster* variance—ie, some proportion of the total variance (within-cluster plus between-cluster) is transferred from *between-cluster* variance to *within-cluster* variance. The object of the Ward procedure is, however, both at this first step and at subsequent ones, to minimise the proportion of variance that is *within-cluster* for the given number of clusters—or, to put it another way, to maximise the homogeneity of the clusters.

The second step in the Ward procedure is to combine the next best pair of clusters, both of which may still be single-case clusters but one of which may be the two-case cluster formed at the preceding step. (Inter-cluster distance where the clusters each have two or more cases is measured between their respective centroids and is calculated as the mean of the distances between each case in one cluster and each case in the other.) Subsequent steps of the Ward procedure operate on the same principle and continue until a predetermined minimum number of clusters is reached. When the Ward procedure was first used in respect of the 1977/78 SCOTS data this minimum number was fixed at 10—ie, at a number somewhat below what was thought might be optimal.

254

There is no objective way of determining what the optimum number of clusters is, for the decision requires an assessment of balance of advantage. A large number of clusters has the advantage of keeping low the proportion of variance that is *within-cluster*, but it also implies that many or most will be very small and the number of them unmanageable. On the other hand, if there are very few clusters, the *within cluster* variance will form a high proportion of the total variance and those included in each cluster will almost certainly have little homogeneity. On a first inspection of the output of the Ward procedure, it appeared that a solution with approximately 20 clusters would afford clusters of acceptable homogeneity. However there was no need to make a final decision at this stage, since a Ward solution has, in itself, an inherent disadvantage.

This disadvantage arises from the fact that the centroids of the clusters in the solution reached have been strongly influenced in their location by that of the first two cases incorporated in their respective clusters, for it will be recalled from what has been said above that the starting point of cluster is just two cases that happen to be close together. (They do *not*, it should be noted, necessarily lie in an area of a general density.) The addition of cases to a cluster or the combination of adjacent clusters does of course involve the movement of centroids and this movement is likely in general to be for the better. However, there is no guarantee that their final positions will be optimal. An optimising procedure is therefore needed—a process commonly known as *relocation*.

A relocation procedure can be started with only one less than the maximum number of clusters—in this case, 127—but it would be very wasteful of computer time. Accordingly, since the Ward procedure provides a semi-optimised solution, one of its solutions with rather more clusters than was likely to be needed yielded a useful starting point—in fact its 30 cluster solution.

(The relocation program used was *not* the one contained in Clustan, but one written by the present writer when a (more limited) series of cluster analyses was being carried out on the 1974/75 SCOTS data. (The Clustan package available to the author at that time did not, in the light of the best information available, permit him to use his own distance matrix as input to its RELOCATE procedure.) The author's program, is, however, believed to produce results identical to those of the Clustan RELOCATE procedure.)

A relocation program requires at the outset to know, or to

calculate, the within and between cluster variance for the starting position. It then takes every case in turn and tries the effect of removing it to each other cluster and effects a transfer to whichever one offers the largest reduction in overall *within-cluster* variance, though if no transfer offers an improvement, it is of course left in its original cluster. (It will be noted that 'founder members' of original clusters are in this way given an opportunity to be detached from early associates.) After all cases have been given a chance to move it is necessary to repeat the process if one or more transfers have been made, since each move changes the situation for all other cases—for every transfer involves moving the centroids of the giving and the receiving clusters. The process is thus an iterative one.

Once the optimum solution *for that number of clusters* has been achieved, the number of clusters is reduced by one in exactly the same way as in the Ward procedure, and the interative relocation procedures restarted. Thus iterative relocation and Ward-type cluster amalgamations occur alternately until the pre-set minimum number of clusters is reached.

In the analysis undertaken, the minimum was again set at 10 clusters, but this time the minimum number of clusters that seemed to provide an adequate degree of within-cluster homogeneity lay in the neighbourhood of an 18-cluster solution.

Unfortunately even this solution could not be regarded as final, since it is known that even relocation procedures can produce somewhat different results with the same basic data if they have different starting points. To overcome this problem, a series of steps were taken.

It would have been legitimate to have re-run the relocation program using random starting points, but it was thought better to use other semi-optimised sets. To this end a wholly different type of clustering procedure was used, an improved type of Mode analysis available in the Clustan package under the name of DENSITY.[4] The DENSITY procedure was used twice using two different 'density estimates' and thus producing two different sets

---

[4] A type of cluster analysis that locates areas of density—as defined by the density-estimate formula employed—and then adds to them cases on a 'nearest-neighbour' basis. A problem of 'nearest-neighbour' analysis is that clusters tend to fuse—often leaving only a single cluster—long before all cases have been added. The Clustan DENSITY procedure does not allow such fusing to occur until all cases have been added, even though the last cases added are much more remote from the clusters to which they are added than other clusters from one another.

FIGURE 6
FLOW-CHART SHOWING SEQUENCE OF CLUSTER ANALYSIS PROCEDURES

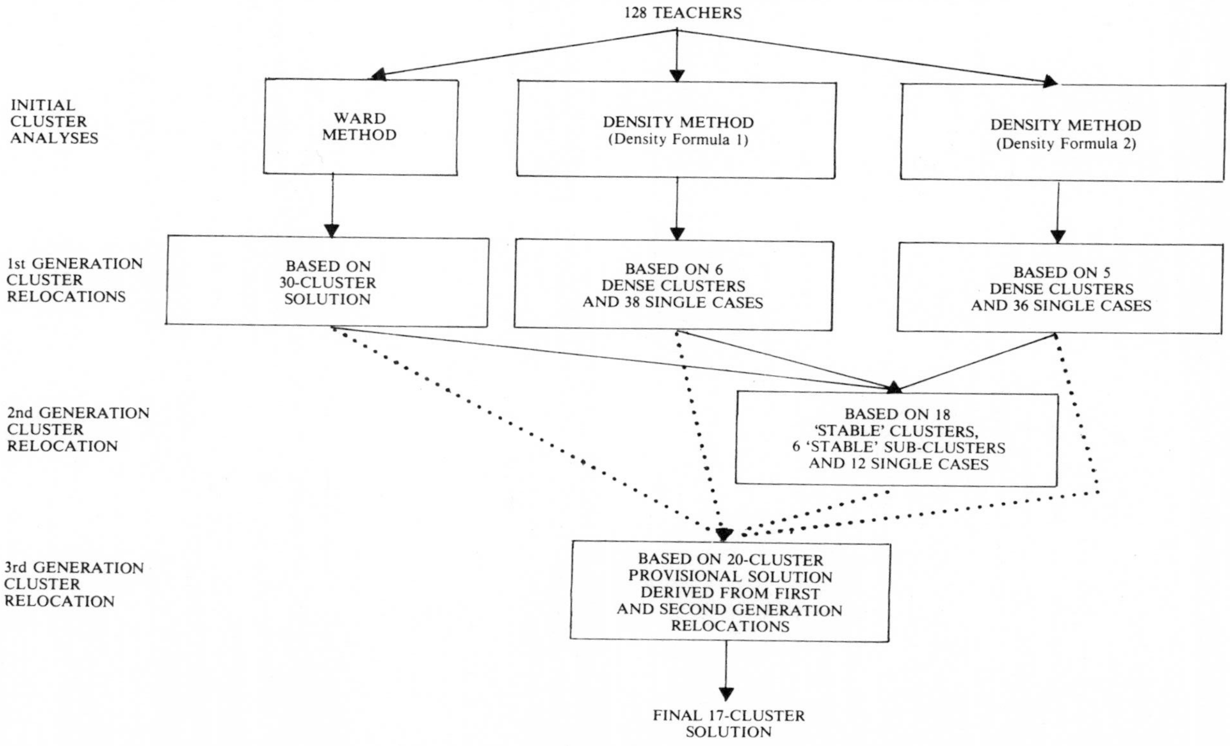

INITIAL
CLUSTER
ANALYSES

128 TEACHERS

WARD
METHOD

DENSITY METHOD
(Density Formula 1)

DENSITY METHOD
(Density Formula 2)

1st GENERATION
CLUSTER
RELOCATIONS

BASED ON
30-CLUSTER
SOLUTION

BASED ON 6
DENSE CLUSTERS
AND 38 SINGLE CASES

BASED ON 5
DENSE CLUSTERS
AND 36 SINGLE CASES

2nd GENERATION
CLUSTER
RELOCATION

BASED ON 18
'STABLE' CLUSTERS,
6 'STABLE' SUB-CLUSTERS
AND 12 SINGLE CASES

3rd GENERATION
CLUSTER
RELOCATION

BASED ON 20-CLUSTER
PROVISIONAL SOLUTION
DERIVED FROM FIRST
AND SECOND GENERATION
RELOCATIONS

FINAL 17-CLUSTER
SOLUTION

of clusters.[5] These two clusterings were then used as inputs to the relocation program and the sets of clusterings produced were compared with the 18-cluster solution from the relocation of the Ward output. These three sets of relocated clusters can be conveniently referred to as 'first generation' clusters. (These and subsequent steps are shown in relation to one another in Figure 6.) The purpose of the comparison was to establish a starting point for a 'second generation' relocation. The comparison of the three sets of clusters showed that many of the cases held together in the same groupings no matter which clustering procedure had been used. Their cluster membership was therefore seen as already safely established. However there remained cases that were differently placed. These were seen as being as yet insecure. They were accordingly separated from their clusters.

Thus it was that the relocation program was re-run with a starting position of 36 clusters. Half of these were the stable cases still clustered as in the earlier relocation results. The remaining 18 were the artificially created ones, 12 of them consisting of single cases and the remainder of sub-clusters (of two-four cases each), which, though stably linked internally, were not so to any of the basic 18 stable clusters.

The fresh set of clusters produced by this 'second-generation' run of the relocation program was then compared to the output of the 'first-generation' relocation based on the original Ward output to provide a starting point for a 'third-generation' relocation intended to resolve the differences between them.

Cases clustered identically were of course left undisturbed, but a decision had to be made about others. The practice adopted was to follow the 'second-generation' output where it was supported by that of at least two 'first-generation' relocations and in a few other instances where there appeared to be a special case for doing so.[6] The result was a 20-cluster input to a third-generation relocation, the outcome of which was accepted as final. From its set of solutions, the 17-cluster solution was selected. The alternatives with less than 17 clusters were seen as failing to provide an adequate degree of homogeneity in every cluster.

[5] The two runs of the DENSITY procedure, each employing a different density formula, produced six and five dense 'nuclei' respectively, and hence that number of clusters. As the last cases added were necessarily out-liers, they were arbitrarily excluded and each treated as a single-member cluster when it came to providing starting-points for the relocation program. The total number of clusters input were, therefore, 44 (6 + 38) and 41 (5 + 36) respectively.

[6] Only three of these 'special case' transfers were supported in the subsequent relocation.

INDEX